DRAMA IN THE CATHEDRAL

By the Same Author

Theatre Books
Choreographing the Stage Musical
Drama Improvised

Plays
Adventure of Sir Gawain and the Green Knight
Beowulf
The Ingoldsby Legends
The Midlands Mysteries
One Child at a Time
The Parting of Friends
Ring of Lead
Sir Gawain and the Green Knight
Snow White and the Seven Dwarfs
Troilus and Criseyde

Drama
in the
Cathedral

A Twentieth Century
Encounter of Church and Stage

Kenneth Pickering

J. Garnet Miller

Copyright © 2001 by Kenneth Pickering

First published by Churchman Publishing in 1986

This Second Edition published by J. Garnet Miller
(A sub-division of Cressrelles Publishing Company Limited)
10 Station Road Industrial Estate, Colwall, Near Malvern,
Worcestershire WR13 6RN

British Library Cataloguing-in-Publication Data
A CIP record for this book is available from the British Library

ISBN: 0-85343-627-4

Printed and bound in England by Polestar Scientifica, Exeter

Contents

Illustrations

For Irene,

Who went with me
To be my guide,
In my most need
To go by my side.

Acknowledgements

I gratefully acknowledge the help given by the following in the preparation of this book:

Dr E. Martin Browne; The Director and Staff of the Sherman Theatre, University College, Cardiff; Mr Fairbrass of S. W. Bligh & Sons, Canterbury; Fisk-Moore Studios, Canterbury; Mr Philip Hollingworth; Mr Laurence Irving; the Librarians at Canterbury City and Canterbury Cathedral Libraries, *Radius*, Sittingbourne College of Education, The University of Kent at Canterbury and especially at University College, Cardiff; *The Times*; and Mr Bob Cheeseman.

My particular thanks to Mr H. M. Quinn at University College, Cardiff and to my wife and family who made this work possible.

I must also record my profound gratitude to the former Dean of Canterbury, The Very Reverend Victor de Waal for his constant help in the publication of this book.

Finally, the Friends of Canterbury Cathedral have provided me with much support, for which I am very grateful. Not least for their kind permission to use Laurence Irving's design for *The Coming of Christ* as the cover illustration for this second edition. He painted this delightful picture at the age of 86, wholly from memory - 55 years after the event!

K. W. Pickering
August 2001

Foreword to the First Edition

by The Very Reverend Victor de Waal, MA, DD,
Dean of Canterbury

The revival, after the lapse of centuries, of drama in churches - something which is once again taken for granted all over the world -owes much to the genius of George Bell, Dean of Canterbury from 1924-1929. In those five years the Cathedral blossomed under his guidance into a renewal which still inspires its worship, its pilgrimage and not least its concern with the arts. The Liturgy of the Cathedral since the enthronement of Archbishop Lang in 1928, which Bell himself devised, has itself included a proper sense of theatre. Best known, however, of his legacies to Canterbury was his founding of the *Friends of the Cathedral* (the first such organisation anywhere), whose Arts Festival became the first festival of its kind in Britain.

It was for the commissioned plays that the Festival became famous and, through the founding of the *Religious Drama Society*, likewise at Canterbury, exercised an important influence on the English theatre, both in content and the new freedoms that production in churches brought to the stage.

As for content, the plays reflect the themes that exercised the best Christian thinkers in Europe of their period, concerns that were central to George Bell's own life and ministry at Canterbury and then as Bishop of Chichester, when he spoke prophetically, sometimes to the nation's discomfort.

So, for example, in T. S. Eliot's *Murder in the Cathedral*, the fiftieth anniversary of whose first performance is marked by the publication of Dr Pickering's book, religious, aesthetic and moral elements are fused in a way which has added permanently to the poetry of the English language, enabled the Church to enter again more deeply into its traditions, and inspired the conscientious opposition to political tyranny.

Those who are concerned with the health of society will ask themselves in what ways today the marriage of the Church and the arts could contribute in a similarly inspiring and creative way to the wholeness of our civilisation. It is a question to which at Canterbury we continue to address ourselves.

Drama in the Cathedral is to be welcomed, therefore, not only as an important contribution to the history of the English theatre, which it is, but also as a book that will help us to enter again into what is best in the tradition of our Church in its focusing of the possibilities of human life together.

Author's note to the Second Edition

This completely revised and updated version of a book originally published in 1986 covers a period in the British theatre when the term 'producer', meaning the person with artistic control over a play, has been gradually replaced by the term 'director'. Both terms are used and it will be obvious from the context that neither refer to the kind of 'producer' who has financial or organisational concerns unless this is clearly stated.

Introduction

English cathedrals make unlikely playhouses: some would even think it blasphemous to think of them as such. Yet some of the more interesting developments in twentieth century drama took place within their walls. Between the years 1928 and 1948 a number of unusual verse plays by Laurence Binyon, T. S. Eliot, Christopher Fry, Christopher Hassall, Laurie Lee, John Masefield, Dorothy L. Sayers and Charles Williams had their first performance in the Nave or Chapter House of Canterbury Cathedral. Among these plays was an acknowledged masterpiece, T. S. Eliot's *Murder in the Cathedral*, which has been performed and discussed widely since it was first seen at Canterbury in 1935. But, apart from the odd revival by amateur church groups, the other plays have virtually disappeared, as if under the permanent shadow of Eliot's great play. Most of these Canterbury plays were not primarily intended for long-term survival, they were written especially for a particular event and, having fulfilled their purpose, were neglected.

The fact that they are rarely performed tells us little about them; many good and interesting plays are left unperformed simply because the whole process of producing them is such an expensive and complicated business compared with, say, the performance of an obscure piece of music. Nevertheless, they constitute a very intriguing episode in the development of British drama which, on account of their unconventional setting, has been largely overlooked by theatre historians. This book examines the antecedents and the consequences of their performance.

Some of the Canterbury plays have been mentioned briefly in surveys of twentieth century drama. They tend to be placed in what Katherine Worth has called "the not very jolly corner labelled verse and religious drama"[1] and are generally felt to have had common weaknesses. Recent critical attitudes towards what is usually thought to have been a 'movement' in religious verse plays are largely dismissive, condescending or even contemptuous. Ivor Brown speaks of "The Crypt of St Eliot",[2] and Arnold Hinchliffe reports Donoghue's jibe that,

Audiences could feel that they had not been to the theatre so much as tricked into attending Church.[3]

Eliot himself seemed to confirm this view by turning to the commercial theatre after the success of *Murder in the Cathedral* and maintaining that his Canterbury play had been written for a particular sort of audience who "go to Festivals and expect to have to put up with poetry."[4] Kenneth Muir, probably taking his cue from Eliot's well-known comment, states similarly that the Canterbury plays were not for "ordinary playgoers", but "for poetry lovers".[5] A fair proportion of the Canterbury audience certainly was conservative, genteel and equally at home in the rarified atmosphere of the Cloisters or of Georgian verse. But there is a good deal of evidence to suggest that at times they were angered by, and at others bewildered by, the plays and that socially and intellectually they were virtually indistinguishable from "ordinary playgoers" of the nineteen-twenties and thirties.

It is frequently asserted that the plays were all part of an elegant amateurism, plays performed by amateurs for an audience of occasional poets. Amateur performance in itself need not, of course, be a bad thing, for as Shaw remarked when asked to distinguish between amateur and professional acting

There are only two kinds of actors - good actors and bad actors.[6]

Even that paragon of drama historians, Allardyce Nicoll, repeats the error of assigning the Canterbury plays to the amateur theatre.[7]

A far more accurate and interesting view of the Canterbury plays is that they were an almost unique example of close cooperation between the professional and amateur theatre, but that they were largely influenced by traditions from the professional theatre. The fact that the plays were intended to be performed in an ecclesiastical setting, and not in an actual theatre building, is somehow felt to constitute a weakness in itself. The feeling that even *Murder in the Cathedral* works better in a church building than on a theatre stage is regretted, and the failure of the remaining Canterbury plays to achieve a substantial run in the commercial theatre is taken as a sign of inadequacy.

In recent years, however, our concept as to what constitutes a theatre and a stage have changed rapidly. Barns, canal barges, disused churches, engine sheds and London buses have all become theatres and, under the influence of Stephen Joseph, Jean-Louis Barrault or Peter Brook, a stage can be anywhere that an empty space can be found - an arena, an avenue, a platform - the possibilities, it seems, are endless.

Looking back to the early productions at Canterbury, we find a building imposing its discipline on playwrights and taxing the imaginations of producers in such a way that the developments in staging techniques employed there pre-empted similar developments in the commercial theatre by some twenty years. The fact that the Canterbury plays did not depend on the stifling restrictions of the proscenium arch and velvet curtains of the commercial theatre in the nineteen-twenties and thirties was their strength; they had to be experimental and non-commercial in order to take advantage of their unusual setting.

There are two critical works that have made a genuine attempt to consider at least some of the Canterbury plays in detail. These are Gerald Weales's *Religion in Modern English Drama* (Philadelphia 1961) and William V. Spanos's *The Christian Tradition in Modern British Verse Drama* (New Jersey 1967). Weales's book is a rather pedestrian affair; he plods dutifully through every play that has appeared on the English stage since 1884 that could in any sense be called religious and rarely considers the plays in performance. For our purposes, Weales's study is incomplete because neither Laurence Binyon's nor Laurie Lee's Canterbury plays qualify for consideration. Nevertheless, the book, which gives almost equal attention to a huge number of plays regardless of quality, provides both valuable background and fair judgement and enables lines of development to be traced, even though the author himself is not always aware of them.

Spanos's book is a far more impressive work although, unfortunately, he also neglects Binyon and Lee. He examines the remaining plays against the theological background of the period, maintaining especially that some of the plays are a response to a special concern with the Incarnation and its significance for time which became the fulcrum for the crisis theology of Barth and Bonhoeffer. Spanos argues that the playwrights he discusses were governed by a "sacramental aesthetic" as were medieval playwrights, but having established this he demonstrates how, one by one, they failed to fulfil the resulting implications. Spanos lacks a sense of theatrical tradition and therefore gives a distorted view of the influences to which the Canterbury playwrights were subject, he also neglects considerations of performance which, in this case, are important for a full understanding of the style of the plays. It is, nevertheless, a most valuable book which deals expansively with post-war developments outside Canterbury.

The most important fact about these two books is that, having given detailed consideration to many of the Canterbury plays, they reach a conclusion that is entirely contrary to the popular critical idea. Spanos speaks of, "A body of verse drama that for popularity and genuine artistic merit ranks as high as any since the seventeenth century."[8] This is an extravagant claim and, if it is supportable, it is essential to look at those plays which Spanos does not mention to see how they fit his case and to explain the origin of all the plays. Gerald Weales refers to the "new professionalism that marked the later development of the movement",[9] and invites a thorough investigation of the relationship between the drama of the Church and of the theatre.

Notes to Introduction

1/2. Katherine Worth, 'Eliot and the Living Theatre', *Eliot in Perspective: A Symposium,* ed. Graham Martin (London 1970) 148.

3. Denis Donoghue, *The Third Voice* (Princeton 1959), 158, quoted by Arnold Hincliffe, 'Verse Drama', *British Theatre 1950-1970* (Oxford 1974), 39.

4. T. S. Eliot, 'Poetry and Drama', *Selected Prose* (Harmondsworth 1953), 72.

5. Kenneth Muir, 'Verse and Prose', *Stratford-upon-Avon Studies IV: Contemporary Theatre* (London 1962), 105.

6. Quoted in *Amateur Stage XXV No. 6* (1970), 58.

7. Allardyce Nicoll, *English Drama: A Modern Viewpoint* (London 1968), 122-4.

8. William V. Spanos, *The Christian Tradition on Modern British Verse Drama* (New Jersey 1967), 16.

9. Gerald Weales, *Religion in Modern English Drama* (Philadelphia 1961), 110.

Part One

The Church, the Stage and the Search for a New Drama

1

Drama and The Church

On Whit Monday, May 1928, John Masefield's play, *The Coming of Christ*, was performed in the Nave of Canterbury Cathedral. This was a remarkable event as no drama had been seen in an English cathedral since medieval times and, moreover, the Church had for centuries expressed its total opposition to drama in any form. Church attitudes towards drama had been slow and difficult to change. More than fifty years of debate and reappraisal concerning the relations between the Church and the Stage had preceded *The Coming of Christ*, and whereas for some the event was a long over-due act of reconciliation between the Church and drama, for others the theatre and all its works still belonged to the devil.[1]

The Church had traditionally based its attitude towards drama on its view of the theatre and actors. A vicar who opposed the opening of the Theatre Royal, Stratford in 1884 on the grounds that "a theatre would not tend to the moral elevation of the neighbourhood" and that it would, therefore, "become the resort of the lowest classes",[2] was merely expressing an opinion that was widely held by clergymen in his day. The Anglican Church tended to lead the way in the adoption of more liberal views; the opposition of the Roman Catholic Church and of the Nonconformists was even stronger and persisted for far longer - in some extreme cases even until the present time. The attitude of the churches was not without justification; it derived, in large part, from theatrical conditions in the first half of the nineteenth century: "the drab and reeking hall where half boozed mummers roared a glee"[3] was a familiar place of entertainment and the auditoria of theatres were a popular soliciting ground for prostitutes. But from about the middle of the century onwards a gradual improvement in the life of the theatre became apparent, and churchmen were increasingly challenged to rethink their position.

Allardyce Nicoll[4] and Donald Hole[5] have suggested a number of factors contributing to a change in the moral tone of the theatre in the second half of the nineteenth century. Firstly, changes in Victorian society itself were reflected in the theatre. The rapid urbanisation of Britain, as a result of the Industrial Revolution, produced a new middle-class, and it was particularly among this new section of society that a strict moral tone emerged. The evangelistic movement, culminating in the Great Revival of 1859, added some two million members to the churches, but from the beginning of Queen Victoria's reign there had been a growing acceptance of more rigid standards of propriety.

The queen herself contributed to the elevation of the theatre. In 1849 she appointed Charles Kean as manager of the Windsor Castle theatricals and, until the death of her husband, she and Prince Albert were regular patrons of the theatre. The greater decorum of the audiences and the greater social status for actors that royal patronage helped to bring about were reinforced by changes in the playhouses themselves.

The pit, the favourite haunt of the more rowdy elements of the audience, was progressively replaced by stalls, and the fashionable dress circle became an established feature for the comfort of the *nouveaux riches*. Laurence Irving has also pointed out that the practice of letting boxes to members of the aristocracy also became common in the middle years of the century, and it enabled actor-managers to mingle with a section of society whose patronage helped their own status.[6] New modes of transport and greater refinement in the theatres themselves gradually brought theatre-going within the reach of a whole new section of society and it is hardly surprising therefore that drama began to be adapted to the tastes and preoccupations of the middle classes.

Even while the Theatres' Monopoly Act was still in force, Madame Vestris achieved a remarkable style of performance at the Olympic Theatre which appealed to a genteel audience. By producing burlettas, which consisted of three acts rather than five, and having an accompaniment from a tinkling piano, Madame Vestris evaded the law defining legitimate drama. Her actors conversed with each other on stage rather than directing remarks at the audience and the whole atmosphere of this small theatre was one of restraint.[7]

We can see that, for a variety of reasons, it became easier for the Church to regard the stage with rather more approval; but these reasons alone do not account for the active support which some churchmen gave to drama from about 1870 onwards. Allardyce Nicoll's suggestion that the Stage found an unexpected ally in the Church in its attempt to achieve respectability is misleading; and his account overlooks the two most important individual contributions to the work of reconciliation: the work of Sir Henry Irving and of Stuart Headlam.[8]

Irving's Initiative

Irving's achievement in winning the sympathy of churchmen has been seriously underrated or entirely overlooked. By 1875, Irving's production of *Hamlet* had established him as London's leading actor; and his meticulous productions were attracting fashionable and middle-class audiences to the theatre. Irving was determined to raise the status of his profession, and he realised that prejudice in church circles was a major obstacle to the achievement of his aim. He had evidence that some clergy were beginning to support the theatre and equal proof that hostile attitudes continued to predominate. An Anglican bishop who attended *Hamlet* wrote to Irving expressing his enjoyment, but added:

> I am and was most careful not to startle clerical or even general public opinion by dropping my incognito; opinion in this matter will change, but it can't be forced.[9]

5

The almost total antipathy of the Nonconformist churches was made clear to Irving when in 1875 a Congregationalist minister, the Reverend Aveling, discovered that in a moment of bravado his son had claimed to be Irving's brother. Acutely embarrassed by the suggestion that he had theatrical connections, Aveling made a vehement public denial and justified it in a telegram to Irving:

> Right or wrong, the great majority of our people look unfavourably on theatrical exhibitions.[10]

Irving was determined to effect a change in the attitudes that the bishop's letter and Aveling's telegram described. His position as a public figure enabled him to carry on his campaign to churchmen by a variety of means; and he never missed an opportunity to make public statements concerning the Church and Stage. The most extraordinary feature of Irving's strategy was that it was not merely defensive. Not only did he refute the charges of moral depravity which the Church had levelled at the theatres; he made the revolutionary claim that the Theatre was a powerful agent of edification. Addressing a conference of the *Church of England Temperance Society* in 1875, Irving said:

> Gentlemen, change your attitudes towards the stage and believe me, the stage will co-operate with your work of faith and labour of love. It will help you in disarming and decimating the forces which make for moral evil, and in implanting and fostering the seeds and energies of moral good.[11]

Irving also reminded his audience of the sympathy that existed between the Church and Stage in medieval times, and issued a plea to the clergy not to inveigh against the theatre from their pulpits.

Predictably, such appeals and claims on behalf of the Stage aroused furious opposition in some sections of the Church and for nearly thirty years Irving contended with periodic outbursts of hostility. As late as 1891 an Anglican clergyman, the Reverend H. Stratton of St Helens, Lancashire, preached a sermon denouncing Irving's claims for the theatre and sent the full text to *The Times*. The Methodist Church was quick to come out in support of Stratton, and in its leader *The Methodist Times* commented:

> It is inevitable that Christian ministers should fix their attention very largely upon the terrible evils that have hitherto been associated with

the theatre. If so attractive and powerful an institution could be saved from the horrible evils which have always been associated with it, and made the vehicle of innocent recreation and elevated instruction, which its advocates describe, we are sure that no one would rejoice more than the young minister who has so bravely and eloquently denounced existing evils.[12]

Such statements demonstrated that there were elements of almost incurable prejudice in some Church circles and that attitudes were still based on tradition rather than on evidence.

Irving, however, was a formidable opponent. The way in which he conducted his own theatre, the generosity of his nature and the loyalty of his company were living proof of the respectability he claimed for the profession. He could always produce a withering reply to counter his critics.

When a Presbyterian, Samuel Smith, published a pamphlet in 1900 denouncing immoral plays and players, Irving wrote to him:

To rely on such evidence seems to be ministering, however unwittingly, to those unworthy prejudices which have for so long hindered the public appreciation of the art of theatre . . . if such statements concerning certain plays are true, my reverence for *The Bible* is not diminished by the grossness of some of its pages.[13]

"Unworthy prejudices" certainly followed the great actor to his death in 1905 - the sister of the Dean of Westminster protested furiously to her brother for giving permission for Sir Henry Irving to be buried in the Abbey, but the Dean and overwhelming public opinion prevailed. This was an indication of Irving's splendid achievement; an address presented to Irving in 1876 by the graduates and undergraduates of Trinity College, Dublin, put it thus:

You have succeeded in commending it [the theatre] to the favour of a portion of society, large and justly influential, who usually hold aloof from the theatre.[14]

In spite of repeated opposition, Irving broke down many of the barriers between drama and the Church. He made almost every production at the Lyceum into a talking point in intellectual circles and helped to establish a more sympathetic attitude towards the performance of drama in the universities.

Signs of actual approval from churchmen occurred with increasing frequency during Irving's career: in 1877 he joined a group of Anglican clergy for a reading of *The Merchant of Venice* at a friend's house,[15] but in 1890 many Anglican priests openly attended Irving's recital at St James' Hall. The audience also included several Roman Catholic priests, who were defying the ban of Cardinal Manning on attendance at any sort of dramatic performance.[16] No doubt many clergymen were influenced by the introduction of drama at Oxford in 1881. Jowett, the Vice Chancellor, not only allowed Frank Benson to perform *Agamemnon* in Balliol Hall, but also sanctioned plays at the New Theatre. Much of the impetus for these innovations came from William Courtney, a fellow of New College, who was a Christian and a devotee of Irving. At Jowett's invitation, Irving himself lectured to the Oxford undergraduates; and the *Oxford Union Drama Society*, which was to include many future clergymen in its membership, was founded in 1885.[17]

The peculiar magnetism that Irving exerted over his audience was responsible for a complete reversal in the attitudes of many leading figures in the Anglican Church. He was regarded with a veneration, which seems almost incredible today, by such different characters as the Reverend C. L. Dodgson (Lewis Carroll),[18] Canon Thorndike (the father of the famous theatrical family of Sybil, Russell and Eileen who contributed to the Canterbury Plays),[19] and William Hutton, Dean of Winchester, who actually wrote a play, *The Dead Heart* (1889), for Irving to produce at the Lyceum.

By far the most spectacular recognition of Irving's achievements, however, came with his knighthood in 1895. But two years later the Anglican Church added a further honour, which was a remarkable prelude to the Canterbury Plays. Dr Farrar, Dean of Canterbury, invited Sir Henry Irving to read from Tennyson's verse play *Becket*, in the Chapter House of Canterbury Cathedral. On May 31st 1897 the reading took place; standing within a few yards of the spot where Archbishop Thomas Becket had been murdered, Irving read from a specially printed, large-type copy of the play mounted on a purple-draped lectern. Eric Jones-Evans maintains that the reading lasted just under three hours,[20] whereas Irving's grandson, Laurence, put it at one and a half hours;[21] both, however, are agreed that a huge audience was held spellbound and responded with tremendous applause.

Figure 1: Sir Henry Irving reading scenes from Tennyson's verse-play *Becket*, in the Chapter House of Canterbury Cathedral, 1897.

Irving had succeeded first in removing much of what W. S. Gilbert called "the unnecessary and unchristian antagonism existing between the Theatre and the Church";[22] secondly, in actively commending the theatre to them; and finally, in bringing drama itself into the precincts of the Church. Without his influence it is doubtful if the Canterbury Plays would have taken place. It probably never occurred to the playwrights of the nineteen-twenties and thirties who wrote for Canterbury that they owed a good deal to an actor whom it had become fashionable to decry.

Influences From Within the Church

So far this account of the attitude of the Victorian Church has given the impression of a conservative and intransigent body, confronting a rapidly changing theatre. This is by no means the complete picture.

In fact the Church responded to the shifting social and cultural conditions of the nineteenth century with extraordinary vigour. A number of movements within the Church revived its spiritual life and contributed to the national morality. Corruption and complacency among the ecclesiastical hierarchy were largely replaced by personal piety and a new mood of confidence. Faced with the enormous social problems caused by massive urban development, the Church also began to acquire a genuine social conscience and to involve itself in the life of the people: particularly in the field of education. As a remedy to the evils of alcoholism and the secularisation which seemed to accompany industrialisation, the Church promoted the great causes of temperance and Sabbatarianism.

One of the most significant movements within the Church for its relations with the Theatre was the Christian Socialism of F. D. Maurice. Maurice attacked the predominant middle-class belief that virtue led to prosperity and that sin led to poverty.[23] Instead, he argued that progress would be achieved if the correct social conditions were created, an idea which rapidly gained support and led to a new interest in social reform. He also called into question the traditional doctrine that unending future torment awaited those who had failed to repent in this life.[24] Maurice's beliefs led to his dismissal from King's College, London in 1853. He had held professorships in English Literature, History and Divinity, but his initiative had already been responsible for the founding of Queen's College for women and after his dismissal he immediately founded the first Working Men's College. He was eventually appointed to a Chair of Casuistry and Moral Philosophy at Cambridge where he exerted a considerable influence on his students. Lively minds within the Church of England followed Maurice in attempting to project a more compassionate and socially concerned image of the Church: the ministry of the Church, therefore, obviously had to extend to the actors, dancers and showmen who often inhabited dreary lodgings in large cities.

Another source of renewal in the Church, which had consequences for the theatre, was the *Oxford Movement*. This Anglo-Catholic revival stressed the importance of the Sacraments in the life of the Church as a means of spiritual nourishment. Sacramentalism "revealed a spiritual meaning underlying the expression of beauty and art"[25] and produced a new enthusiasm for the Liturgy. Clergymen with a flair for ritual and ceremony began to rediscover the dramatic elements of the worship of the Church, particularly in the Mass. The Anglo-Catholic branch of the Church became the most sympathetic in its attitude to the theatre, and it was Anglo-Catholic theology which was eventually to inspire many of the writers, actors and producers who contributed to the Canterbury Plays of the 1920s and '30s.

One clergyman who could produce a superb performance in the celebration of the Mass was Reverend N. D. Nihill of Shoreditch. His concern to render the great service to perfection attracted the attention of liturgical enthusiasts and they came from great distances to attend worship in his church.[26] In 1871, Rev. Nihill visited the *Passion Play* at Oberammergau, and his imagination was immediately fired by the possibilities of dramatic performance as a means of evangelism and worship. On his return, he organised *Bethlehem Tableaux* in St Michael's School, Shoreditch - this is the first recorded dramatic activity sponsored by a clergyman in England in modern times.[27] From this modest beginning a great deal was to emerge.

11

The Reverend Stuart Headlam

Among the crowds who attended Rev. Nihill's celebration of Mass was a young theological student, Stuart Headlam. Headlam is another of those figures whom drama historians have tended to ignore.[28] Irving is, at least, credited with having been honoured with the outward signs of a changed attitude towards the stage, even if his active contribution has not been appreciated. But Irving himself once remarked to Ben Greet:

> People sometimes maintain that the Stage is indebted to me for the greater esteem in which it is now held, but really, did they but know it, actors owe far more to that man Headlam.[29]

An interesting and revealing portrait of Headlam is incorporated in the figure of the Rev. James Mavor Morell, the Christian Socialist cleric of George Bernard Shaw's play *Candida*.[30] Shaw and Headlam became fellow Fabians, and after Headlam's death Shaw said of him:

> Headlam belonged to a type of the clergy peculiar to the latter half of the nineteenth century. These clergymen . . . were up in revolt against the conventional idea of a parson. They wanted the clergyman to be able to go to the theatre, to say d—n if he wished to do so, to take a large interest in social and political questions, to have dancing in his house if he chose, and to affirm the joyousness and freedom and catholicity of the Church at every turn. Headlam certainly made it difficult for a bishop to offer him promotion. He liked the ballet; he left none of his views unspoken. Naturally he was always in hot water with stupid people.[31]

Headlam became one of the most controversial figures in the Church and Stage debate. He was a man of superb courage,[32] a clergyman who dared to stand bail for Oscar Wilde, at the risk of antagonising even his closest friends. He was undoubtedly something of an eccentric, with a gift for dramatic gestures of defiance and, as Archbishop Randall Davidson once said of him: "went straight ahead, with blinkers on."[33]

Neither Headlam's biographer, F. G. Bettany, nor those who have recorded Father Nihill's enthusiasm for drama,[34] have suggested any link between Headlam's admiration for Nihill and his later involvement with the theatre. But it seems reasonable to

suggest, particularly as Headlam eventually became Nihill's curate, that something of Nihill's influence accounts for Headlam's
dramatic flair.

Headlam, however, was quite clear as to the main source of his
inspiration: it was the Christian Socialist teaching of Maurice with
his focus on the Incarnation and the Sacraments.[35] In his Fabian
paper, *Maurice and Kingsley*, Headlam acknowledged his debt to his
old tutor:

Maurice however . . . acted as a liberator to our young minds.
The Fatherhood of God with, as its corollary, the eternal Sonship of
Christ and consequently the Brotherhood of Man. It was from the doctrines of the Incarnation - God made Man - and the Atonement - Man
reconciled to God, made one with God by the Sacrifice of His Son - that
he derived what unifies his social teaching. He was a Puritan, though
he was at the same time in the truest sense a sacramentarian . . . People
have talked of my fads and complained that I was interested in such a
variety of disconnected things in Bradlaugh, and the stage and
education . . . The doctrine of the Incarnation is their warrant.[36]

As we shall see, Incarnational Theology provided the basis for a
good deal of the Christian drama which became possible in later
years,[37] but Headlam's concern for the theatre began in a very
practical way. His first curacy was at St John's, Drury Lane (1870-
3), and here he found a large number of actors, actresses and
dancers amongst his parishioners. As a diligent, pastoral clergyman, he made frequent visits to their lodgings, and he began to
attend the ballet at the Alhambra. On one occasion, he recognised
two of the girls on stage as communicants and, in speaking to them
after the performance, he was horrified to hear them imploring him
not to tell other members of his congregation how they earned their
living.[38] Headlam was outraged and determined to break down the
prejudice with which the Church regarded the stage. He was
convinced that the Church was failing in its pastoral responsibility
to theatre people, who often moved from parish to parish. He was
certain that the irrational suspicion of the churches cut off many
needy theatrical individuals from its ministry and sacraments.

Headlam decided to make a point of frequent theatre attendance himself, in addition to speaking openly of his disquiet con-

cerning the Church's attitude. His Bishop, however, was already beginning to find him an irritant and was probably glad when Headlam's sermons gave him an excuse to dismiss him. The Bishop actually claimed that he was disturbed by Headlam's preaching, which opposed the idea of Hell as eternal judgement and contained other echoes of Maurice's teaching.[39] There is no doubt, however, that Headlam's sympathy for the theatre was the root cause of his being forced to resign in 1873 and to take another curacy at Bethnal Green.

Headlam was not easily diverted from his purpose and he at once continued his efforts on behalf of the theatre; he went to see Irving in *Hamlet* and his enthusiasm for drama, particularly for Shakespeare, was soon passed on to some of his parishioners. The new curate was made responsible for the training of pupil teachers, one of whom later recalled Headlam's influence and approach:

We sat round a table and studied with him history ... and literature (we read Tennyson I remember) and the plays of Shakespeare. Headlam would allot the parts in the plays to different members of the class ... there would be a discussion of the drama and of the characters ... occasionally he made up a party for the pit of the theatre.[40]

But the event which marked the turning point in Headlam's career was his lecture, *Theatres and Music Halls*, which he delivered at the Commonwealth Club on Sunday 7th October 1877. The lecture might never have come to the attention of his superiors had not an actor in the audience asked for a copy of the text. We do not know this actor's name, but he claimed to have seen ministers of religion outside his theatre, trying to dissuade the audience from going in, thus attempting to deprive him of a living. Headlam's words had seemed so refreshing to the actor that he arranged for the lecture to be published in *Era*; and from that moment Headlam was at the very centre of the Church-versus-Stage controversy.[41] The passage in Headlam's lecture which particularly shocked his Bishop contained a suggestion that all young women should be positively encouraged to go to the theatre, to see the vivacity of the dancers and actresses: "John Bunyan speaks somewhere with regret of 'the young woman whose name was dull'", said Headlam.[42]

This was too much for the puritanical Bishop Jackson; and Headlam received notice to leave his curacy on 4th January 1878.

Headlam, however, was not alone in his defence of the stage. Progressive thinkers within the Church, aware of changing social conditions and interested in popular culture, were concerned to bridge the gulf which separated the Church from various sections of society. They saw drama as having possibilities for making Christianity relevant to modern life. One such clergyman was John Oakley, who later became Dean of Manchester. He was delighted by the content of Headlam's *Theatres and Music Halls* lecture and wrote him a letter of support:

> I know nothing more desirable than to shock out of their stolid complacency the slow-witted respectability of the whole class of old-fashioned, unobservant, unenterprising church people, lay and clerical, bishops, rural deans, squires, tradesmen and the rest of them.[43]

Headlam was greatly encouraged by this and other sympathetic letters which he received, and he decided that the next step was to widen his dispute with his superiors, from a parochial to a national issue; and to unite both the elements within the Church and the theatre who were working for a better understanding.

As a first move, Headlam preached a sermon on *The Church and the Stage* and then entered into a defiant correspondence with Bishop Jackson concerning his dismissal from his curacy. In order to draw attention to his views, Headlam audaciously published, in pamphlet form, the Bishop's correspondence and his own replies. It was a masterstroke and convinced a good number of clergy that the Bishop was not a representative of a faith whose founder had been frequently seen with "publicans and sinners". Bishop Jackson had written:

> Not for the first time has it caused me to ask pardon of our great Master if I erred, as I think I did, in admitting you to ministry. It is, of course, vain to argue with one who prefers so unhesitatingly his own judgement, backed by the approval of actors and the proprietors of music-halls, to that of his incumbent and Bishop, neither of whom can be considered Puritans. But I do pray earnestly that you may not have to meet before the Judgement Seat those, whom your encouragement first led to places where they lost the blush of shame and took the first downward step towards vice and misery.[44]

Headlam's published reply and comments made reference to the fact that many of the Bishop's own regular congregation were also frequent visitors to the theatre, but showed no signs of depravity.

Secondly, Headlam demonstrated the extent to which his views were beginning to command support by reissuing his *Theatres and Music Halls* as a pamphlet, with a preface and a selection of the encouraging correspondence he had received. The lively preface included quotations from the Psalms, the Athanasian Creed, Wordsworth and Palgrave: and among those who read it with some sympathy was Archbishop Tait of Canterbury.[45]

In the same year, 1879, after consultation with some of his leading allies, Headlam founded *The Church and Stage Guild*. Its aim was to bring about a better understanding between the two traditional antagonists. Headlam had originally suggested the title Guild of Christ at Cana, a response to a passage in Oakley's letter, in which he had referred to Christ's mixing with all sections of society.[46] *The Church and Stage Guild* continued its activities until the end of the century; it was never a particularly large body, although by the end of its first year of existence it had nearly five hundred members, drawn almost equally from the clergy, laity and the theatre. But it provided a focus for the debate on Church attitudes to the Theatre and enabled Headlam, its first secretary, to conduct his campaign with the backing of an organisation that was difficult to ignore.

Because of Headlam's particular enthusiasm for ballet, the *Church and Stage Guild* failed to attract many leading figures from the Theatre into its membership - there was a general feeling of antipathy towards dancers and music hall artists among actors. Irving, particularly, was something of a disappointment to Headlam. Although the two men expressed considerable admiration for each other, Irving apparently resented the legitimate theatre being discussed alongside the music hall and ballet.[47] Irving was therefore never actively involved in the *Guild* and the actors' membership tended to be restricted to those with High Church leanings.

The work of the *Guild* was, however, important and out of all proportion to its size. Its main regular function was its series of 'At Homes' and 'Conversaziones' held in the foyer of the Drury Lane

Theatre. At these monthly meetings, there was an opportunity for clergymen to fraternise with dancers and actors, which Headlam felt would achieve the desired breakdown of prejudice. Headlam was criticised by some church members for devoting too little time at meetings to prayer and evangelisation, but Headlam thought that personal contact was more important. Another major feature of the *Guild's* meetings were the papers read by prominent and progressive thinkers: these included George Bernard Shaw who spoke on three occasions. Shaw's papers were: *Acting, by One Who Does Not Believe In It*, or *The Place of the Stage in the Fool's Paradise of Art* (1889), *Ibsen's Didactic Plays* (1890) and *Parsifal* (1894). Other famous speakers included William Poel, who spoke in 1884 and 1887, acquainting the members with his revolutionary ideas on the staging of Shakespeare.[48]

The business meetings of the *Guild* enabled the members to survey the progress that was being made in the campaign for better Church-Stage relations and to plan accordingly. Wherever the *Guild* felt that a formal protest was desirable, Headlam was authorised to write. An example of this aspect of the work was the dispute with Canon Liddon of the *Oxford Churchmen's Union*. Headlam wrote to Liddon requesting that the *Union's* rule forbidding its members to attend the theatre be rescinded. Liddon, however, responded with the charge that "theatres maintained their popularity by trifling with evil" (1891).[49]

The *Guild* had met with similar inflexibility when it sent a deputation to meet Dr Temple, the new Bishop of London, in 1885. Ben Greet, the actor-manager who contributed to every aspect of the movement for religious drama, arranged this meeting - of which a full and colourful account appears in Bettany's *Stuart Headlam*.[50] The Bishop was both ignorant of and hostile to the theatre. But he sat, *New Testament* in hand, denouncing the terrible temptations for young men presented by the unseemly dresses of the dancers! There was a lively exchange between the Bishop and two of the dancers in the deputation; and Temple only just coped with the situation as he was pressed to be more specific about the temptations of their attire! Headlam was forthright and unwavering in his replies to the Bishop's allegations of the theatre's evils but, at the meeting, there was scarcely a sign that attitudes would change.

In later years, Headlam felt that the meeting had achieved its purpose for, in saying goodbye to one of the dancers, the Bishop said: "I am sure you are a good woman; I hope you don't imagine I think any harm of you." To which the startled dancer replied, "I should hope not."[51] Headlam's conviction that people had only to meet for prejudices to gradually disappear, was probably not unfounded.[52]

Headlam's career was astonishing in its energy and diversity. After his dismissal from Bethnal Green, he briefly held a curacy with Father Nihill at Shoreditch (1881-2); but again he was dismissed and his licence to preach removed altogether. Headlam, at Ben Greet's suggestion, reapplied for a licence, but Bishop Temple was particularly unsympathetic after the deputation and refused. It was not until 1898 that the new Bishop of London, Dr Creighton, granted Headlam a licence to preach in the diocese, and Headlam felt it to be a moment of triumph.[53]

Among his many activities Headlam also founded *The Guild of St Matthew*, concerned with the improvement in the standard of the services of the Mass;[54] he edited *The Church Reformer* (1884-95)[55] which had Dr Dearmer[56] as its drama critic and included articles by Sidney Webb and Ramsey Macdonald. *The Anti Puritan League*[57], with G. K. Chesterton among its members, was established at Headlam's home, and Oscar Wilde[58] was brought to that home after his trial. Headlam enjoyed the friendship and support of Ruskin;[59] and thousands of London school children had their first experience of Shakespeare in performance as a result of Headlam's influence on the London School Board. This initiative was responsible for the schools' Shakespeare performances by the Ben Greet Company.[60] Headlam was, in fact, a major contributor to the advance of amateur and educational drama which we will examine briefly in Chapter Two. T. G. Williams wrote:

> The important place that acted drama has come to occupy in the curriculum of the *Evening Institute* is due, principally, to the advocacy of the late Rev. S. G. Headlam, who was convinced of the cultural value of the theatre and of its importance as a religious, social and

educational force. He fought down the prejudice that regarded play-acting as degenerate idling ... The introduction of the study of acted drama, and particularly Shakespeare, into the *Evening Institutes of London* is directly traceable to the championship of its claims and the *Stuart Headlam Shakespeare Association of London* is a fitting memorial to his courageous espousal of the cause.[61]

Religion in Drama

It may seem surprising that the Christian Church, with its central beliefs based in the dramatic events of the *Old* and *New Testaments*, had not, since the Middle Ages, devised plays as a means of evangelisation and celebration. In some predominantly Catholic countries, traditional medieval plays had survived and were performed regularly in the nineteenth century,[62] but no branch of the Church had evolved a new form of stage drama. Victorian Britain had never even seen the performance of a medieval play and, with its distrust of the theatre, there seemed to be little hope of the churches creating a new Christian drama.

No doubt the main reason for the lack of enthusiasm which the churches showed for drama was the general puritan reaction to the theatre. But, in fact, the dramatic potential of the Christian faith had been realised by the Protestant churches and had been formed into an unique and impressive type of unstaged drama: the oratorio. Originally, Handel had composed his *Esther* (circa 1720) as a biblical drama to be staged with full costume, but the Bishop of London objected to the advertised performance at the Haymarket Theatre, and so the score was revised for performance without action.[63] The demand for such musical dramas, which dispensed with the theatrical elements, grew rapidly among the middle classes and reached a peak during the Victorian era. Not only was Handel's *Messiah* extremely popular; Mendelssohn rediscovered the great passion drama of Bach, *The St Matthew Passion*, and wrote his own *Elijah* and *St Paul*. Many lesser composers hastened to cater for the dramatic sense of Victorian Christians; and such compositions as Gaul's *Ruth* enjoyed immense vogue during the late part of the nineteenth century. The drama of the Passion was a favourite subject for oratorio and works like Sir John Stainer's *The Crucifixion* and J. H. Maunder's *From Olivet to Calvary* brought the oratorio within range of the modest ability of the average church choir. The popularity of these two works is scarcely diminished today, particularly in Nonconformist churches and, although musically they owe a good deal to Mendelssohn and even to the parlour song, they have a direct, dramatic quality which is both devotional and moving. The Nativity was another popular subject for oratorio, and the shepherd's plays from the medieval cycles had their Victorian equivalent in Thomas Adams's *The Holy Child* or the numerous works entitled *Bethlehem*.

The Victorian oratorio, or cantata as the shorter works were known, was a product of the Protestant concern with the importance, and sometimes literal interpretation, of *The Bible*. These unstaged dramas invariably consisted of narrative description of events and dramatic dialogue interspersed with meditation and comment from the chorus; and sometimes with hymns for the active involvement of the audience or congregation. The text was always selected from the Scriptures and supplemented by devotional verse.

To some extent this format was imitated when, eventually, a new series of religious plays came to be written for performance in church. J. H. Maunder, the composer of *From Olivet to Calvary*, produced an interesting transitional composition with his cantata *Bethlehem* (1910). Maunder, as well as being a well-known organist, also trained the choir at the Lyceum Theatre; and his *Bethlehem* contains elaborate stage directions and scene settings, together with many dramatic effects such as sheep bells, shepherd's pipes and the sound of an approaching camel caravan.

A renewed interest in the dramatic possibilities of the Christian faith was certainly helped by the oratorio, but two important developments in the commercial theatre also contributed significantly. With the growing middle-class interest in the theatre and a tendency for plays to be increasingly concerned with contemporary problems, it was inevitable that religion would become a topic for the playwright. The Victorian era paid enormous attention to, at least, the outward trappings of religion and the Church had considerable significance as a social and cultural force. Drama could no longer ignore this aspect of life.

Henry Arthur Jones's *Saints and Sinners*, which opened at the Vaudeville Theatre on September 25th 1884, was the archetype for a large number of plays which had sentimental, religious themes.[64] It dealt with the tribulations of a Nonconformist minister, confronted by the degradation of his daughter and the uncharitable behaviour of two of his deacons. Forced into making a public confession of his daughter's shame, the minister loses his chapel and he and his daughter almost starve to death. But finally, the daughter's first, true love returns from Australia "rich with money and forgiveness"[65] and rescues them both. In the original version, Letty, the daughter, dies before she can accept the final offer of marriage, but Jones changed to a happy ending after public protest!

Gerald Weales's *Religion in Modern English Drama*[66] contains an extensive survey of the many plays which followed *Saints and Sinners* in dealing with some aspect of church life. They were invariably melodramatic, usually involved a clergyman and were concerned with behaviour rather than dogma. Jones himself was adamant that the Church was not immune from the exposure of drama, but that the stage was no place for theological issues. In response to the accusations of blasphemy which followed the production of *Saints and Sinners*, Jones wrote an essay, 'Religion and the Stage' which appeared in *The Nineteenth Century*. He criticised those protesting playgoers:

> The idea of human life as being about six-sevenths secular and one-seventh sacred keeps possession of them, and they do not wish to have this convenient fiction disturbed or examined.[67]

On the whole, however, the new brand of religious plays became very popular and had the approval of many clergymen. The plays were strongly moral in tone and good was shown to triumph over evil. If some of the plays attacked puritanism and rigid attitudes within branches of the Church, they probably preached only to the converted because, even by the close of the century, the extreme Catholic and Nonconformist churches still avoided the theatre.

Undoubtedly the religious content of a growing number of plays did enable liberal-minded clergymen to attend the theatre more openly and to recommend their congregations to do the same. Strict censorship during the Victorian age still forbade biblical drama in the theatre, but in 1895 the actor and playwright Wilson Barrett gave clergymen the opportunity to commend unreservedly the evangelical qualities of the theatre. *The Sign of the Cross*, Barrett's drama of the early Church was, in Shaw's words:

> The spectacle of a hardy Roman prefect, a robust soldier and able general, gradually falling under the spell of a pale Christian girl, white and worn with spiritual ecstasy.[68]

H. B. Irving, the son of Sir Henry, played the part of Marcusa Superbus, and Laurence Irving (H. B.'s son), who contributed so substantially to the Canterbury plays, wrote:

> Barrett was the first, perhaps, to discover the box office value of an entertainment that administered the purge of quasi-religious experience in the appetising jam of voluptuous orgies and titillating tortures.[69]

The Sign of the Cross, which Henry Arthur Jones described as "holy-mouth diarrhoea",[70] nevertheless caught the imagination of many churchmen. Dean Hole of Rochester called on the clergy to give their "presence and commendations" to "this most pathetic tragedy";[71] and the Bishop of Truro claimed that Barrett had "purified the stage".[72] *The Sign of the Cross* gave Shaw the original idea for *Androcles and the Lion*,[73] but its immediate successors were a number of spectacular plays of similar style - *Ben Hur*, *The Christian King*,[74] *The Daughters of Babylon*, *The Judgement of Pharaoh*, *Quo Vadis* and *The Sorrows of Satan* - all of which have had their more recent equivalents in Hollywood. These melodramas enjoyed brief popularity at the turn of the century and may well have convinced churchmen of the desirability of expressing their faith in dramatic form.

With actors playing the parts of clergymen or Christian martyrs; clergymen extolling the virtues of the theatre; and a growing awareness of drama as an educative force, the Anglican Church was ready to create its own drama. The first play written for church performance in modern times was the Rev. H. Cresswell's *The Conversion of England*, which was produced in St Peters, Vauxhall in 1898 - the year after Irving's reading of *Becket* in the Chapter House at Canterbury. "It has come at last," said Shaw, reviewing a second performance of the play in Church House, Westminster for *The Saturday Review*, "The parson has carried the war into the enemy's country."[75] *The Church Times* remarked:

> It is a step towards the re-establishment of relations which originally existed between the Church and Stage. Perhaps a great future lies before Religious Plays, for the unimaginative Englishman learns far more readily through the eye than through the ear.[76]

Although we must concede Gerald Weales's point that Shaw's review contains "no understandable account of the play itself",[77] Shaw does provide sufficient information to deduce that *The Conversion of England* was a play in two parts, and consisted of a series of scenes depicting the spread of Christianity in England, played against a background produced by painted backcloths. It is not possible to tell from the tone of Shaw's review whether he is patronising or serious in his approval of the play; but the review raises some important issues concerning the nature of religious drama, and warrants quotation both for these and the more amusing aspects of the production. Speaking of his long-held conviction that the Services of the Church rival many plays for sheer theatricality, Shaw continues:

> He [the cleric] is acting them with scenery, costumes, 'limelight', music, processions and everything complete in Church House great halls which hold £200 easily. Not that he charges for admission . . . And the view is not obstructed by matinée hats; for before the performance a clergyman, clad with the whole authority of the Church of England, steps before the curtain and orders those hats to come off![78]

Shaw then introduces a typical attack on the contemporary theatre as he moves to an interesting topic:

> To say that the clergymen who enact the miracle plays speak better than actors is nothing; for at present, all the professions and most of the trades can make the same boast. But the difference is something more than a technical one. The tone of a man's voice is the tone of his life - the average clergyman's utterance betrays his ignorance, his conceit, his class-narrowness, his snobbery . . . But the clergymen who are coming into the field against the [theatre] managers are not average clergymen. *The Conversion of England* on their playbills means

something more than the title of an entertainment, and that something is not the conversion of England's follies and vices into box office returns. At the Westminster performance last Saturday the actors spoke as men speak in the presence of greater matters than their own personal success. You may go to the theatre for months without hearing that particular effect.[79]

Shaw adds that there was no applause at the performance and that the effect was "highly beneficial."[80] He then turns to the substance of the play, but claims he is unable to make a balanced judgement because:

I came to it from a round of duties which included such works as *Never Again* at the Vaudeville, so that the mere force of contrast made it perfectly enthralling to me. When the British Bishop, objecting to the Roman missionaries, exclaimed: 'The whole world is heretic! There is no knowledge of the truth anywhere except at Bangor', I shrieked with laughter. No doubt it was not a first-class joke; but after the dreary equivoques of the farcical comedians it was manna in the wilderness.[81]

Shaw then gives a further sample of the dialogue and suggests that the character of Queen Bertha was a caricature by Cresswell "of some Mrs Poudie who opposed him in his early curacies",[82] Shaw's review then leaves the play for wider issues and he fires broadsides at censorship and prejudice towards the actors:

The Conversion of England evades censorship by not taking money at the door. Otherwise the Lord Chamberlain would probably suppress it, unless Mr Cresswell consented to cut out the religious passages.[83]

Then, with the suggestion that Christ,

would not have objected to go to the theatre on Sunday with Mary Magdalene if Jerusalem had been Paris",[84]

Shaw concludes with a Headlam-like challenge to the clergy:

Never mind the mote in the actor's eye: you will find plenty of beams behind the spectacles of your own congregations.[85]

The Conversion of England had a number of implications for the future development of religious drama in Britain. From the outset, drama for church performance was not generally to be governed by financial restraints and was therefore free to evolve along experimental or commercially less popular lines. The absence of applause and the suggestion that actors were dealing with "greater matters than their own personal success" indicates an unusual and unique attitude to the performance, both from the audience and the players; the play takes on the quality of an act of worship - and therefore becomes difficult to judge by theatrical standards.

Because of the non-theatrical nature of church buildings, the emphasis is on simplicity of staging and sincerity of performance and Christian history emerges as a rich source of dramatic material. There are also signs that Christian plays may lead the way to a more sensible attitude to censorship. Many who watched the play may well have asked with Henry Arthur Jones: "If the Pulpit loses its power, will the Drama take its place?"[86]

The Church and the Stage in the Twentieth Century

The closing years of the nineteenth century provided substantial evidence of the change of attitude that was necessary before an event such as Masefield's play, *The Coming of Christ*, could take place. Irving's knighthood and his reading in the Chapter House; Headlam's renewed licence to preach; Barrett's *The Sign of the Cross*; and Cresswell's *The Conversion of England* were all indications that the Church and Drama were moving closer together.

Headlam's *Church and Stage Guild* quietly ceased functioning just after its twenty-first anniversary, on Ascension Day 1900. Surveying the *Guild's* achievements, Headlam explained the cessation of its activities:

The 'new charity,' as Ruskin called it, made headway, and by about the beginning of the century we could consider our work done - prejudice against the stage removed, the arts of the theatre vindicated, friendly relations between clergy and players established, and the ban against the clergyman's association with stage-folk and frequenting the playhouse or music hall lifted. But it was a long battle lasting twenty-one years.[87]

Headlam was, of course, speaking only of the Anglican Church, and the controversy surrounding Irving's burial in Westminster Abbey suggests that his claims may have been slightly exaggerated. But Ben Greet, whose professional company performed at one of the Canterbury Cathedral festivals,[88] was convinced of the importance of Headlam's work for the stage:

The *Guild* did a great deal of good to my profession, especially to the younger actors, and it is not too much to say that its founder helped largely to remove prejudice against the stage and the stage-player. [89]
The Canterbury Plays relied heavily for their success on professional actors and producers, and would have been impossible to stage had it not been for Headlam's achievement.

A new organisation, the *Actors' Church Union*, was established shortly after the start of the century and continues its work today. It provides chaplains who are available for the needs of actors throughout the country. The Union appointed the Rev. Donald Hole as its first, full-time organising secretary and between 1900 and 1920 he toured the country preaching, as Headlam had done, on 'The Church and the Stage'. Leading figures from the theatre such as H. B. Irving and Sybil Thorndike helped to establish and support the *Union*; and this organisation, like its predecessor, tended to attract actors and clergy with High Church leanings.[90]

Shortly after the founding of the *Actors' Church Union*, Randall Davidson became Archbishop of Canterbury. Davidson had been a member of the *Young Clergy Society* with Stuart Headlam and when Headlam was establishing the *Church and Stage Guild*, was himself Archbishop Tait's chaplain. Davidson had similar socialist sympathies to Headlam and had even persuaded Queen Victoria to read Henry George's *Progress and Poverty*, "which she found difficult."[91] He had supported Headlam in his work for the *Church and Stage Guild* and had been Bishop of Rochester when the Thorndike family were living in the Cathedral precincts.[92]

Archbishop Davidson did not go to the theatre frequently, but he was not ashamed to do so. He liked Shakespeare and Gilbert and Sullivan, but it was not until the last few years of his life that he saw a modern play, Drinkwater's *Abraham Lincoln*. He was also present at one of the first performances of Shaw's *St Joan* in 1924 and wrote of his appreciation to Sybil Thorndike, with whom he had kept in touch since his Rochester days. The actress responded in a rambling letter in which she acknowledged the encouragement that Davidson's presence in the audience had represented to those who were seeking to establish a truly Christian drama:

26

It [*St Joan*] is the first great Christian play I've ever known, we wish we could find more such plays - but they will come, I feel, because people want them.[93]

Randall Davidson's career as Archbishop spanned a period of considerable advance in Christian drama. Shortly before he resigned his archbishopric, a Board of Education report, *Drama in Adult Education* (1927), mentioned the churches as one of the chief agents for the encouragement of drama:

In the Middle Ages the Church was the protagonist of the drama and used it as a means of religious education. It would almost appear that this situation is arising today. [94]

But there were some developments about which even the liberal-minded Davidson was not too happy: particularly the advent of the biblical play. As Archbishop, Davidson was frequently consulted by the Lord Chamberlain on the question of stage censorship. Until 1913 there had been a total ban on stage plays dealing with biblical subjects. For some years there had been pressure on the Lord Chamberlain to reverse this ruling. As early as 1893 Henry Arthur Jones had written:

I see no reason why the great human stories of *The Bible* should not be utilised on our stage . . . The English Theatre could not possibly make a worse use of *The Bible* than the sects have done, or misunderstood it so completely. [95]

In 1913 a licence was granted to Beerbohm Tree for a production of Louis N. Parker's *Joseph and His Brethren*. The position of the censor had been somewhat weakened by the Parliamentary Committee under Sir Hubert Samuel, which had investigated stage censorship in 1909, following a storm of protest when Shaw's *The Showing Up of Blanco Posnet* failed to obtain a licence.[96] A greater liberality was also brought about by the revival of medieval drama at the beginning of the century and by the showing of the American film version of the life of Christ, *From the Manger to the Cross*, at the Albert Hall in 1912. The film was not subject to censorship and, as *The Times* pointed out, "helped to prove that irreverence and blasphemy are not essential features of a theatrical display."[97]

A trickle of biblical plays followed *Joseph and His Brethren*: Arnold Bennett's *Judith* (1919), Clemence Dane's *Naboth's Vineyard*

(1925) and D. H. Lawrence's *David* (1926) were all given a licence. But Randall Davidson expressed his disquiet in a letter to the Lord Chamberlain which showed a very clear grasp of the issues involved:

The Archbishop of Canterbury to the Earl of Cromer
13th November 1924

I return herewith the Play *Judas Iscariot*. I wish they did not write these plays, for the men who write them are not men qualified to handle these great subjects greatly. This good man has handled it feebly but quite harmlessly unless we were to say that nothing of the kind could be on the Stage at all, and that position can no longer be sustained. So far therefore as I am concerned I should raise no criticism to your giving him a licence. My belief is that the Play is so thin that it could not attract great attention. One dare not, however, say this when the title is of so sensational a sort and the whole subject is so unfamiliar to quantities of our fellow country-men that they imagine Mr Thurston to be an original theological thinker, which is very far from being the case ... I am rather glad that Bernard Shaw does not take a Play of that sort in hand for he might raise for us much more perilous issues.[98]

As we shall see in the chapter on verse drama, a number of writers of very serious intention and technical originality were, by 1924, beginning to write religious plays. One of these playwrights was John Masefield. Two years later the Archbishop also had his first dealings with Masefield, in his rôle of adviser to the Lord Chamberlain. Masefield had submitted his play *The Trial of Jesus* to the Lord Chamberlain for a licence. This play, however, raised a problem that had not previously been encountered in a modern work: it involved the appearance of the person of Christ. *The Trial of Jesus* was accordingly sent to Davidson for his comments and it is obvious, from his letter to the Lord Chamberlain, that he was greatly exercised as to the right course of action. Finally, though conceding that the play had been written with great reverence and scriptural accuracy, the Archbishop concluded that:

I do not think protest would be awakened by the definite ruling that the Figure of our Blessed Lord Himself must not be produced in any drama which you sanction.[99]

In 1924, Randall Davidson had also taken the step which was to bring about the performance of *The Coming of Christ* and the other Canterbury Plays. He appointed George Bell, his chaplain, to the vacant office of Dean of Canterbury. In the same year, Davidson was reminded of the progress made by the Church in its attitude to drama when he heard of the serious illness of his old friend, Stuart Headlam. The Archbishop wrote to Headlam of his admiration for the work he had done in education, with the trade unions and the Church and Stage Guild; and expressed his concern for Headlam's health. Headlam was deeply moved and wrote to Davidson, "Now I can say I have won" and on November 18, 1924 he died.[100]

Davidson had made a substantial contribution to the deeper sympathy which the Church had gradually extended towards drama. But he had reached the limit of his vision. It was therefore against his advice that the new Dean of Canterbury and John Masefield collaborated in the remarkable production of *The Coming of Christ*. Headlam would doubtless have approved.

Randall Davidson, Stuart Headlam and the new Dean of Canterbury, George Bell, were all examples of clergymen to whom Shaw referred in his review of *The Conversion of England*. They were not average clergymen: they created, rather than followed, public opinion. The importance of their work is not confined to a better relationship between Church and Stage although, in their day, the approval of the Church was vital to the theatre. Their main contribution was in creating a new type of audience, who went to the theatre expecting the drama to deal with serious issues. The Canterbury plays were only a small product of this expectation.

The battle against prejudice was not yet won, however: in 1936, for example, the great pioneer of Drama-in-Education, Peter Slade, approached Westminster and Ely Cathedrals for permission for his Parable Players to perform there, but the authorities there were "shocked by such an idea"[101], even though London schools and churches had hosted performances.

Notes to Chapter One

1. Laurence Irving confirms this. Tape Recording 1, see Bibliography.
2. Peter Leyson, *London Theatres::A Short History and Guide* (Lon. 1970), 50.
3. Laurence Irving quotes this contemporary description of the C19th music hall, The Vic at Oxford in *The Successors* (London 1967), 134.
4. Allardyce Nicoll, *A History of English Drama 1660-1900, Vol. V, Late Nineteenth Century Drama* (Cambridge 1967), 15-17.
5. Donald Hole, The *Church and the Stage* (London 1934).
6. Laurence Irving, *The Successors* (London 1967), 237-238.
7. See Patrick Howarth, *The Year is 1851* (London 1951), 114.
8. Allardyce Nicoll, *A History of English Drama 1660-1900, op. cit.,* 17.
9/10/11/12/13/14/15/16. Laurence Irving, *Henry Irving: The Actor and His World* (London 1951), 251, 257, 534, 634, 277, 288, 524.
17/18. See L. Irving, *The Successors* (London 1967), 67-8, 134-5, 70-1.
19. Elizabeth Sprigge, *Sybil Thorndike Casson* (London 1971).
20. Eric Jones-Evans, 'Henry Irving in Kent', *Kent Life X, 11* (1971), 29-30.
21. Laurence Irving, *Henry Irving* (London 1951), 608.
22. W. S. Gilbert, *A Stage Play* (Laurel) and *British Drama: The Nineteenth Century* (New York 1967), 160.
23. Stuart Headlam, *Church Reformer III, 121,* June 1884, attacked Archbishop Benson for expressing this view.
24. See especially Alex R. Vidler, *F. D. Maurice & Company,* (London 1966).
25. Donald Hole, *op. cit.,* 14.
26. F. G. Bettany, *Stuart Headlam* (London 1926), 75.
27. Kathleen Bainbridge-Bell & June Ottaway, *A Brief Historical Sketch of the Religious Drama Society of Great Britain* (London 1957), 4.
28. Allardyce Nicoll, *A History of English Drama 1660-1900,* op. cit., 17.
29. F. G. Bettany, *op.cit.,* 103.
30. See especially the introduction to Act 1.
31. F.G.Bettany, *op. cit.,* 125.
32/33. See Roger Lloyd,*The Church of England 1900-1965* (Lon. 1966), 290.
34. See Kathleen Bainbridge-Bell and June Ottaway who erroneously refer to the 'Rev.N.O.Nihill' instead of 'Rev.N.D.Nihill'.
35. See Alex R.Vidler, *F. D. Maurice & Company* (London 1966), 264 & 277.
36. Quoted in F. G. Bettany, *op. cit.,* 20-21.
37. See Chapter 8.
38. F. G. Bettany, *op. cit.,* 28.
39. *Ibid.,* 32.; also Geoffrey Rowell, *Hell & the Victorians* (London 1974), 76-89.

40/41/42. Bettany, *op. cit.*, 37, 43-44.

43. *Ibid.*, 98; also quoted in Donald Hole, *op.cit.*, 16.

44/45/46/47/48. Bettany, *op. cit.*, 58, 97, 59, 101, 104-5.

49. *Ibid.*, 107. A paper in reply to Liddon by the actress Ella Dietz, was published as a pamphlet.

50. *Ibid.*, 54-68. The meeting was reported in the *Church Reformer*, October, 1885, of which Headlam was the editor.

51. Bettany, *op. cit.*, 68-69.

52. *cp.* Headlam's attitude to the conduct of meetings of the Guild.

53. Bettany, *op. cit.*, 70-71.

54. See Bettany, *op. cit.*, 84-89 and Roger Lloyd, *op. cit.*, 290-1.

55. Bettany, *op. cit.*, 109ff, and the introduction to Shaw's *Candida*.

56. Husband of Mabel Dearmer, founder of the *Morality Play Society*, see below, p41.

57. Bettany, *op. cit.*, 128-9.

58. The first person to meet Wilde from jail was Ricketts, designer of the first Canterbury Play, see Appendix.

59/60. Bettany, *op. cit.*, 102, 196-200

61. T. G. Williams 'Drama as Education', *Theatre and Stage*, ed. Harold Downs (London, undated), 1, 242.

62. e.g. The *Pastorelas*, popular in Spanish-speaking countries.

63. Percy A. Scholes, *The Oxford Companion to Music* (London 1955), 729.

64/65/66/67. Gerald Weales, *op. cit.*, 3, 3-37, 4.

68/69. Quoted in Laurence Irving, *The Successors* (London 1967), 258.

70/71/72. Gerald Weales, *op. cit.*, 25, 26.

73. See Laurence Irving, *The Successors* (London 1967).

74. A review of this play appears in J. T. Grein, *Dramatic Criticism 1902-3* (London 1904), 197-200.

75. G. B. Shaw, *Our Theatre in the Nineties* (London 1932), iii, 293.

76. Quoted in Kathleen Bainbridge-Bell & June Ottaway, *op. cit.*, 4.

77. Gerald Weales, *op. cit.*, 94.

78/79/80/81/82/83/84/85. G. B. Shaw, *op. cit.*, 293, 294, 295, 297.

86. Henry Arthur Jones, *The Renascence of the English Drama* (London 1895), 131.

87. Bettany, *op. cit.*, 108.

88. See Chapter 4.

89. Bettany, *op. cit.*, 103. See Allardyce Nicholl's view that the *Guild* was merely an expression of, and not a cause of, the changed attitude. Nicholl, *op. cit.*, 17.

90. See Donald Hole, *op. cit.*

91. Bettany, *op. cit.*, 84.

92/93. See G. K. A. Bell, *Randall Davidson - Archbishop of Canterbury* (London 1935), ii, 1212.

94. Quoted in S. S. Shrubsole and S. Beddow, *Dramatic Production, A Practical Guide for Free Churchmen and Others* (London 1932), 9.

95. Henry Arthur Jones, *op. cit.*, 123.

96/97. Gerald Weales, *op. cit.*, 32.

98/99. See G. K. A. Bell, *op. cit.*, 121-4.

100. Bettany, *op. cit.*, 243.

101. Peter Slade in a letter to the author, i/08/2000.

2

From Medieval to Modern Morality

An important incentive to playwrights and churchmen who were trying to establish a new form of Christian drama at the beginning of the twentieth century, was the renewal of interest in the performance of medieval religious plays. The existence of these Christian verse-dramas was known to nineteenth century scholars and men of the theatre, and a number of mystery and morality plays had been published, although no agreement had been reached on the precise definition of the two terms, in collections of old plays.[1] Irving referred to such plays when he appealed to churchmen for a renewal of the friendly relations between Church and Stage.[2] Shaw spoke of "mystery plays" when he reviewed the performance of a modern play in a church.[3] However, neither Irving, Shaw nor any of the scholars who debated the nature and origins of the morality play, had ever seen a medieval play in performance. The plays were merely interesting curiosities that were presumed to have no commercial possibilities or contemporary relevance.

The man who was responsible for a change not only in this view, but in the whole direction of modern theatre performances, was

William Poel. Poel made his first appearance as an actor in 1876, but he was never, according to Lewis Casson,[4] a good actor, and it was as a producer and scholar that he made his mark. His main determination appears to have been to break away from the proscenium arch and to re-create the conditions of the Elizabethan theatre. He was concerned that, in every respect, modern performances of old plays should reproduce, as far as possible, the original conditions and this led to his passionate regard for the accuracy of the text, and an insistence that a play's original form should be respected. His objectives brought him into direct opposition to the current trends in the commercial theatre of his day but, undeterred, he founded the *Elizabethan Stage Society* in 1894.[5]

Poel was the producer of the first modern performances of Marlowe's *Dr Faustus* and Milton's *Samson Agonistes*, but in some respects he was a rather surprising source for the revival of medieval Christian drama. He was something of a sceptic, generally anti-clerical and violently anti-Catholic. Yet he apparently had a deep respect for the person of Christ.[6] After the sudden death of his mother in 1901, Poel was recommended by his friend, A. W. Ward, to find comfort in reading the medieval play *Everyman*. Poel was greatly moved and resolved to produce the play in suitable surroundings.[7] He had already utilised a number of halls and courtyards and it was a comparatively small step for him to visualise the dramatic potential of ecclesiastical buildings. He first approached the Dean and Chapter of Westminster Abbey for permission to stage *Everyman* in the cloisters, but ignorance and bigotry prevented that august body from identifying itself with the revival of a remarkable Christian play, and permission was refused.[8]

Had Poel's next approach been successful, the course of drama at Canterbury might well have been different, for Poel contacted Dean Farrar of Canterbury, who had previously arranged for Sir Henry Irving to read from Tennyson's *Becket* in the Chapter House.[9] Farrar, a liberal-minded clergyman and popular author, was enthusiastic about the idea of a performance of *Everyman* in Canterbury Cathedral, but this scheme met with strong opposition from the Chapter and Farrar's acceptance of Poel's proposition was over-ruled. Poel was still determined that *Everyman* should be performed under suitable conditions, and he eventually arranged for his *Elizabethan Stage Society* to introduce medieval drama to the modern world in the Master's Courtyard of the London Charter-house; once a monastery but now a home for pensioners.[10]

Everyman was first performed on July 13th, 1901. The style of this open-air production was in marked contrast to the current trends in the commercial theatre at that time and created a sensation. The commercial theatre was still dominated by the pro-scenium arch and the footlights, which clearly separated the actors on stage from the audience; but Poel's staging was an imaginative combination of mansions and levels, representing Heaven, Earth and specific locations, such as the grave. At no point were the audience far from the action and entrances were made through the auditorium.[11] Almost thirty years later, the Canterbury Plays were staged in very similar conditions to Poel's *Everyman* and many features of their production can be traced back to his pioneering work.

Everyman was an unqualified success and, together with *The Sacrifice of Isaac* from the *Chester Cycle*, which Poel added to the programme, received reviews testifying to a moving and unique theatrical experience.[12] The production was repeated the following weekend and, because of increasing public demand, again the next week. A fortnight later, *Everyman* was performed in the quadrangle of University College, Oxford and in the autumn at the Royal Pavilion, Brighton. By the following season, *Everyman* was established as a stage classic and was being staged commercially at both St George's Hall and the Imperial Theatre, London.

After the success of *Everyman* in London, Poel appears to have lost interest in the play; and the production was taken over by Ben Greet, an extraordinary character whose name appears in every one of the chapters in this book which trace the origins of the Canterbury Plays.[13] Greet organised a lucrative tour of the provinces with *Everyman*, a task for which he was ideally suited because of his long experience as a travelling actor-manager with Shakespearian productions, and his establishment of the open-air performances in Regent's Park.

When the American impresario Charles Frohman arranged a tour of the United States of America for *Everyman*, Greet took with him the young actress Sybil Thorndike to play Beauty or Good Deeds. The play opened in New York in October 1902 with Edith Wynne Matthison as Everyman, a part which, rather surprisingly, she had played ever since Poel's first production. The choice of a woman as Everyman, which would no doubt meet with considerable approval today, not only provided Shaw with the idea for the character of Ann Whitefield in *Man and Superman* (1903),[14] but also enabled Sybil Thorndike to play her first leading rôle in a religious play when Edith Wynne Matthison fell ill.[15] Russell Thorndike, Sybil's brother, joined Greet on a subsequent tour and all three were to make a contribution at Canterbury.[16]

After an unpromising start, *Everyman* was as popular in the United States as it had been in England;[17] and Greet added to his programme a nativity play, *The Star of Bethlehem*, which he had adapted from the *Wakefield Shepherd's Play*.[18] Both *Everyman* and *The Star of Bethlehem* remained great favourites of Greet and in 1915, and for twelve years following, he included one or other of them in the repertoire at the Old Vic,[19] a theatre which provided many of the professional actors who took part in the Canterbury Plays.

Granville-Barker wrote to E. Harcourt Williams[20] describing another offshoot of Poel's original production of *Everyman*.[21] Granville-Barker, a disciple of Poel in his advocacy of the platform stage, had visited Saltzburg where the German director, Max Reinhardt, had staged Hofmannsthal's *Jedermann* in the Cathedral square. *Jedermann* was a direct result of *Everyman*, for Reinhardt had seen Poel's production at the Charterhouse in 1901 and had returned to Germany to persuade Hofmannsthal to join him in a similar venture. The performances of the play in Saltzburg became an annual event and formed the basis of the Saltzburg Festival.[22] Granville-Barker felt that *Jedermann* failed to achieve the deep, spiritual experience of *Everyman*. "At no time did I want to go on my knees," he wrote to Harcourt Williams, "and I could hardly keep from it when old Poel first did it."[23] Nevertheless, it was the Saltzburg Festival which provided George Bell, Dean of Canterbury in 1928, with the idea of establishing a Canterbury Festival in which drama would play a large part.[24]

The first Canterbury Festival of 1929 included a performance of *Everyman* directed by another important associate of Poel, W. Nugent Monck, who had taken part in the original Charterhouse production of 1901. Monck became, probably, the most important exponent of medieval plays after Poel's initial breakthrough. In 1905 he formed the *English Drama Society* which gave the first modern performance of the interlude, *Youth* - a highly successful venture, which culminated in a performance at Court before Queen Alexandra. In 1906 Monck produced the nativity plays from the *Chester Cycle*, but in 1909 he achieved notoriety, and received a sharp reminder of lingering anti-stage puritanism, when he considered staging the *Ludus Coventriae*. His production would have involved introducing the figure of Christ and Monck was actually threatened with prosecution under the Blasphemy Act. It was not, in fact, until 1952 that he managed to obtain the Lord Chamberlain's permission for a public performance of the play.[25]

Monck could consider himself unfortunate in being threatened with prosecution, as the appearance of God in the original production of *Everyman* had never become an issue in England. But, as we shall see, the question of enacting Christ or the Deity became a major concern to those seeking to establish a new Christian drama.[26] To some extent, the problem could be overcome by private performances;[27] and it is reasonable to suggest that whenever the Deity or Christ was represented by an actor in the years between 1901-1930, the hostile were usually quietened by the reverence and taste of the performance. The issue was, however, only part of the much wider impact made by the rediscovery of medieval drama, an impact which can be conveniently summarised as *intention, style* and *staging*.

The intention of the medieval morality was essentially didactic, and this feature had a particular significance for the theatre at the beginning of the twentieth century. Drama, it was claimed by progressive thinkers, was an educational force and a means of social teaching; the newly-discovered morality play *Everyman* was a supreme example of the effectiveness of a drama of ideas. Indeed, the very characters themselves were an embodiment of an idea, and even when the action was localised, it was universal in significance.

If the religious truths which *Everyman* and the mystery plays tried to teach were to be profound, it was, of course, necessary to present the idea of God or Christ in a compelling, dramatic form. But as Robert Potter points out, this presupposes a very different type of theatre from the predominant style of English theatre at the turn of the century. Audiences in the commercial theatre expected to see an actor identifying himself with, and almost becoming, the character he was playing. In medieval drama, the actor was to 'present' a character:

... to an audience whose attention is directed towards a higher, and invisible, hypothetical truth which the visible actors present.[28]

The act of presenting a character, who might be the embodiment of an idea, enables complex religious beliefs to be presented in dramatic form. The focus is no longer on the behaviour or motivation of the character, but on the truth he stands for. It is therefore unnecessary for the actor to create a believable 'person' - instead, he must draw attention to the statements he is making in action or in words. Action may, in fact, be minimal and symbolic and the words spoken in a highly formalised way. Thus removed from naturalism and the need to 'become' the part he is playing in a human sense, the actor can, if necessary, even present God.

This approach to acting ran contrary to the naturalistic style that concentrated on characterisation and truthfulness in performance pioneered by Stanislavsky. Although his ideas had not become the basis of an actor's training in England at the turn of the century, there was already in the theatre an emphasis on creating believable characters. One obvious result of this difference in approach was that amateur actors, speakers of verse and even clergymen were probably better equipped than some professionally experienced actors, to act in medieval plays.

Many playwrights who wrote religious plays in the wake of *Everyman* also found that the figures of God or Christ were essential to their purpose or that, in some way, it was necessary to represent the transcendent. The idea that an actor was merely presenting the figure and not claiming to 'be' the character was particularly important for the acceptability of their work. What the didactic aspect of the newly-discovered medieval drama amounted to was a deliberate attempt to discuss and present religious doctrine; a topic which both the nineteenth century Church, as a whole, and the Victorian theatre considered to be beyond the scope of, and inappropriate to, drama. After the revival of *Everyman* it therefore became increasingly difficult for clergymen to condemn drama as a thing of wickedness and, indeed, an increasing number of clergymen began to see evangelical possibilities in revivals of other medieval plays and in the writing of new 'moralities'. Christian playwrights were equally convinced that doctrinal aspects of their faith could occupy a central position in their work for the stage.

But, as Granville-Barker's letter to Harcourt Williams testifies, the intention of *Everyman* was not merely didactic. The original play, and Poel's careful production, constituted an actual religious experience in which the actors and audience joined in devotion and worship. Other medieval plays revived in the following years proved to have the same quality, a blend of recounting an event and celebrating it. The traditional barrier between actors and audience ceased to exist and the experience of the play itself was shown to be more like a ritual in which a known and loved truth is re-affirmed. This feature of the medieval plays had immediate importance for playwrights like Yeats and Bottomley, who were investigating the ritual elements of theatre[29] but, at the same time, it suggested to other playwrights and to high churchmen that the roots of medieval drama, and of any new religious drama, lay in the Liturgy.[30] Thus in the years succeeding Poel's *Everyman*, we have Bottomley's experiments in ritual verse drama; Eliot's *A Dialogue on Dramatic Poetry* (1928), in which he discusses the relation of drama to the Mass; and, in the same year, the first Canterbury play, Masefield's *The Coming of Christ*, at once a play and an act of worship and described as "a new morality."

In practical staging terms, the different relationship between actor and audience envisaged by medieval plays was particularly suited to the platform stage of which Poel was an advocate. The situation in which actors address and teach their audience and join with them in an act of worship suggests that actors and audience can see each other and are in physical proximity. The dividing line between actor and audience, as it exists on a proscenium stage, is replaced by an intermingling of the cast and spectators.

In *Everyman,* Poel extended his use of the platform stage to encompass a series of platforms and acting areas. Producers who followed his lead, were therefore inspired to explore the staging possibilities offered by ecclesiastical buildings. Generally, they found that chancel steps, pulpits and the rood screen provided a variety of effective levels and backgrounds. The main feature which contributed to the quality of the Canterbury Plays was that the building itself added a dimension to the drama; but the revival of medieval plays coincided with, and partly created, a fashion for split-level staging. Such purpose-built, small theatres as John Masefield's at Boar's Hill reflected this influence.[31] The absence of wing space in non-theatrical buildings also required a different approach to the important question of effective entrances and exits for actors. In the early years of this century, therefore, there was a great deal of experiment with entrances through the auditorium,[32] processions[33] and finally with plays specifically written to exploit these qualities.

Stylistically, medieval drama had three most noticeable influences on twentieth century playwrights. The revival added an important stimulus to the growth of new verse-drama because of the impact made by the lively, irregular and non-literary language of the early plays. Medieval verse was entirely different from the pseudo-Elizabethan, blank verse which was common in the Victorian theatre. Its most obvious quality was its apparent simplicity and yet it combined both biblical paraphrase with a simulation of colloquial speech. The language of *Everyman* certainly made a profound impression on Masefield, whose play *The Coming of Christ* shows many similarities with the medieval play, and on Eliot, who used the neutral verse of *Everyman* as a linguistic model for his Canterbury play, *Murder in the Cathedral.*

One particular device which religious playwrights borrowed from medieval plays was the opening speech by God or angels: a celestial survey of the earthly scene. The purpose of the heavenly prologue to the earthly action was to show that the life of mankind is part of God's plan and the problem of presenting this concept in dramatic form recurs throughout the Canterbury plays. The use of an area of the stage to represent Heaven and the introduction of God into the drama created problems of censorship and provoked accusations of blasphemy, but several playwrights evaded the issue by placing man's destiny in the hands of innocuous angels.[34]

A further line of development suggested by medieval plays, especially by the moralities, was the inclusion of allegorical characters. The immediate effect of a drama which included such figures as Death, Beauty or Goods and Riches was to universalise the significance of the action. Playwrights also became increasingly aware that the action of a play need not consist of the behaviour of the characters with their various motivations. Ritualistic action could point to a meaning beyond and could, in some respects, have far greater significance than realistic action. In the same way the heightened, ritualistic language of Liturgy could be seen to create meanings outside the scope of naturalistic dialogue.

The various influences which the revival of medieval drama had on Christian writers at the beginning of the twentieth century can be seen first, at a fairly crude level, in the work of Laurence Housman and of two women playwrights, A. M. Buckton and Mabel Dearmer. As we have already seen, the nativity plays from the mystery cycles were among the first medieval plays to become popular in modern times, and it was with their modern nativity plays that these three playwrights achieved their initial success. Housman's *Bethlehem* (1902), Buckton's *Eager Heart* (1904) and Dearmer's *The Soul of the World* (1911), together with Robert Hugh Benson's *A Mystery Play in Honour of the Nativity of Our Lord* (1907) were all primarily intended for performance in church or hall and, like the increasing number of popular and unsophisticated church oratorios,[35] envisaged an audience who joined in the devotions and the hymn singing.

Housman, the writer of the first modern nativity play (if we exclude Reverend Nihill's *Bethlehem Tableaux*[36]), immediately ran into trouble with the censor and failed to obtain a licence for public performance of his *Bethlehem*.[37] Housman was, however, determined to show that it is possible for the drama to come near, without irreverence, to the central truths of Christianity[38] and he formed the *Bethlehem Society* in order to enable Edward Gordon Craig to produce the play at a private performance in the Great Hall of London University. Housman's intention that the play should

... startle men's minds to a realisation of whether for them Christianity is a curious relic of the past or a truth still living and central[39]

probably holds true for many subsequent playwrights using biblical material and certainly for the Canterbury playwrights. But, as Gerald Weales has indicated, Housman's attempts to give contemporaneity and humanity to the play through the rustic simplicity of his shepherds is a great weakness that has often been repeated.[40] When Masefield, with his penchant for "old gaffers"[41] came to write his Canterbury nativity, *The Coming of Christ*, he tried a novel solution to the problem by presenting his shepherds as articulate mystics or revolutionaries.[42]

Unlike Housman, who produced a substantial body of religious drama between 1902 and 1950, A. M. Buckton's only surviving published work is *Eager Heart*. Such was the popularity achieved, however, that it became, in the words of Percy Dearmer, "almost an institution."[43] *The Incorporated Society of Eager Heart* ensured annual performances of the play (including a special production by Ben Greet at Sadlers' Wells in 1933) until the outbreak of World War II. With its characters, Eager Fame and Eager Sense who try to divert Eager Heart from her purpose, and its prologue and epilogue pointing the moral and challenging the audience to respond, the play is clearly derivative of *Everyman*. This does not mean its success was entirely undeserved. The plot is simple but dramatically effective; the character of Eager Heart herself is genuinely appealing. She has made preparations for the coming of a new king whose appearance she sincerely expects; but, when a poor and desolate family call at her house, she feels impelled to share with them the food and shelter she has made ready. When she leaves the house she meets the shepherds and the wise men, all of whom have failed to understand the true significance of the expected king. Eager Heart brings them to her home where they find the poor family grouped in a tableaux of the traditional nativity scene.[44] The significance of the scene appears also to have eluded the Lord

Chamberlain. For, as Laurence Housman rather bitterly commented, the play obtained a licence because "he never noticed that the Holy Family was in the cast."[45]

It was after producing a performance of Housman's *Bethlehem* at St Mary's, Primrose Hill, that Mabel Dearmer decided to write her own religious plays. She was married to the vicar of St Mary's, Dr Percy Dearmer, a well-known hymn writer and drama critic for the Rev. Stuart Headlam's *Church Reformer*;[46] she always preferred to be known as Mrs Percy Dearmer. Mabel Dearmer's first play, *The Soul of the World*, was the opening production of her newly formed *Morality Play Society* which later included works by Clifford Bax and W. B. Yeats in its repertoire. *The Soul of the World* has certain important similarities with Masefield's Canterbury play, for it is a nativity play which opens in Heaven. Here Eternity indicates that an event will shortly take place that will enable Eternity to enter Time.[47] The whole play is, in fact, set against a debate between Time and Eternity as to who rules the world. To this interesting idea, Mabel Dearmer adds another element that was explored in such Canterbury plays as Christopher Hassall's *Christ's Comet* - for the wise men and the shepherds come eventually to Calvary where Mary explains to them, and the audience, the significance of Christ's birth and death.

After writing another Christmas mystery, *The Playmate* (1911), Mabel turned to the *Old Testament* story of Joseph which also provided Louis N. Parker with the subject for the first biblical play to obtain the Lord Chamberlain's licence, *Joseph and His Brethren* (1913)[48] and more recently formed the basis of the first *Old Testament* rock musical, *Joseph and the Amazing Technicolour Dreamcoat* (1968). Mabel Dearmer's play, *The Dreamer* (1912) sees Joseph as a Christ-figure, but she also stated in her preface,

... he is necessarily a type also of every man who attempts to follow Christ on the path of spiritual life.[49]

The point is somewhat laboured in the play, but we can see quite clearly Mabel's intention of showing God's involvement in the life of Man. The play significantly opens with discussion among the angels who appear on the upper level of the stage which represents Heaven. And this was precisely the technique which Masefield and Dorothy Sayers employed for their Canterbury plays. Mabel Dearmer also created a precedent by interesting a leading church musician, Martin Shaw, in her plays so that her angels were provided with impressive fanfares from an original score.

Mabel Dearmer and the *Morality Play Society* were both casualties of the 1914-18 war.[50] Her plays, though interesting in form, were doomed by the awkwardness and quaintness of the verse.[51] But she had begun to explore the possibilities of the morality play for modern times. After the First World War, the taste for such simple piety as expressed in *Eager Heart* or Mabel Dearmer's work changed markedly and Christian writers who were also serious lay theologians began to look for new approaches to the writing of religious drama. Unfortunately, however, the ideas provided by the renewed interest in medieval drama were never fully followed up and there has probably yet to be an entirely successful modern morality. John Masefield's *The Coming of Christ*, the first Canterbury play, was, in many ways, the most notable achievement in this direction, but thereafter the Canterbury playwrights tended to move towards the history play.

When, in the 1980s, the Dean of Canterbury sought to re-establish the idea of drama in the Cathedral, it was a series of spectacular productions of medieval mystery plays which eventually fulfilled his vision. This achievement is described in the final chapter of this book.

Notes to Chapter 2.

1. See Robert Potter, *The English Morality Play* (London 1975), 192-221.
2. See Chapter 1.
3. See pp. 5-10, Chapter 1.
4. Elizabeth Sprigge, *Sybil Thorndike Casson* (London 1971), 79-81.
5. For details of Poel's career, see Robert Speaight, *William Poel and the Elizabethan Revival* (Cambridge, Massachussetts 1954). Speaight was one of the leading actors at Canterbury.
6. Gerald Weales, *Religion in Modern English Drama* (Philadelph. 1961), 94.
7. Robert Potter, *op. cit.*, 1-2.
8. *Ibid.* and Gerald Weales, *op.cit.*, 55.
9. See previous Chapter and illustration.
10. Robert Potter, *op.cit.*, 2-4.
11. William Poel, *Monthly Letters: Essays on the Drama* (London 1929), 82-84. Poel cites Reinhardt and Craig as following his lead.
12. Reviews quoted Robert Potter, *op.cit.*, 2-4.
13. See Appendix.
14. Robert Potter, *op.cit.*, 226.
15. Elizabeth Sprigge, *op.cit.*, 56-58, 60-64.
16. See Appendix.
17. Robert Potter, *op.cit.*, 223-25.
18. Elizabeth Sprigge, *op.cit.*, 60-64.
19. Kathleen Bainbridge-Bell and June Ottaway, *A Brief Historical Sketch of the Religious Drama Society of Great Britain* (London 1957), 5.
20. See Appendix.
21. A letter of 1936 to Harcourt Williams in C. B. Purdom, *Harley Granville-Barker* (Cambridge, Mass. 1956), 246.
22. Robert Potter, *op.cit.*, 230-1.
23. C. B. Purdom, *op.cit.*, 246.
24. The connection between Saltzburg and George Bell has been overlooked by Potter and Weales.
25. See June Ottaway, "Nugent Monck of Norwich", *Christian Drama II* (1953).
26. See below, p. 91.
27. cp. below, p. 66.
28. Robert Potter, *op.cit.*, 3-4.
29. See Chapter 3.
30. See below, p. 18.
31. See below, pp. 63-7.

32. cp. Martin Harvey's production of *Oedipus Rex*, see below, p. 89.

33. See below, p. 105.

34. For a fuller discussion see Chapters 9 and 10.

35. See above, pp. 19-20.

36. See above, p. 11.

37. See Gerald Weales, *op.cit.*, 98, 121-124.

38/39. L. Housman "In Spite of the Censor", *Critic XLII* (1903), 141.

40. Gerald Weales, *op.cit.*, 124.

41. See especially Edith Sitwell on the Georgians and their enthusiasm for "old gaffers" (a reference to Masefield's *The Everlasting Mercy*) in Robert Ross, *The Georgian Revolt* (London 1965), 196.

42. See Chapter 5.

43. Percy Dearmer, "Religion and Drama", *The Times*, May 23, 1922, 16.

44. Gerald Weales, *op.cit.*, 98-99.

45. Laurence Housman, *The Unexpected Years* (Indianapolis 1936), 212.

46. See above, p. 18.

47. The basis of William V. Spanos's book: *The Christian Tradition in Modern British Verse Drama* is that the Nativity as the event which reconciles Time and Eter nity, is the single most important inspiration of the twentieth century Christian verse play.

48. See above, p. 27.

49. Mrs Percy Dearmer, *The Dreamer: A Drama of the Life of Joseph* (London 1912), 7.

50. Gerald Weales, *op.cit.*, 103.

51. For a consideration of Mrs Dearmer's verse see Stephen Gwynn Preface, v; Mabel Dearmer, *Three Plays* (London 1916), 5-6.

3

The Canterbury Plays and the Development of Verse Drama

The Canterbury plays have been seen as part of a revival of verse drama, a new movement which started in the 1920s and thirties and which culminated in the post-war plays of T. S. Eliot and Christopher Fry. One critic, Derek Stanford, even sees this movement as the fourth phase of a recurrent pattern in poetic drama, which involves "the phase of experiment, the phase of maturity, the phase of decline and the phase of revival."[1] But this view of the Canterbury plays as "revival" is misleading, since it implies that verse drama and the Romantic Theatre which largely depended on it, were virtually dead. It is sometimes assumed that towards the end of the nineteenth century:

> . . . the drama abandoned the Arthurian Court for the modern industrial slum, the shining pre-Raphaelite romance for a passionate interest in the rights of women, public hygiene and the disastrous results of failure to divorce.[2]

This idea has grown up because Ibsen's abandonment of verse in favour of the "very much more difficult art of writing the genuine, plain language spoken in real life" is often represented as a great watershed in European drama.[3] Romanticism and verse drama in England are therefore thought to have retreated rapidly with the impact of Naturalism, once the first performance of an Ibsen play had taken place in 1880.

In fact, a continuous line of verse drama can be traced through to the twentieth century, though perhaps the plays were not particularly successful or impressive. A number of leading figures in the theatre in the early years of the twentieth century still believed in the possibility of successful verse drama, developed from nineteenth century attempts. This school of thought was strongly represented in the actors and producers who came to Canterbury.

E. Harcourt Williams, for instance, was a Bensonian who acted in and produced two of the Canterbury plays.[4] He had seen Irving in Tennyson's *Becket* and had acted in the verse plays of Stephen Philips and Gilbert Murray's translations of Euripides when they first appeared just after the turn of the century. Russell Thorndike, who was chosen for the leading rôle in the Canterbury production of *Becket* in 1932 had, ten years earlier, played the part of Peer in the Old Vic's first British production of Ibsen's last verse play.[5] All the Canterbury plays were acted by casts who were experienced in the handling of verse in the commercial theatre.

The Legacy of the Nineteenth Century - a General Survey

The nineteenth century is not a promising source of inspiration for verse drama. Whereas the poetry and novels of the period continue to attract serious attention as living works of art, very little of the drama has survived. This is not simply because in the ephemeral art of the theatre very little does endure, but because nineteenth century plays were of an exceptionally poor quality; and of the verse drama in particular, most critics would agree with Macready when he said of Browning's *Strafford*: "Feeble rant. It is not good!"[6] Nicoll has argued that the nineteenth century poets whose lyric poetry is, deservedly, admired were temperamentally unsuited to the writing of drama.[7] Coleridge, Keats, Shelley and Wordsworth all wrote plays, but their efforts were uniformly tedious and only Coleridge (*Remorse*, Drury Lane, 1813) succeeded in having a play staged in his lifetime. The failure of these poets to produce good stage plays was almost certainly due to their total ignorance of the theatre. The more flamboyant Byron, who actually enjoyed his association with the theatre, wrote plays that were correspondingly more successful.

Conditions in the theatre throughout the nineteenth century were certainly unhelpful to poets. The huge theatres, which held a legal monopoly until 1843, and the crude stage and auditorium lighting had given rise to an acting style that lacked any sort of subtlety or refinement. Poets of genuine sensitivity were unlikely to want their lines declaimed loudly to the accompaniment of expansive gestures; and audiences, which at the beginning of the century had been rowdy, licentious and squalid, seemed to gain no better taste with their increased decorum and continued to hanker after spectacle, sentimentality and melodrama.

With the advent of new, smaller theatres producing legitimate drama, new acting styles emerged, but the actor-managers, who completely dominated the theatre for the second half of the century, relied on their own magnetic and powerful personalities for their success. Plays were, to some extent, merely used as a basis for the virtuoso display that the public expected. In Shaw's view this tendency debased the art of the playwright and therefore discouraged the genuine artist. He said of Irving, England's leading actor-manager:

> I am not exaggerating when I say that he regarded an author as a person whose business it was to provide plays at five shillings an act, and, in emergencies, to write the fifth act whilst the fourth was being performed . . . [8]

There is, however, a good deal of evidence to suggest that the period's leading poets could have benefited from disciplining their work to Irving's requirements.

The success which some of the actor-managers achieved with third-rate material, indicates that the opportunities did exist for good stage verse to be written. Charles Kean, for instance, created one of his most popular rôles in Boucicault's blank verse dramatisation of Delavigne's *Louis XI* (1885). Eric Bentley in *The Life of the*

Drama uses a description of Irving's later interpretation of the part to illustrate what great acting can achieve in an apparently bad play.[9] Boucicault succeeded where better poets failed because he knew what his public wanted - memorable lines and spectacle:

> Who that ever heard them will ever forget the lines Irving used to speak as the rascally old king in *Louis XI* to Martin Harvey as the gay young Dauphin.
> 'Three Kingdoms, boy, could sit upon this head
> As light as that silk cap on thine.'[10]

Irving therefore could raise "a melodrama of no importance and a surprisingly bad historical play into dramatic masterpieces"[11] and "could give importance and a noble melancholy to any sort of drivel that was put into his mouth."[12] It is fascinating to think what he might have achieved if a great play had been written.

Revivals of Nineteenth Century Verse Plays

The reasons for the failure of verse drama in the nineteenth century have been fully discussed by Nicoll, Kenneth Muir, Donoghue and others. They have really added nothing new to the two important statements quoted by William Poel in 1923. In his *Letters* this famous Elizabethan scholar and pioneer producer of medieval drama says:

> As Russell Lowell, the American poet, has so well expressed it, 'As soon as there is a gap between the speech of books and that of life, the language becomes, as far as poetry is concerned, as dead as Latin.' George Lewes, our greatest dramatic critic, says that every actor must endeavour to give the poetry he is speaking on stage some resemblance of the intonations used in conversation or no reality can be created.[13]

Generally speaking, the verse drama of the nineteenth century seems to have been accompanied by both the serious faults indicated by Poel.

Concluding his discussion of the shortcomings of nineteenth century verse plays, Allardyce Nicoll remarks that Browning's *Strafford*, Stephen Phillips's *Paolo and Francesca*, Shelley's *The Cenci* and Tennyson's *Becket* are all alike in one respect, they are:

. . . removed from the life of their day, wilfully ignorant of the demands of contemporaries, each of these is imitative in essence, not of life, but of past literary models.[14]

Yet it was precisely these plays which suggested the possibility of establishing a lively verse drama in the following century.

Shelley's *The Cenci* (1819) was never performed during the poet's lifetime. He had very clear ideas of what he wanted in theatrical terms and asked a friend to offer the play to Covent Garden. The rôle of Beatrice he felt "precisely fitted Miss O'Neill" and he was "very reluctant that anyone but Kean should play the Count."[15] But Shelley had overlooked the stringency of theatrical censorship and the play, with its theme of incest, was banned. It was not until March 1886 that *The Cenci* was seen in performance at a private production by the *Shelley Society* in the Great Theatre, Islington. Obviously the audience was partisan, but many were surprised and delighted by the play. But whilst the subject matter remained unacceptable for the Lord Chamberlain's Licence there was little chance that Shelley's play would be widely known.

In 1922, however, one hundred years after Shelley's death, the play received a public performance with Sybil Thorndike as Beatrice Cenci. There were obvious weaknesses: the play contained echoes of *Macbeth*; the verse was good, but the construction of the play clumsy. Shelley himself seemed to have handled his theme nervously and the action tended to lose impulse after the death of the Count. The play was, nevertheless, greeted with considerable enthusiasm. Audrey Williamson's reaction, written some years later, was that the play:

. . . comes to grips with theatrical technique, sharply characterised and packed with needle-nerved suspense - and shows a genuine attempt . . . to shape the verse into dialogue which seemed natural for stage purposes.[16]

It was also discovered that, in his preface, Shelley had written perceptively on the problems of verse drama,[17] and his play demonstrated the possibilities of the medium. The 1922 production was, however, above all notable for the superb performance of Sybil Thorndike. Shaw was so moved when he realised that he had discovered the very actress for whom to write his *St Joan* and the trial scene in his play was suggested by Sybil Thorndike's playing in the trial of Shelley's play.[18]

Sybil Thorndike's success in *The Cenci* fired her enthusiasm, and that of the rest of her family, for verse drama. Its reinstatement as a living theatre form became a major concern for them in future years. Eileen, Sybil's sister, produced three of the Canterbury plays; Russell, their brother, acted in one. Sybil's children, Ann, Christopher and Mary Casson all became professionally involved in the theatre and acted at Canterbury and she herself delivered an address at a Canterbury Festival.[19]

In a similar way, a revival of Browning's *Strafford* had repercussions in the twentieth century. The twenty-four year old poet wrote a play at the suggestion of Macready, but when the great actor read it he was disappointed. It had "neither power nor nature nor healthful fancy"[20] he wrote in his diary, but he honoured his agreement with Browning and presented the play at Covent Garden in 1837. Browning was apparently enraptured by the performance, but neither Macready nor the public shared his enthusiasm and the play was dropped after a mere five performances.

In 1889, the year of Browning's death, William Courtney, a fellow of New College, Oxford, who had contributed a great deal towards promoting a sympathetic attitude to drama in the University,[21] prepared an acting edition of *Strafford* for a revival of the play. The production, to be staged by *Oxford University Drama Society*, had the young H. B. Irving, son of Sir Henry, in the leading rôle. H. B. Irving's own son, Laurence, became one of the most influential figures in the Canterbury festivals and he has described the revival of *Strafford* in his book, *The Successors*.[22] Both Laurence Irving and Robertson Davies[23] maintain that the play with its psychological, rather than physical, action would be very acceptable in the modern theatre.[24] Browning, by "dispensing with a plot" and using his characters "to personify the political and personal conflicts"[25] had suggested a style which could be developed with advantage. At least one Canterbury playwright, T. S. Eliot, was, however, far from impressed by Browning's work. "What personage, in a play by Browning," he asked "remains alive in the mind?"[26]

The nineteenth century play which perhaps had the greatest significance for Canterbury was Tennyson's *Becket*. Tennyson was sixty-five when he wrote his first play *Queen Mary* (1876) and submitted it to Isobel Bateman, under whose management Irving was the leading actor at the Lyceum. This play was to form the third part of an historical trilogy that would "complete the line of Shakespeare's English chronicle-plays," and was, like all his subsequent plays, painstakingly researched.[27] Browning declared *Queen Mary* to be "astonishingly fine"[28] when he read it. In spite of the consequent improvements, the play only ran for twenty-three nights, yet Irving retained some faith in Tennyson and, four years later in 1880, Irving gave a lavish production of *The Cup*.[29]

Tennyson, with his son and biographer, Hallam, visited Canterbury in 1877 and, like so many visitors before and since, stood in the various spots associated with the martyrdom of Thomas Becket.[30] No English city is so clearly identified with the martyrdom of a saint as is Canterbury with Becket; there are as many reminders of Becket in Canterbury as there are of Shakespeare in Stratford-on-Avon. Probably no single historical act is popularly felt to have been so outrageous as the murder of an Archbishop in his own Cathedral and no event so completely symbolises the struggles between Church and State and between a man and his conscience. For most English people also, the idea of pilgrimage is inseparable from Canterbury, and pilgrimages to Canterbury have, ever since Becket's death, led literally or metaphorically to his tomb.

It is hardly surprising, therefore, that the martyrdom has caught the imagination of writers and has inspired several novels, at least one great series of poems and plays by Douglas Jerrold (1829), George Darley (1840), Tennyson (1879), Eliot (1935), Anouilh (1961) and Fry (1961). There are also plays by Binyon, Ray Lawler and James Goldman which continue the story of Henry II or explore the continuing effect of Becket's death.

Tennyson researched carefully into the available twelfth century writings following his visit to Canterbury and by 1879, three years after his first notes for the play, he had completed *Becket*. The poet sent the play to Irving who, with the excuse that it would be too expensive to stage, refused it. Later events showed that Irving felt drastic alterations to be necessary and to these, he was certain, Tennyson would never agree. Tennyson, however, was obviously disappointed by Irving's refusal and although Hallam Tennyson says that his father "considered the time was not ripe for its publication," it was probably Irving's action which delayed the publication of the play until 1884.[31]

The Earl of Selborne, to whom *Becket* was dedicated, described the dedication as "the greatest real honour that has ever been done me,"[32] and the Right Honourable J. Bryce felt that: "One cannot imagine a more vivid, a more perfectly faithful picture than it gives of Henry and Thomas."[33] Praise for the play's historical accuracy and the vividness of the characterisation continued to flow from readers who enjoyed *Becket* in the quietness of the study. But there seemed to be little possibility of the play being staged.

There is a conflict of evidence over the next stage in the development of *Becket*. Laurence Irving maintains that his grandfather waited until Tennyson's death in 1892 before seriously considering the staging of *Becket*.[34] But Hallam Tennyson testifies that Irving wrote to Tennyson in 1891 asking permission to produce it, saying that:

... the taste of the theatre-going public had changed in the interval [since 1879] and that it was now likely to be a success.[35]

It is certain that Irving was genuinely sensitive to a good deal of late Victorian taste and to the likely offence that his cuts in the play would cause Tennyson. He may well have felt that the ageing Laureate would be less concerned than in earlier years or that it was worth acquiring the right to perform the play at some time in the future, knowing that he could make a success of it.

In the event, Irving had not long to wait, for Tennyson died in 1892 and the play was immediately put into rehearsal. With many revisions to the text, and music based on Gregorian melody by C. V. Stanford, *Becket* opened in 1893. Since Irving came to London no play, not even *The Bells*, met with such approval from his audience. Hallam Tennyson spoke of "the indescribable tenderness" of Irving's speech;[36] Harcourt Williams described his visit to see the performance as "a circumstance that shaped the course of my life."[37] S. R. Littlewood, who attended the first performance of

Murder in the Cathedral, was also present on the opening night of *Becket* at the Lyceum[38] and E. V. Lucas, who saw *Becket* revived at Canterbury compared what he saw there with the indelible experience of seeing Irving.[39] It is hardly surprising that later writers saw in *Becket* possibilities of a genuine religious drama for, as Irving wrote to Hallam after the fifteenth performance:

> To me, *Becket* is a very noble play, with something of that lofty feeling and that far-reaching influence, which belongs to a Passion Play ... I know that such a play has an ennobling influence on both the audience who see it and the actors who play in it.[40]

Becket remained Irving's favourite rôle until his death. Laurence Irving has given a moving account of how the play acquired great personal significance for his grandfather as he approached the end of his life. As we have seen, it was *Becket* which Irving read in the Chapter House at Canterbury, in a dramatic demonstration of the growing tolerance of the Church towards the theatre in 1897.[41]

A recent discovery of a wax cylinder recording of Irving speaking lines from *Becket* has shown that he used a remarkably naturalistic technique in his approach to the play. Irving is often represented as having had a most stilted style of diction and movement and as having completely subjected the text to his own personality. The short recording, however, was mistaken at first for an impromptu account of a walk with Henry Stanley (the explorer and friend of Irving) and was only later recognised by Jones-Evans as Irving's very unforced and carefully naturalistic rendering of lines from *Becket*.[42] This is, admittedly, slender evidence, but it does suggest that Irving was capable of allowing the quality of the text to speak for itself and that the writing was not so contrived and removed from real life as has often been supposed.

The Twentieth Century - Stephen Phillips (1864-1915)

The meteoric rise and fall of Stephen Phillips have become almost a legend.[43] When his *Paolo and Francesca* was produced by George Alexander at the St James's Theatre in 1900, with the golden-voiced Henry Ainley as Paolo, a new age of poetic drama was thought to have dawned. The sober critic, William Archer, considered the play "a thing of exquisite poetic form";[44] another critic spoke of "necklets of perfectly matched pearls";[45] and the critical ecstasy reached a climax when Churton Collins claimed that Phillips was entitled to "kinship with the aristocrats of his art - with Sophocles and Dante".[46]

Similarly extravagant praise was lavished on Phillips's *Herod*, which Alexander produced the same year at Her Majesty's Theatre. Max Beerbohm found it:

> ... so fiery coloured; so intense, the character so largely projected, the action so relentlessly progresses till the final drops of awe are wrung from us, that only the greatest of dramatic poets could accompany with verse quite worthy of it.[47]

George Alexander, therefore, had no hesitation in mounting a third play by Phillips, *Ulysses*, in 1902; and because of the success of *Herod* and *Ulysses* he sold the rights to *Paolo and Francesca* to H. B. Irving, who was establishing himself in theatre management.

With Harcourt Williams[48] as Paolo and Dorothea Baird,[49] H. B. Irving's wife, as Francesca the play was performed in 1906. "Their natural good looks and their ability to give mellifluous utterance"[50] were enough, according to Laurence Irving, to ensure the success of the production in an age which attached enormous importance to the sound and rather less to the content.

The vogue for Phillips's plays passed almost as rapidly as it had started. By 1914, H. B. Irving was trying to rescue Phillips from destitution and total disillusionment and agreed to mount *The Sin of David*. War had just been declared when the play opened at the Savoy. Laurence Irving suggests: ". . . my father must have known that those who had the heart to go to the theatre could not be distracted by Phillips's sombre tragedy."[51] One critic showed some enthusiasm and declared "The joy of it to welcome Stephen Phillips back to the stage",[52] and it is just possible that without the war Phillips might have had the financial success he so desperately needed. The late Ben Travers, famous as a writer of farce, was an apprentice to Phillips's publisher at the time, and tried to point out to the poet that H. B. Irving's heavy-handed, Lyceum-style production was strangling the play, but Phillips, "sadly dishevelled, his pale flabby face void of expression" was too "far gone in dissipation",[53] and within a year, both he and his plays were dead.[54]

Phillips, however, had many poor imitators, among them Mrs Percy Dearmer, and he inspired the much-maligned Comyns Carr to write for the theatre again. Perhaps most surprising of all was the fact that when William Archer's *Three Plays* were published posthumously in 1927 it was found that even he, the great advocate of Ibsen and realism, had attempted to write in blank verse. The desire to write in verse clearly persisted.

Gilbert Murray (1866-1957)

The failure of verse drama to seem relevant to contemporary life and the increasing impact of naturalism meant that an ever decreasing number of theatre managers were prepared to stage verse plays. After the brief success of Stephen Phillips, verse drama seemed likely to disappear from the commercial theatre and there was a growing tendency for it to be a minority, élitist interest.

An event which had considerable significance for the theatrical élite and for the subsequent development of verse drama was the production between 1904 and 1908 of Gilbert Murray's four new translations of Euripides's plays at the Court Theatre. The famous Vedrenne-Barker management were, to some extent, able to experiment with drama of minority interest because of the enormous success they had achieved with productions of Shaw's plays.

Gilbert Murray, the brilliant young professor of Greek on whom Shaw modelled the character of Adolphus Cusins in *Major Barbara*, had a genuine passion for the theatre and some experience as a playwright before he turned to Euripides. His *Carlyon Sahib*, described by William Archer as a "curiously grim and powerful but unskilful piece of work which moved me very much",[55] had been produced by Mrs Patrick Campbell in 1899, with the young Granville-Barker in the cast. A second play, *Andromache* appeared in 1901. Although Archer, by now a close friend of Murray, found *Andromache* "a noble, beautiful and very moving figure",[56] neither of Murray's original plays were received with general enthusiasm. But the translations from Euripides, Shaw remarked, "came into our dramatic literature with all the impulsive power of original works."[57] Murray combined his infectious enthusiasm for Greek drama with his considerable knowledge of the contemporary theatre to create plays which, though not always strictly accurate as translations, were strikingly effective theatrically. He decided that verse was the most appropriate medium, but abandoned blank verse in favour of a freer form of verse which has some of the characteristics of the Georgian poets. T. S. Eliot was one of Murray's chief disparagers, dismissing him as "a very insignificant follower of the pre-Raphaelite movement", who had elected the "William Morris couplet" and "the Swinburne lyric"[58] as his substitute for the magnificence of Greek dramatic verse. Nothing, however, prevented Murray's translations from achieving unparalleled success and at the time of his death 400,000 copies had been sold.

William Archer realised that Murray's great achievement was to have made Euripides stageworthy by conceiving the plays as live theatre, and by using "subtly modulated, free-moving verse"[59] he had broken away from the deadening influence of pseudo-Elizabethan, blank verse. Murray also opened up new possibilities by his use of the chorus, the effectiveness of which depended upon the supply of well-trained speakers. This had repercussions which we shall examine later,[60] but it is interesting to note that Eliot anticipated a criticism that was frequently levelled at his own play, *Murder in the Cathedral*, when he wrote in 1920 of *Medea*:

> . . . the refined Dalcroze chorus had mellifluous voices which rendered their lyrics happily inaudible. All this contributed toward the highbrow effect which is so depressing . . .[61]

Familiar names associated with other forms of verse drama, whom we have already discussed, were also connected with Murray's translations. Harcourt Williams played opposite Edith Wynne-Matthison in *Electra* (Court Theatre 1907),[62] Sybil Thorndike achieved one of her great successes in *Medea* which she continued to play from 1908 and throughout World War I. Laurence Irving had his first experience of actors entering through the aisles at Martin Harvey's production of *Oedipus Rex* (Covent Garden 1911)[63] and Ann Casson appeared as Electra and Medea at various times.[64]

It is generally felt that Murray's translations of Sophocles and Aeschylus were less successful than his Euripides, but for the first twenty years of the century he created, from all his work, a type of drama which depended upon the spoken word, just when the commercial theatre appeared to be moving in the opposite direction. His work has become unfashionable now; taste has turned against his "luscious rhythms and decorative Georgian style", yet his achievement helped to ensure an audience and performers for poetic drama.[65]

Voice, Verse and the Actor

One of the factors which contributed to the continued interest in verse for the theatre was the change in the pattern of training for actors throughout the late nineteenth and early twentieth centuries. The latter half of the nineteenth century saw the gradual disappearance of the old, stock companies in which young actors had traditionally received their early training and experience. The only alternative for aspiring actors was to go to a private teacher of elocution and this, coupled with the growing interest in self-help and adult education, caused a rapid increase in the number of such teachers. Various private schools of elocution also began to appear and in 1896 Ben Greet founded an Academy of Acting, just off the Strand.[66]

The effect of this development was to focus attention on the human voice as a speaking instrument[67] and, gradually, elocution became recognised as a complex art with a scientific basis. As lessons were held either individually or with small groups, the speaking of dramatic verse became the most common material on which to work and it was not long before recitation became a recognised part of an actor's craft. Recitation even included the duologue, in which an actor played two parts alternately, using differing voices and postures.

To cater for the new interest in elocution, a steady stream of handbooks appeared in the eighteen-eighties and nineties: *Bell's Standard Elocutionist* (from which Irving would recite) was the most famous, and both *Millard's Grammar of Elocution* (1882) and Henry Neville's *Voice, Gesture and Elocutionary Art* (1897) were very popular. All such textbooks included large sections of verse for recitation and the emphasis was always on the dramatic. So popular did the idea of recitation become that, in 1902, Percy Cross Standing published an anthology entitled *Favourite Recitations by Favourite Actors* which included Thomas Hood's *Eugene Aram*, the poem with which Irving could enthral an audience.

In order to give added status to the study of elocution, the various musical academies began to include it as a subject for diploma examinations. The importance of verse as a foundation for good speech was thought to be paramount and such institutions as The London College of Music (founded 1887), The Royal Academy of Music (1822), Trinity College of Music (1872) and the Guildhall School of Music and Drama (1880) included the study of versification and prosody in their Licentiateship and Associateship diploma examinations in elocution. In the case of London College this practice persists to the present day.[68]

Ben Greet's example in establishing an academy dealing solely with the needs of actors and actresses was followed by Elsie Fogertie, a specialist in speech training who organised classes in elocution at the Crystal Palace School of Art. She established her Central School of Speech Training and Dramatic Art in 1906 and quickly made choral speaking an important feature of her work. Her book *The Speaking of English Verse* (1923) contains a great deal of material on the speaking of the Greek chorus[69] and she not only responded to the opportunities provided by Gilbert Murray's translations but she also trained the famous chorus for Eliot's *Murder in the Cathedral*.[70]

In 1909 the *Poetry Society* was founded, and this organisation encouraged private teachers to enter their pupils for examinations in verse-speaking which included a section of verse drama. Stephen Philips, as editor of the Society's *Poetry Review,* and the young John Masefield were both involved in the *Poetry Society,* which became a favourite target of the critic, A. R. Orage, editor of *The New Age* (1908-1921).[71]

The situation which developed in the early years of this century was that verse speaking was the basis of training for actors and actresses who would find the commercial theatre emphasising naturalism. This factor helped to preserve an acting style which belonged to the romantic theatre and, at its worse, included a type of voice production best described as 'lowing.' It is no exaggeration to say that for many amateur actors, at this time, the concept of acting simply meant mellifluous speech: and even the naturalistic professional stage depended on a kind of highly selective, imitative realism for its success.

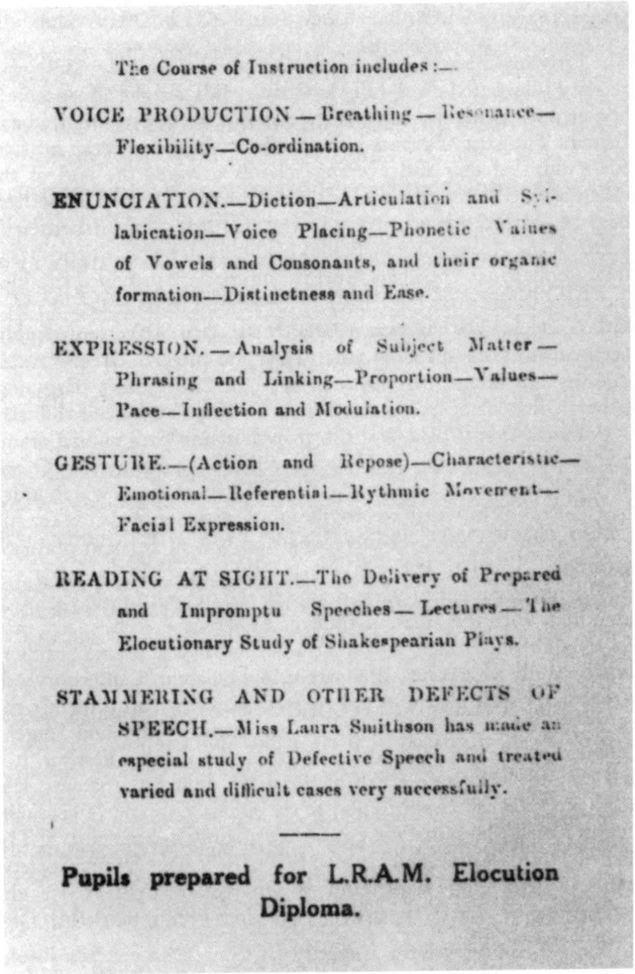

The Course of Instruction includes :—

VOICE PRODUCTION — Breathing — Resonance— Flexibility—Co-ordination.

ENUNCIATION.—Diction—Articulation and Syllabication—Voice Placing—Phonetic Values of Vowels and Consonants, and their organic formation—Distinctness and Ease.

EXPRESSION. — Analysis of Subject Matter — Phrasing and Linking—Proportion—Values— Pace—Inflection and Modulation.

GESTURE.—(Action and Repose)—Characteristic— Emotional—Referential—Rythmic Movement— Facial Expression.

READING AT SIGHT.—The Delivery of Prepared and Impromptu Speeches — Lectures — The Elocutionary Study of Shakespearian Plays.

STAMMERING AND OTHER DEFECTS OF SPEECH.—Miss Laura Smithson has made an especial study of Defective Speech and treated varied and difficult cases very successfully.

———

Pupils prepared for L.R.A.M. Elocution Diploma.

Figure 2: Syllabus offered by a typical teacher of Elocution, Voice Production and Dramatic Training, 1913-20.

Amateur Drama

The growing interest in theatre-going as a respectable middle-class activity, and the advancement of education generally, helped the development of amateur drama in Britain. The idea of drama in performance began to creep into the curriculum of day and evening schools towards the end of the nineteenth century. Progressive schoolmasters, who perhaps had been at Oxford when or since Jowett had first allowed Benson to perform the *Agamemnon* in Balliol Hall (1881), began to encourage their pupils to act.[72] Gilbert Murray's translations provided an added incentive to the growing tendency for schools to stage Greek plays. In London, school children were introduced to Shakespeare by the performances organised by Stuart Headlam and Ben Greet;[73] and, in middle-class homes, parents such as Sybil Thorndike's clergyman father - a devotee of Irving - might read Shakespeare to their children.[74]

After World War I, the growth in non-professional drama accelerated. The Board of Education published a survey: *The Drama in Adult Education* and the *British Drama League* was founded by Geoffrey Whitworth in 1919 to provide an advisory service, a library and a focal point for the ever-increasing numbers of amateur dramatic societies.

The development of verse drama in the twentieth century is often identified with the amateur theatre. Many professionals brought their skills and traditions to verse drama, but there was certainly a great deal of amateur involvement. Canterbury was particularly well-placed in this respect, because it had probably the oldest dramatic society in the country - the Old Stagers, founded in 1842 to give performances at the Cricket Festival.

It is too easy to underrate much of the work done by amateurs; it is really not a valid criticism of a play to say (as it is so often of twentieth century verse plays) that it is performed "mainly by amateurs."[75] The *British Drama League* and a similar body, the *Village Drama Society*, helped to encourage high standards among amateur groups. The work done by Little Theatres[76] has often been remarkable. Guy Boas wrote in 1937:

Since the war a vast enthusiasm has welled up in the soul of England for amateur drama. In almost every town, college, school, village and country house the amateur's desire to act a play and to act it well has become passionate.[77]

In the same year, Una Ellis-Fermor produced an interesting survey, *Village Drama 1350-1937*, which concluded that drama was once again becoming an important part of community life. This, probably more than anywhere else, was the case at Canterbury and it was this fact which made the plays we are to consider in detail a possibility. Ellis-Fermor maintains:

... the part played by the present amateur movement is seen to be vital to the twentieth century dramatic renaissance. Indeed, the modern amateur movement, with its inevitable referendum to the people, is bringing back again many of the characteristics of the medieval attitude to drama and, in linking them to a highly evolved and technically expert professional art, such as the middle ages did not possess, stands on the verge of seemingly incalculable theatrical possibilities.[78]

The Boars Hill Dramatists

Abercrombie, Binyon, Bottomley and Masefield are usually seen as belonging to a group of writers whose attempts to reinstate poetic drama were so esoteric that they warrant the label 'coterie dramatists'. Binyon and Masefield are of particular interest as they were the first two living playwrights to have their plays performed at Canterbury. Priscilla Thouless maintains that they were also the last English playwrights to write in the romantic tradition.[79] To coterie and romantic, a third label, 'Georgian', is often added and the appearance in 1911 of Masefield's poem *The Everlasting Mercy*, with its new, robust realism, is often felt to have marked the beginning of the Georgian movement.[80] All three labels have acquired something of a tone of condescension and it has become a little too easy to pigeon-hole these writers and forget them.

While it is probably fair to say of Binyon that he wrote for the romantic theatre, Masefield is a much more complex figure. He was by no means as limited as recent attitudes to his work suggest. His knowledge of the theatre was extensive. His book, *William Shakespeare*, described by L. A. G. Strong as "the best book about

Shakespeare which has been written in our time",[81] approaches the playwright from the standpoint of the producer and actor[82] and his *A Macbeth Production* shows a perceptive approach to the problems of rehearsal and performance.[83] Masefield also researched into the more progressive aspects of the theatre of his day and pressed for the adoption of the advanced ideas of Edward Gordon Craig. He had a vision for a new type of London theatre, a National Theatre, combined with an art gallery, which would be devoted to producing classic plays.[84] Although this was never realised, he encouraged new writing for the stage by building a theatre in his garden at Boars Hill, Oxford.

In the early nineteen-twenties, Masefield regularly produced Shakespeare, translations from classical French dramatists and plays by contemporary playwrights in his small theatre. Many of the actors were drawn from Oxford University, but friends and members of his own family also took part.[85] The theatre itself was designed to be as flexible as possible, but the open stage, with its steps into the auditorium across its whole breadth, was particularly suited to accommodating a chorus. The complete stage was nineteen feet deep with a traverse curtain which left a front stage of five feet in depth.[86] In many ways, the stage resembled the chancel steps and platform on which Masefield produced his play *The Coming of Christ* in Canterbury Cathedral.

Not only was Masefield involved in the problems of production, he was also very aware of the pitfalls of writing verse-drama. He was a brilliant storyteller and in constant demand as a lecturer,[87] and speaking to the *Scottish Association for the Speaking of Verse* he summarised the problems of the playgoer with typical sparkle:

When they have gone to listen to poetry upon the stage, they have often heard actors speaking the verse as though it were not only prose but very bad prose; or when they wearied of that method, speaking it as though it were a very bad form of church service, the solemnity of which was made worse by being expensive.[88]

Masefield had a very clear idea of what he wanted to avoid in his own writing. He rebelled against the blank verse tradition perpetuated by Tennyson and Stephen Phillips and even produced a brilliant parody of a nineteenth century verse play, remarking:

The play had better be in blank verse as it is so much easier to write than prose and easier to speak than rhyme.[89]

The great difficulty in discussing Masefield's own drama is the wide variety of styles with which he experimented. If he is remembered at all today it is probably for his first prose play, *The Tragedy of Nan* (1909) which was last seen at the Mercury Theatre in 1943. This play, which Donoghue describes as "one of the most embarrassing plays in the modern theatre",[90] is Masefield's attempt to draw upon the rhythms of his native Herefordshire speech in the way that Yeats and Synge exploited Irish speech patterns. William Poel, referring to a performance of *Nan* in Birmingham (1918) said:

Let it be granted that Masefield's play is morbid, and that when acted it fails to excite genuine tragic emotion. Yet like Ford's *Broken Heart*, the play is of the literary and dramatic quality which has its place in the history of drama, and cannot be put on the shelf simply because it does not please everybody.[91]

Probably the best feature of the play is the way in which the Severn, rising threateningly, is represented almost as a living character and as recently as 1970 an article appeared suggesting that *The Tragedy of Nan* deserved revival.[92]

After another prose play, *Pompey the Great* (1910), Masefield turned to verse, and wrote *Philip the King* in heroic couplets. Here he uses the Greek device of the Messenger bringing dramatic tidings of disaster, but in this case of the defeated Armada.

Several influences have been detected in Masefield's work. He appears to owe something to Lady Gregory and to Yeats with whom both he and Binyon had a personal friendship.[93] The impact of the Pound-Fenellosa 'No' plays, published in 1913 and 1916, also affected Masefied's style and he made increasing use of ideas from classical drama, deriving partly, no doubt, from the success of another personal acquaintance, Gilbert Murray. All three main sources of inspiration became more apparent in the plays written in, and after, 1915.

The Faithful (1915), a play with a Japanese theme, was followed in 1917 by Masefield's first overtly religious verse play, the unfinished *Good Friday*. By this time, Masefield was reconciled to the fact that verse plays were unlikely to achieve much popular success in the commercial theatre. His reaction, however, was to take advantage of the possibilities of a private performance, particularly the absence of censorship. For the first time since the medieval period, therefore, we have a playwright introducing the figure of Christ.

The play *Good Friday* was not particularly remarkable. Arnold Bennett wrote in his journal:

A terribly dull and portentous thing in rhyme. I was most acutely bored. I found that all the 'élite' said they liked the damn thing.[94]

Again there is the Greek Messenger, this time he is the centurion, Longinus, who brings Pilate news of the crucifixion. Gerald Weales contends that "the verse is too weak for the work it has to do",[95] but there is a moment of effective simplicity when Longinus says:

Good, Lord, it is a slow way to make die
A man, a strong man, who can beget men.

Masefield's next phase was his classical French period during which he adapted and translated both Racine's *Berenice* and *Esther* (1922). Then he returned to original verse tragedy with *A King's Daughter* (1923) and *Tristan and Isolt* (1927), and between these he wrote his most impressive pre-Canterbury religious play, The *Trial of Jesus* (1925).

As we can see, it is almost impossible to make a general statement of any validity about Masefield's work. He increasingly combined verse and prose and experimented with the use of a chorus. He took advantage of the upsurge of amateur drama to ensure performance of his plays and four of them were included in the *Village Drama Society's* list of recommended plays.[96] Far from simply preserving a tradition, he seemed determined to experiment, even when this meant that his plays appealed only to an élite. It is probable though, that Masefield wrote so copiously and in so many varied forms, that it was a matter of comparative indifference to him whether one single work of his was well received or not.

There are, however, two very obvious qualities in Masefield's plays: the unpretentious clarity of the verse and the seriousness of the intention. The theatre critic, J. C. Trewin, who never missed an opportunity to praise Masefield, found his work refreshing in comparison with Eliot or Charles Williams: "Masefield's simplicity is a lesson to the self-consciously cerebral dramatist."[97]

Masefield's simplicity is deceptive, it never amounts to naïvety, but his verse, though sometimes capable of brilliant flashes, never commands the emotional range to suit the subject matter. Although Masefield could be witty in the formal situation of a lecture or in writing a parody, he was, as E. Martin Browne remarked, "a man of immense seriousness" who lacked humour and was concerned mainly with the emotions of pity and terror.[98] His preface to *The Tragedy of Nan* showed his position clearly:

> Tragedy at its best is a vision of the heart of life. The heart of life can only be laid bare in the agony and exaltation of dreadful acts. The vision of agony or spiritual contest, pushed beyond the limits of the dying personality, is exalting and cleansing.[99]

It is not surprising, therefore, that when Masefield decided to express his own mystical Christianity in drama he always concentrated on Christ's suffering. The 1914-18 war, which left very deep scars of bitterness in his mind, intensified his belief in the death of Christ as a tragedy rather than as a triumph.[100]

Laurence Binyon

Binyon, like Masefield, had plays performed both at Boars Hill and at Canterbury. A quiet, self-effacing man, he was one of Gilbert Murray's students at Oxford in the 1890s and he won the Newdigate Prize for Poetry. Binyon was a cousin of both Stephen Phillips and Frank Benson and so he had a strong family tradition of romantic theatre. For most of his working life he was Keeper of Oriental Prints and Drawings at the British Museum, and he produced several authoritative books on the subject. It is doubtful, however, if his verse would have become known outside a comparatively small circle of friends but for the sudden success of his poem, *For the Fallen*. This sensitive poem, with its restrained grief and effective reworking of a text from the *Book of Joshua*, just caught the mood of numbed shock at the catastrophic slaughter of the First World War, and appeared on memorials all over the Empire.

Binyon's plays really belong with him in a museum, they are, as Ernest Reynolds has noted, "not much more than historical fustian."[101] True to romantic tradition he chose larger-than-life figures as his heroes and heroines: Attila the Hun; Paris and Oenone; the beautiful, oriental princess, Ayuli; Henry II with his disturbing gift for sudden appearances; and King Arthur.

As a young man, Binyon was introduced by Robert Bridges (who also lived at Boars Hill) to the work of Hopkins, and he became interested in various experimental forms of versification.[102] But in his plays he never broke free from blank verse and, although his language is not obviously pseudo-Elizabethan, it retains a rather faded and rarified tone.

Attila was produced at Her Majesty's Theatre in 1907 by Oscar Asche, who had taken over the management from Tree. Asche had recently achieved the longest run in theatrical history at that time with his spectacular *Chu Chin Chow* and he gave the same sort of lavish production to Binyon's play, employing Charles Ricketts as designer and playing Attila himself. The music was by Stanford, who had composed the music for Tennyson's *Becket* at the Lyceum. A. A. Milne, who dubbed the play 'How I Brought Back the Asches', was greatly impressed:

> It is a fine story finely told; and it is finely told because in telling it you have forgotten that you were a poet and remembered only that you [Binyon] were a dramatist.[103]

Binyon, who insisted that, "verse is to me a much more natural medium than prose",[104] rarely achieved anything more than a graceful style and a romanticised view of historical figures. His attempts at philosophical utterance were trite and his aim was to dramatise literature rather than to make a statement of his own. The final moments of *Attila* are typical of all his work; it shows an awareness of theatrical effect, but more than a hint of melodrama:

> **Rorik** (*a Hun*): Attila is dead,
> And God has slain him, God has smitten him.
> (*They pass out into the crowd without; wails and furious cries repeat themselves into the far distance.*)
> **Idico** (*a Princess. Listening transfixed*):
> The pillar of the world is broken down:
> And yet heaven has not fallen! O Attila . . .
> Gods of my country, now you are avenged!
> *Curtain.*[105]

The performance of Binyon's *Arthur* at the Old Vic in 1923 was perhaps the last example of the type of romanticism that had been popular in Victorian days. It was produced by Sir Martin Harvey, the last surviving actor-manager to have received his training with Irving at the Lyceum, and was provided with incidental music by Sir Edward Elgar. In almost every way, therefore, the occasion resembled Comyns Carr's *King Arthur* and even one of Binyon's admirers described the event as an act of 'heroism' by the management.[106]

The play was almost absurdly out of keeping with the taste of its time; the spirit of theatrical romanticism had long since gone into the musical. Only a reviewer for *The Bookman*, viewing the play from the safety of his study, was able to enthuse over the "noble speech, aching with sorrow and regret, but balanced by hope" and the "simplicity, directness and restraint" of "this strong tragedy".[107] Certainly, the verse was considerably better than Comyns Carr's, but the sentiments were much the same.

Binyon was not entirely out of touch with the commercial theatre and appears to have been rather unfortunate in his attempts to co-operate with some of its leading figures. H. B. Irving asked Binyon to write a play with Richard III as protagonist, but the invitation came just after the outbreak of war in 1914 and neither the play nor its promised production ever materialised.[108] Many years later, in 1938, Binyon published an unfinished play, *Brief Candle*, described by Nowell Smith as a "subtle and vivid fragment . . . about Richard III and his mother",[109] which was, presumably, the outcome of Irving's request. It showed far more promise than his plays on legendary figures and might well have brought him a popular success.

In 1922, Sybil Thorndike and Lewis Casson asked Binyon, a close personal friend, to write a play about Joan of Arc. Binyon enthusiastically agreed and made a start on the play. Shortly after this, however, Lewis Casson read in the press that Shaw also intended to dramatise the life of Saint Joan and he wrote to Shaw explaining the predicament. Shaw replied on a postcard as usual, in typically uncompromising fashion:

Nonsense! Of course Sybil plays my St Joan - Let so and so do the other one. I warned off Masefield and Drinkwater but I forgot Binyon.[110] It was characteristic of Binyon's retiring nature that he said "Shaw will write it much better than I can" and quietly withdrew.[111]

Withdrawal from reality increasingly affected his work. He was far happier writing pieces for Masefield's *Oxford Recitations* than for the commercial theatre, and he wrote to Gordon Bottomley: "I long in my heart to get away from the Museum and write a magnum opus."[112] He never realised his ambition, but an incomplete part of his projected drama about Merlin was published posthumously as *The Madness of Merlin* in 1947.

Probably both Masefield and Binyon wrote their best plays for Canterbury, which suggests that the Canterbury event imposed favourable conditions on these two playwrights. These features and the plays themselves will be considered in detail later. It is interesting to note, however, that Priscilla Thouless, in an otherwise comprehensive account of their work up to 1934, mentions neither of these plays,[113] and this tends to presuppose that only plays written for the commercial theatre are worth consideration.

Gordon Bottomley and Lascelles Abercrombie

In November 1917, Edward Marsh published his second anthology of Georgian verse, and the two major pieces which he included were the poetic dramas *King Lear's Wife* by Gordon Bottomley and *End of the World* by Lascelles Abercrombie. "The Georgian temper was essentially dramatic",[114] Robert Ross maintains and their revolt was against the enervation of the *fin de siècle* verse, which never got beyond the confines of the study. It was, therefore, not surprising that it was Bottomley and Abercrombie who made the most concentrated and carefully argued attempt to restore poetry into drama in the early part of the twentieth century.

Both Bottomley and Abercrombie presented a strong case for the reinstatement of verse into the theatre, but their concern with form and language tended to take precedence over subject matter. They rarely seemed to question whether verse was appropriate to their theme; rather, they looked for a theme that was appropriate to verse. It now seems all the more remarkable, therefore, that the main criticisms aimed at *Georgian Poetry II* centred on the brutal and unnecessary realism of the two plays and not on the strangeness of their subjects.[115]

Bottomley, who tried out many of his plays at Boars Hill, had given permission for John Drinkwater[116] to produce *King Lear's Wife* at the Birmingham Repertory Theatre in 1915. Yeats, Wilfred Gibson and Abercrombie were all present, and among the small literary coterie there was a general feeling of delight, "the only really great literary event" of the year, Edward Marsh told Rupert Brooke.[117] But audiences did not share their enthusiasm and became disappointingly small; they took particular exception to the unpleasant corpse-washer's song at the end of the play in which a louse is pictured crawling around under the shift of the dead Queen Hygd!

Bottomley seemed totally unconcerned about the unfavourable reaction to his play and the Censor's objection to the louse song - he simply laughed "out of his great beard"[118] and continued with his dreams of "a different kind of theatre".[119] Indeed, between 1900, when his first play *The Crier by Night* was performed at the Portmanteau Theatre, USA, and 1918, when he published *Gruach*, Bottomley developed an attitude to drama which made success in the commercial theatre of his day impossible.

His first concern was for speech and sound, and he felt that poetic drama should move towards the formality of opera and not try to emulate prose drama. He envisaged a type of theatre in which there would be no scenery, though he was struck by the possibilities of moveable screens.[120] The Victorian and Edwardian verse drama had failed, he argued, because it had tried to exist in theatre settings which created a sense of realism. The language, he insisted, must create both setting and atmosphere.

E. Martin Browne pointed out that Bottomley's great contribution to verse drama was his success in establishing a new approach to the writing of stage language:

   . . . he studied the diction of his own time for its rhythms. And he
   evolved a type of verse for his dialogue, which in its structure based on

stress with no reference to the number of syllables and its free use of other than iambic feet, broke the new ground . . .[121]

In this Bottomley was true to his declared aim, for he had noted with dismay the widening gulf between stage dialogue and ordinary speech, and declared that: ". . . if poetry is to regain its right of entry to the theatre it must learn again to base itself upon contemporary speech rhythms."[122]

Many of Bottomley's ideas on the theatre were extremely interesting. He demanded richly costumed figures to speak his lines who would stand out from, and not be overwhelmed by, their background. He experimented with light and sound and, in terms of stage technique, would have found more acceptance in the experimental theatre of the present day. There were some critics who even suggested that early reactions to his plays were misguided. R. L. Megroz wrote in 1923, "*Gruach* is a play that is as dramatic as it is poetically beautiful" then, turning his attention to the full range of Bottomley's work, he continued:

> It passeth the wit of men to understand why only one other of Gordon Bottomley's plays has been acted . . . [his] plays are well charged with dramatic action. The characters . . . are rich blooded human beings . . . there is scarcely a play published . . . which would not . . . thrill and delight . . .[123]

Allardyce Nicholl's *British Drama* contains a careful and fair analysis of most of Bottomley's plays,[124] but we should mention here his one play written for a cathedral performance. This was *The Acts of Saint Peter* written for the octocentenary celebrations of the Cathedral Church of St Peter, Exeter in 1933 and performed again in 1934, under E. Martin Browne's direction, at St Margaret's, Westminster. In this play, particularly, Bottomley worked for clear, uncomplicated poetic language based on speech rhythms. It was probably the first religious play in modern times which did not distort the syntax to fit the verse form and it impressed E. Martin Browne, who was to become a key figure in the further development of verse drama, by this quality.

The second production of the play was sponsored by *The Religious Drama Society* and attracted a good deal of attention. *The Times* considered it better than the average religious play[125] and although

The Acts of St Peter rarely rose to enormous heights it did avoid the almost perverse, esoteric quality of some of his other plays. It could, however, be argued that in writing for a cathedral audience, Bottomley was merely catering for another kind of élitism. It was only when the Canterbury Cathedral plays involved leading figures from the commercial theatre that this problem began to disappear and a wider audience were forced to take notice.

Lascelles Abercrombie, whilst anxious to reinstate poetry into drama, was far less concerned than Bottomley with how he could achieve this in theatrical terms. His main achievement was to use blank verse without any appearance of antiquity:

> . . . to liberate once more this, his favourite measure, from the restrictive and academic devitalization of melodious, but too pedantically precise, Victorian practice.[126]

Abercrombie maintained that every sentence in poetry contains two sorts of energy: kinetic energy, that is onward movement, and potential energy, which is generated by the juxtaposition of images and sounds.[127] From this premise he argued that verse was a much more subtle means of expression than prose and that only verse with its "rich elaboration"[128] could adequately express the "inmost spirit of human action."[129]

Although many of Abercrombie's poems were written in dramatic form, only *End of the World* was remotely stageable. Even this play only achieved performances in small, amateur theatres. The tiny, fifty-seat Contemporary Theatre Club performed *End of the World* in 1938; this was a particularly sensitive production of what Edward Marsh had once described as "a sublime work, in its fusion of poetry and comedy there has been nothing like it."[130] Una Ellis-Fermor reviewed the 1938 production:

> All these actors could speak verse and reverenced it. They appreciated, even delighted in, their medium and the substance of the play. Sure of the dramatist's imaginative knowledge (that inner conviction without which no actor can trust himself as a vehicle of poetic expression) they became the characters of the play . . . They reached what is perhaps the greatest achievement possible to a team of actors in poetic drama - to make that poetry 'real and familiar.'[131]

Some General Tendencies

It is important at this stage to draw together certain features of the work done by the 'Boars Hill Playwrights' because of their considerable significance for later dramatists writing for Canterbury. As individuals, they occupied important and influential positions - Masefield as Poet Laureate and the bestselling poet of his day, Binyon as President of the English Association, Abercrombie as Professor of English at London University. As a group, they, together with Yeats and Gilbert Murray,[132] dominated the English Association, the stronghold of the centrist position in poetry for nearly two decades.

Their influence on subsequent verse dramatists was at least as great as Eliot's. Charles Williams, for instance, though superficially affected by Eliot's style, was first and foremost an admirer of Abercrombie; and Christopher Fry has far more in common with Bottomley than with Eliot. But the main consideration must be to explain why, precisely, this group of writers were concerned to write poetic drama at all; because, whatever we may now see in retrospect, they themselves were convinced of the importance of this task and others were equally convinced that the whole future of poetry in the theatre lay in their hands: "the play in verse," A. N. Monkhouse wrote in 1925, "has yet an estimable present with Mr Abercrombie, Mr Binyon, Mr Bottomley . . ."[133]

The Boars Hill dramatists were forced, with Yeats, to introduce an entirely new dimension into the writing of verse drama. Nineteenth century writers had certainly made conscious efforts to create new and interesting verse drama, but these efforts had been based on a largely unconscious and unarticulated feeling that it was the right thing to do. In the years between the wars however, the idea of a popular verse drama had become almost inconceivable, so that Nowell Smith could write with some conviction:

Modern verse drama will never pay its way on the stage except in an educated Utopia.[134]

As Christians, faced with rationalist humanism, the Boars Hill dramatists centred their attack on the subject matter and style of naturalistic theatre. Pointing to the ultimate Truth, which lay, not in the temporal and mundane, but in the transcendent and eternal, they maintained that the proper concern of the theatre was not in the re-creation of everyday life. They doubted, in fact, if drama was really, at its best, a representation; it was rather a form of presentation; and in this belief they were reinforced by the example of the No plays of Japan.

Naturalistic language was their particular target. To some extent this attitude grew from the Georgian view that poetry was a public art, and that a poem was something to be read aloud.[135] But, in maintaining that the external was not easily confined within the bounds of naturalism, they argued that only poetry was capable of exploring the spiritual depths. The range of expression was much wider in verse, with its rhythms capable of generating excitement,[136] its kinetic and potential energy. Lascelles Abercrombie suggested:

> The thing about poetic diction is that it somehow manages to hold more meaning, more of its originating intention than other kinds of language.[137]

Gordon Bottomley even attributed the contemporary theatre's "almost exclusive pursuit of actualism"[138] to the concentration on the re-creation of everyday speech patterns:

> It is true that in the theatre a form of speech is still used - a halting, colloquial usage in the service of a naturalistic convention that aims to present life as we know it and live it: in it, however, language has taken a secondary place, it is not the master force on the stage, it is an accompaniment of the action.[139]

The implication in practical, theatrical terms was that the Boars Hill dramatists wanted "more speech and sound"[140] than was common in most plays of their time. In this they were assisted by the fashion for choral-speaking and they countered any suggestion that physical action was often reduced to a minimum in their plays by further claims for the nature of poetic language. "Most essentially of all," said Gordon Bottomley, "poetry differs from other uses of language on the stage in being, in itself, action."[141] Then, in a dangerous generalisation, he added, "words do not even need to be reinforced by movement, and drama at its highest reaches is a sound in stillness."[142]

Bitterly, Clifford Bax complained of the apparent ignorance of the theatre shown by the poet-dramatists:

> They believe that an audience will listen enraptured to 'choruses' which contain, it may be, sentences that overrun five, six or seven lines. They never consider the strain of listening . . . they fondle their lines and phrases and forget that a play must for ever move onward . . . Has the audience assembled to hear a recitation of verse or see a story unfold?[143]

But, for Bottomley at least, the unfolding of a plot in the naturalistic sense, was not the function of poetic drama:

> The poetic drama is, indeed, not so much a representation of a theme as a meditation upon it or a distillation from it . . . the evocation and isolation for our delight of the elements of beauty and spiritual illumination in the, perhaps, terrible and always serious theme chosen. [144]

The belief that theatre should deal with themes that could not be touched upon in contemporary, naturalistic settings led to the choice of subjects of an historical or mythological nature. This was partly due to a shared enthusiasm for pre-Raphaelite art and for medievalism of the painter and brilliant stage designer, Charles Ricketts.[145] But the Boars Hill dramatists were adamant that the quality of contemporary life could be discussed more effectively in drama, when the subject was not recognisably modern. It was only possible, Bottomley argued in defence of Binyon's subject matter, to see great design and the operation of providence from a distance. Shakespeare, Bottomley maintained, had come to the same conclusion when he presented the drama of Elizabeth and Essex in *Anthony and Cleopatra*.[146]

Historical settings immediately created the problem of an appropriate style of language and in some ways this defeated the brave intentions of adapting blank verse to modern usage (Abercrombie and Binyon's approach), or of basing stage verse on modern speech rhythms (Masefield and Bottomley). It is for this reason that many of the poets' plays are most successful when a sense of complete timelessness is created. And it was with the conviction that the timeless and eternal could only be represented in verse that they turned to write religious plays.

We have, therefore, a group of Christian writers, deeply concerned with new approaches to verse drama. The experimental nature of much of their work had led them to revolutionary ideas about language and the theatre which suggested quite different developments from those in the commercial theatre of their day. They were particularly committed to simplicity of staging, well-spoken verse and the spiritual experience of drama. Conditions at Canterbury were ideal for further development along these lines.

Notes to Chapter 3

1. Derek Stanfield, *Christopher Fry: An Appreciation* (London 1951), 172.
2. Audrey Williamson, *Theatre of Two Decades* (London 1951), 129.
3. Mary Morrison, ed. *The Correspondence of Henrik Ibsen*, letter dated 25th May 1883 (London 1905), 367.
4/5. See Appendix.
6. Quoted in Laurence Irving, *The Successors* (London 1967), 145.
7. Allardyce Nicoll, *A History of English Drama* (Cambridge 1955), IV, 60-63.
8. Stanley Weintraub, ed. *Shaw, an Autobiography 1856-1898* (London 1970), 231.
9. Eric Bentley, *The Life of Drama* (London 1966), 172-5.
10. S. R. Littlewood, 'Poverty, Poetry and Plays', *English VI*, No. 31. (1946), 25-37.
11. G. B. Shaw, *Pen Portraits and Reviews* (London 1949), 161,5.
12. G. B. Shaw, *Ellen Terry and Bernard Shaw. A Correspondence* (London 1932), Preface, xxv.
13. William Poel, *Monthly Letters. Essays on the Drama* (London 1929), 14.
14. Allardyce Nicoll, *op. cit.*, 214.
15. Quoted in M. R. Booth, et. al., *op. cit.*, 196.
16. Audrey Williamson, *op. cit.*, 128. Refers to a later broadcast version with Sybil Thorndike and Rosalie Crutchley, but overlooks the 1922 performance.
17. Preface to the published edition, 1819.
18. The events are described in Elizabeth Sprigge, *Sybil Thorndike Casson* (London 1971), 145-7.
19. See Appendix.
20. Quoted in Laurence Irving, *The Successors* (London 1967), 145.
21. See above, p. 8.
22. *op. cit.*, 144-5.
23. D. Donoghue, *The Third Voice* (Princeton 1959), Chapter 2, 23. He suggests that Browning, in his desire to please Macready, wrote inferior dramatic verse. But Browning, Donoghue maintains "came closer than any other poet-dramatist to the invention of a theatre form answerable to the dominant motives of his time."
24. M. R. Booth, et al., *op. cit.*, 197.
25. Laurence Irving, *The Successors* (London 1967), 145.
26. Quoted by T. R. Barnes, 'Shaw and the London Theatre' in *The Pelican Guide to English Literature VII. The Modern Age.* (Harmondsworth

1961), 220.

27/28. Hallam Lord Tennyson, *Alfred Lord Tennyson. A Memoir by His Son* (London 1897), II, 131, 181.

29. For details see Laurence Irving, *Henry Irving* (London 1951), 367.

30/31/32/33. Hallam Lord Tennyson, *op. cit.*, 131, 198, 199.

34. See especially *TR1*, (Bibliography, D).

35/36. Hallam Lord Tennyson, *op. cit.*, 196.

37. Harold Downs, ed. *Theatre and Stage* (Lon., undated circa 1947), II, 901.

38. S. R. Littlewood, 'Dramatic Notes', *English VI*, 34 (1947), 202.

39. See above, p. 8.

40. Hallam Lord Tennyson, *op. cit.*, 196.

41. See above, p. 8.

42. Radio programme: *The Voice of Henry Irving*, broadcast BBC Radio 3, October 1975.

43. See especially J. C. Trewin, 'Tall Troy's Down', *We'll Hear A Play* (London 1949), 85.

44/45. Quoted in L. Irving, *The Precarious Crust* (London 1971), 113.

46/47. Quoted in Allardyce Nicoll, *English Drama 1900-1930: The Beginnings of the Modern Period* (Cambridge 1973), 284.

48. See Appendix.

49. See below, p. 89.

50/51/52/53. L. Irving, *The Precarious Crust* (London 1971), 113, 236.

54. For a detailed consideration of Phillips's plays and of his close collaboration with Tree see Pricilla Thouless, *Modern Poetic Drama* (London 1934), 10-29.

55/56. Sybil Thorndike, 'The Theatre and Gilbert Murray', in Smith and Toynbee, ed., *Gilbert Murray: An Unfinished Autobiography* (London 1960), 152.

57. Quoted in Smith & Toynbee, ed., *op. cit.*, 17.

58. T. S. Eliot, 'Euripides and Professor Murray' (1920) in *Selected Essays* (London 1951), 62.

59. Quoted in Sybil Thorndike, *op. cit.*, 153

60. See below, p. 103.

61. T. S. Eliot, *op. cit.*, 64.

62. Edith Wynne-Matthison played the title rôle in the first modern performance of *Everyman* (1901). See below, p..

63. See below, p. 89.

64. See Appendix and below, p. 97.

65. E. R. Dodds in Smith & Toynbee, ed., *op.cit.*, 17.

66. See Appendix.

67. Dr W. A. Atkin's seminal work *The Voice* (London, 1900) was the basis of many textbooks of elocution.

68. See above, p. 61 for an example of the type of training in elocution common in the twenties and thirties.

69. Elsie Fogertie, *The Speaking of English Verse* (London 1923), 32-44.

70. See Marion Cole, *Fogie: The Life of Elsie Fogertie* (London 1967).

71. See John Holloway, 'The Literary Scene', *The Pelican Guide to English Literature VII. The Modern Age.* (Harmondsworth 1961), 88.

72. See above, p. 8.

73. See above, p. 18.

74. Elizabeth Sprigge, *Sybil Thorndike Casson* (London 1971).

75. See for instance Kenneth Muir, *op. cit.*, 105 or Allardyce Nicoll *English Drama - A Modern Viewpoint* (London 1968), 122-4.

76. Una Ellis Fermor 'The Little Theatres', *English I*, 5, (1937), 427.

77. Guy Boas, 'Amateur Drama', *English II*, 5, (1937), 384.

78. Una Ellis Fermor 'Village Drama 1350-1937', *English I*, 6 (1937), 558-561.

79. Priscella Thouless, *Modern Poetic Drama* (London 1934), 40.

80. See Robert H. Ross, *The Georgian Revolt: the Rise and Fall of Poetic Ideal* (London 1965), 37.

81. L. A. G. Strong, *John Masefield* (London 1952), 6.

82. John Masefield, *William Shakespeare* (NY 1911, London, revised 1954).

83. John Masefield, *Thanks Before Going: With Other Gratitude for Old Delight Including 'A Macbeth* Production' *and Various Papers not Before Printed* (London 1947).

84. Edward. G. Craig, *Scene: with Introduction and Poem by John Masefield* (London 1923).

85. E. Martin Browne, *Verse in the Modern English Theatre* - the *W. D. Thomas Memorial Lecture* delivered at the University College of Swansea, 28th Feb. 1963. (Cardiff 1963), 8.

86. For details and plan see G. Bottomley, A *Stage for Poetry* (London 1948).

87. See for example *The English Association Bulletin XL* (1920), 28; or *XLVIII* (1921), 39.

88. John Masefield, *With the Living Voice: an Address Given at the First General Meeting of the Scottish Association for the Speaking of Verse*, 24th Oct., 1924 (London 1925), 10.

89. John Masefield, *Recent Prose* (London 1924), quoted in J. C. Trewin, *Verse Drama Since 1800* (London 19656), 24.

90. Denis Donoghue, *op.cit.*, 29.
91. William Poel, *Monthly Letters: Essays on the Drama* (London 1929), 98.
92. Frank Dibb, 'Some Neglected Dramatists: No. 2 - John Masefield', *Amateur Stage XXV* 6 (1970), 28-29.
93. Yeats referred to Masefield as "my murderer", not for any literary reasons but because he had once confessed to Keats that as a child he had attacked his governess with a knife. See *English II*, 11 (1939), 273.
94. Arnold Bennett, *The Journal of Arnold Bennett* (New York 1933), 617.
95. Gerald Weales, *Religion in Modern English Drama* (Philadelphia 1961).
96. Published 1928.
97. J. C. Trewin, *Drama 1945-1950* (London 1951), 30.
98. E. Martin Browne maintains that Masefield "was a man of immense seriousness" T.R.2., see Bibliography D.
99. John Masefield, *The Tragedy of Nan and Other Plays* (London 1909).
100. cp. below, p. 131.
101. Ernest Reynolds, *Modern English Drama:A Survey of Theatre from 1900* (London 1949), 80.
102. Nowell Smith, 'Laurence Binyon', *The Dictionary of National Bibliography 1941-1950*, eds. L. G. Wickam-Legg & E. T. Williams (London 1959), 80-81.
103. A. A. Milne, 'Attila, My Attila', *Punch* September 11th (1907), 186.
104. Laurence Binyon, Preface to *Brief Candles* (London 1938).
105. Laurence Binyon, *Attila - A Tragedy in Four Acts* (London 1907), 134.
106. R. L. Megroz, 'Gordon Bottomley', *Bookman LXIV* 382, (1923), 177.
107. W. L. R., '*Arthur* by Laurence Binyon ', *The Bookman LXIV*, 379 (1923), 44-45.
108. Laurence Irving, *The Precarious Crust* (London 1971), 283.
109. Nowell Smith, 'Thoughts on Laurence Binyon's Poetry', *English IV* 23 (1943), 144-5.
110/111. Sybil Thorndike's memory of the message - the original card having been destroyed in the war, see Elizabeth Sprigge, *Sybil Thorndike Casson* (London 1971), 154.
112. Quoted in Nowell Smith, 'Laurence Binyon', *loc. cit.*, 80- 81.
113. Priscilla Thouless, *op.cit.*
114/115. Robert H. Ross, *op.cit.*, 142, 146-51.
116. W. W. Gibson and John Drinkwater were part of the 'coterie' and both wrote verse plays.
117/118. Robert H. Ross, *op.cit.*, 153, 152.
119. Gordon Bottomley, *A Stage for Poetry* (London 1948), xiii.

120. *Ibid.*, 28. The use of screens was a favourite device of Charles Ricketts and employed very effectively by Laurence Irving at Canterbury.

121. E. M. Browne, *Verse in the Modern English Theatre* (Cardiff 1963), 10.

122. Gordon Bottomley, 'Poetry in the Contemporary Theatre', *Essays and Studies by Members of the English Association XIX* (Oxford 1933), 141.

123. R. L. Megroz, 'Gordon Bottomley', *The Bookman LXIV*, 382, (1923), 177-8.

124. Allardyce Nicoll, *British Drama* 4th Edition (London 1947), 476-81.

125. *The Times*, March 21st 1934, 12.

126. W. W. Gibson, 'Lascelles Abercrombie', *English II 9*, (1939), 211-13.

127. Lascelles Abercrombie, 'Poetry and Contemporary Speech', *English Association Pamphlet No. 27* (London 1914), 5.

128/129. L. Abercrombie, 'John Drinkwater', *English II 5* (1937), 387.

130. Robert H. Ross, *op.cit.*, 153.

131. Una Ellis Fermor, 'Review of *The End of the World*', *English II 8* (1938), 109-11.

132. They were both Vice-Presidents.

133. A. N. Monkhouse, 'The Words and the Play', *Essays and Studies by Members of the English Association XI* (1925), 32-48.

134. Nowell Smith, 'Thoughts on Laurence Binyon's Poetry', *English IV 23* (1943), 145.

135. Most of the Georgians read their verse well, Masefield founded'The Oxford Recitations'.

136. See John Masefield, *With the Living Voice, loc. cit* (London 1925), 13.

137. Lascelles Abercrombie, *Poetry and Contemporary Speech, loc. cit.*, 4.

138/139. Gordon Bottomley, 'Poetry in the Contemporary Theatre', *Essays and Studies by Members of the English Association XIX* (1933), 138.

140. Gordon Bottomley, *A Stage for Poetry* (London 1948) xiii.

141/142. G. Bottomley, 'Poetry in Contemporary Theatre', *loc. cit.*, 140.

143. Clifford Bax, 'Plays in Verse', *Theatre and Stage*, ed Harold Downs, *II* (London undated, circa, 1939), 737.

144. Gordon Bottomley, 'Poetry in Contemporary Theatre', *loc. cit.*, 139-140.

145. See Appendix.

144. Gordon Bottomley, Introduction to The *Madness of Merlin* by Laurence Binyon (London 1947), vi.

Part II

Drama in Nave
and Chapter House

4

George Bell and Drama at Canterbury

George Kennedy Bell (1883-1958) was appointed chaplain to Archbishop Davidson in 1914. Davidson may well have been influenced in his choice by Bell's literary ability because he was seeking a biographer. Bell did not disappoint in this respect and eventually produced a three-volume work, *Randall Davidson*, which traces most of the important developments in the Anglican Church during the first twenty-five years of the twentieth century.[1] The young chaplain had shown an enthusiasm for poetry since his school days:

... preferring to read and write verses, and enjoying at Balsall Heath a private study from which were often heard sounds of his declamations of Shakespeare.[2]

At Westminster School he published his first poem, *The Splendour and Power Have Passed Away*, which was a tribute to the celebrations of Queen Victoria's Diamond Jubilee in Westminster Abbey. The school's Latin play in 1899 provided Bell with his first experience of a public performance - the young A. A. Milne was another of the players. Five years later, while in his third year at Christ Church College, Oxford, Bell won the coveted Newdigate

Prize for English Verse with his poem *Delphi*. This success prompted the publishing house of Routledge to appoint Bell as general editor for their projected series of *Golden Anthologies*: the first five volumes of which he edited entirely, namely: *Poems of Love, Poems of Nature, Poems of Life and Death, Poems of Patriotism* and *The Golden Book of Ballads*. Bell's biographer Ronald Jasper observes:

> It says much for his perspicacity that in the second of these four he included a poem, *I Have a Desire to Go* by Gerald Manley Hopkins, for at this time Hopkins was still unrecognised as a poet.[3]

Bell wrote later: "The first Hopkins I ever read and the lyric cry of it still thrills me."[4] It was Bell's recognition of disturbing new talent that was to be his great contribution to literature. E. Martin Browne gives a revealing insight into Bell's influence on T. S. Eliot in his book *The Making of T. S. Eliot's Plays*.[5]

Bell gained a first in 'Mods', and a second in 'Greats' at Oxford and went on to Wells Theological College. Here he developed an interest in the ecumenical movement and he devised a litany for use in services of Intercession for Christian Unity; he was evolving that concept of the rôle of the Church which led to his involvement with the theatre. His work with the worldwide, ecumenical movement culminated in his election as president of the World Council for Life and Work in 1932.

Such was Bell's dynamic ability in his position as Archbishop's chaplain that it came as no surprise when, in 1924, he was elevated to the vacant office of Dean of Canterbury. He at once demonstrated his concern that the Church should reach outwards. The Cathedral, he insisted, was to remain open for increasingly longer periods; admission charges were abolished and vergers instructed to permit ladies without hats to enter the building. A thorough revision of the Sunday services was undertaken, thus enabling the King's school boys (whom Bell consulted) to be spared the two-hour sequence to which they had been subjected. The first ever radio broadcasts from a cathedral were negotiated by Bell and, in 1925, he was already considering the revolutionary idea of the Cathedral sponsoring some form of Christian drama. With this in mind, he wrote to Geoffrey Whitworth, the founder of the British Drama League, requesting a selection of plays suitable for performance in church. Among the plays sent was John Masefield's verse play, *The Trial of Jesus*, which must have impressed Bell considerably for it was to Masefield that he was to turn when he had formulated his ambitious plans. As a first move, however, he persuaded the Roman Catholics to unite with the Anglicans in a celebration of the seven hundredth anniversary of the coming of the Grey Friars which included a reading by Laurence Housman from his *Little Plays of St Francis*.[6] Bell was himself a keen organiser of play readings and an enthusiast for verse speaking, having taken lessons in voice production as a curate at Leeds Parish Church because he was anxious about the audibility of his sermons.

Bell, like Stuart Headlam, was too involved in the practical concerns of the Church's mission to achieve particular distinction as an original theologian. As Dean of Canterbury he took a lively interest in local affairs, housing, education and unemployment, but at the same time showed a clear grasp of the Church's internal organisation. Bell was greatly concerned about the divisions in the Christian Church which, he felt, prevented it from being an effective body and, as his career progressed, he became increasingly aware of the theological writings of Bonhoeffer who, since 1927, had been developing similar ideas of the nature of the Church. "The Church is Christ", said Bonhoeffer, "existing as community and is to be understood as a collective person."[7] Consequently, when Bell became Bishop of Chichester in 1929, one of his first moves was to present a resolution at an international, ecumenical meeting at Eisenach, which called upon all Christian communities to renounce war and to bring pressure on their governments to settle international disputes by arbitration.

Bell's resolution was later described as "one of the most courageous and far-sighted actions that the ecumenical movement has ever taken",[8] but it was only the beginning of considerable controversy which surrounded the Bishop for much of his life. He rapidly developed a close friendship with Bonhoeffer and their subsequent correspondence reveals the nature of progressive ecumenical thinking during the period of emerging Nazism. During the war, Bell denounced obliteration bombing by either side and many churchmen thought that this, more than any other reason, accounted for the appointment of Fisher and not Bell to the vacant Archbishopric of Canterbury in 1945. Professor. D. M. Mackinnon summed up the feelings of many of Bell's supporters:

> The historians of the Church of England may yet recognise that the worst misfortune to befall its leadership at the end of the war was less the premature death of William Temple than his succession by Fisher of London and not by Bell of Chichester.[9]

Bell appears, however, to have harboured no bitterness and at his last appearance in Convocation he returned to, perhaps, his favourite theme. He moved a motion that the Church:

> ... offers a special welcome to the work done in recent years by poets, artists and producers in the revival of religious drama.[10]

Bell was looking back, self-effacingly, on a revival that he had helped to create.

The Coming of Christ

Writing at the time of Bishop Bell's death, E. Martin Browne wrote: "To George Bell the Church was above all things a creative body."[11] Perhaps the most significant expression of this vision was Bell's desire that drama should be staged in the Mother Cathedral of the Anglican Communion. Bell recalled the realisation of his idea in a sermon he preached in Wittersham Parish Church during Advent in 1953:

> I well remember the origin of the play. John Masefield stayed at the Deanery in Canterbury, one summer's night in 1927. As Dean, I took him round the Cathedral after supper with Ruth Spooner. He was thrilled with all he saw, and the light in which he saw it. Showing him the great nave and the long flight of steps with their separating platforms leading up to the choir . . . I told him of my dream of a nativity play in Canterbury Cathedral on that very place . . . A few weeks later after consulting the Archbishop of Canterbury I wrote and invited him to write a nativity play for Canterbury Cathedral.[12]

Masefield responded by a telegram (now in the British Museum): "Will gladly do all I can to help" and, during a stay in Cornwall throughout August, wrote his play, *The Coming of Christ*. The poet was later to acknowledge his fascination with the life of Christ as a subject for verse in his *Grace Before Ploughing: Fragments of Autobiography*.[13] Here he describes a nineteenth century poem, *The Man Born to be King* by an anonymous woman writer, as "a guide and a marvel for over eighty years." The title was used again by another Canterbury playwright, Dorothy L. Sayers, for her remarkable radio drama that was broadcast during the Second World War.

The Chapter of Canterbury, which twenty-six years earlier had refused Poel's offer to stage *Everyman* in the Cathedral, was now confronted with a more daring proposal by its own Dean. Even the Archbishop, with his declared sympathy towards the stage, had advised Bell against the project; but Bell made his determination clear and, with some reluctance, the Chapter gave him the permission he requested. Bell at once asked Masefield to invite Gustav Holst to compose a score. Holst had already produced a most effective setting of the choruses from Gilbert Murray's translation of Euripides's *Alcestis*. Not only was Holst enthusiastic about the Canterbury project, he also agreed to provide a choir for the performance as difficulties had arisen over the use of the Cathedral Choir.

Bell next contacted Laurence Irving, Sir Henry's grandson, who lived nearby at Whitstable. This was an inspired move as Irving was not only a theatre designer of repute, but was steeped in almost every aspect of the theatre of his day and was keenly aware of its various movements. He had seen his grandfather in Sardou's version of Dante's *Inferno*[14] and attended Martin Harvey's production of *Oedipus Rex* at Covent Garden when players crossed the footlights into the auditorium.[15] His mother, Dorothea Baird, had created the part of Trilbee in Gerald du Maurier's famous play and of Mrs Darling in J. M. Barrie's *Peter Pan*. She had acted with Ben Greet in the verse plays of Stephen Phillips. Laurence Irving's father, H. B. Irving (1870-1919), achieved particular fame for his performance as the Admirable Crichton and became a supporter of the Actor's Church Union, whilst his uncle, L. S. Irving (1871-1914), the playwright, translator and actor, had maintained a lively correspondence with Shaw and had shown a genuine understanding of naturalistic acting, particularly in his Ibsen rôles.

Something of Laurence Irving's infectious enthusiasm, which Bell came to value so much, is reflected in his later autobiography:

Such was the inner life of the Theatre that as a boy I found wonderful
. . . and when the unforeseen time came for me to participate in the
creation of theatrical illusion I found it an abiding wonder that
sophistication never staled and familiarity with it never bred
disenchantment.[16]

When he and his wife Rosalind were invited to a dinner at the
Deanery in 1927, Irving's artistic work had already been seen the
previous year in the London production of *Vaudeville Vanities* and
in his illustrations for John Masefield's *Philip the King*.[17] Bell surprised the Irvings, neither of whom were experienced actors, by
asking them to undertake acting rôles in the play, explaining that
costumes would be provided by Masefield from his wardrobe at
Boars Hill. Irving's professionalism reacted strongly; the Irvings
agreed to act, but suggested that the quality of the designer should
be in keeping with the prominence of the poet and musician. Irving
accordingly obtained the services of his 'master', Charles Ricketts,
probably the most talented theatrical costume designer of his day.

It was Ricketts who alone had gone to meet Oscar Wilde on his
release from prison and had designed the costumes for Wilde's
Salome. His most memorable work was perhaps for the first performance of Shaw's *St Joan* (1924) but he had already produced
designs for Shaw's *Dark Lady of the Sonnets* (1910) and the playwright, who was sparing with such praise, described him as "noble
and generous . . . a natural aristocrat as well as a devoted artist."[18]
Ricketts's designs for Shakespeare's *King Lear* (1909) and *Henry VIII*
(1925) were "sumptuous and scholarly," according to Thomas
Lowensky,[19] and he had collaborated with both Laurance Binyon
on *Attila* (1907) and John Masefield on *Philip the King* (1914).

Ricketts responded to the Canterbury assignment with characteristic gaiety, protesting that "as a good atheist he could not
approve"[20], and was so amazed that Bell should embark on so large
a venture with so little guaranteed security that he remarked "The
spirit of St Francis is indeed abroad!"[21] With his usual sensitivity
and incredible speed, Ricketts produced a set of designs which
exemplified those qualities of boldness in decoration and unity of
colour scheme which had achieved a revolution in theatrical costume and had inspired Yeats to describe him as "the magician."[22]

Working from Ricketts's designs, a team of volunteers, led by Bell's wife, made the costumes, which *The Times* critic labelled as "The plain yet sumptuous medieval finery of which Ricketts was master."[23] Photographs of the 1928 production (now in the British Museum) show how successfully Ricketts took account of the vastness of his theatre, the play having been staged on the Chancel steps. The photographs reveal a pre-Raphaelite flavour; Spanos maintains that this in some way reflects George Bell's tastes,[24] but as I have shown, it was Laurence Irving and Charles Ricketts who were entirely responsible for this aspect of the production.

The original costumes made a brief reappearance for a revival of *The Coming of Christ* in 1953, but to get a good impression of the full effect which Ricketts achieved in the 1928 première we must now rely on the photographic records. These show an abundance of flowers and foliage; lilies are scattered on the stage; leaves and fruit curl and cluster around the Virgin's throne. The angels hold flowers in gauntletted hands while they bend on wings bright with circular and feather-shaped motifs. The kings, in full-sleeved robes, are attended by knights bearing huge shields emblazoned boldly with eagle, leopard and snake; the knights wear tabards of geometric patchwork design and their banners are startling with devices of flying arrows.

The production of *The Coming of Christ* was scheduled for 5.30pm and 8.00pm on Whit Monday, 1928. The cast was to be drawn from local amateurs and from Masefield's own Boars Hill company and would include his daughter Judith as the Virgin Mary. Masefield himself agreed to produce the play and, Laurence Irving recalls, always wore a dinner jacket for this purpose!

From the moment that a first reading of the play was held in the Deanery, three daunting problems became apparent: the first was that some of the sentiments expressed by the shepherds might easily upset members of the audience, which would almost certainly include army officers. Secondly, Masefield had introduced a representation of the Deity in the figure of Anima Christi - a factor which might well antagonise further an already unsympathetic group within the Chapter.

Figure 3: The Angels of the Host of Heaven survey
the infant Christ, *The Coming of Christ*.

Bell remained adamant, however, that Masefield was a serious artist and that if his cherished idea that "The Poet and Artist re-enter the Church" was to be achieved, there must be freedom of expression for those involved. The text, it was decided, could not be cut and Bell was prepared to face the consequences of the anti-war sentiments expressed in the play. To the problem of the Anima Christi, Bell applied a similar solution to Poel in the production of *Everyman*. There would be strict anonymity for the whole cast, and Bell even refused to disclose the identity of the actor playing the Anima Christi to the rest of the cast. In both his method and its outcome Bell appears to have been remarkably successful: the only cast list surviving is an incomplete set of pencilled names on the back of the production photographs and in the minds of the few surviving actors. The part of Anima Christi was, in fact, played by Bernard Storrs, a young regular soldier, but in *The Daily News* review the part was attributed to the Precentor. Masefield's play certainly may have offended a small minority of the audience, but the enthusiastic reception it received generally suggested that Bell's confidence and approach were justified.

The third problem, however, was less easily dealt with and this was the very difficult acoustics of the Cathedral. Laurence Irving recalls vividly that Masefield went to great lengths to train his cast in slow and careful diction. He would take a line like "And the men I employ, all are mine" and insist that Irving listened to the resonance of each word before speaking the next. Bell also took advantage of the enormous interest that the forthcoming produc-tion had generated to warn the audience of the problem. To the six thousand people who applied for tickets he sent two notices: one informing them of an extra performance of the play; and a second stating:

> It will be understood that while every effort will be made to help the proper hearing of the spoken words - as well as the music - the acous-tics of the Cathedral present special difficulties. Ticket holders are urged to procure and read copies of the Play beforehand.

Bell included details of the special Cathedral Edition of the play that would be published in Canterbury and, greatly encouraged by the demand for tickets, made the final preparations.

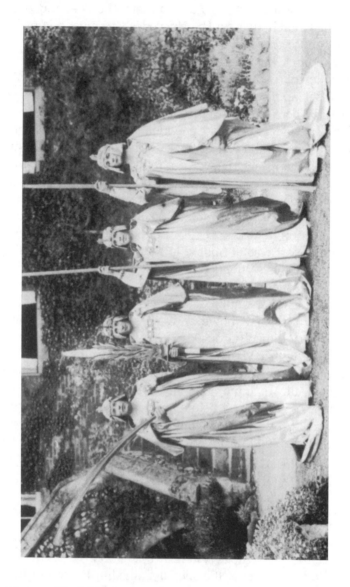

Figure 4: The Male Spirits - The Power, The Sword, The Mercy and The Light, *The Coming of Christ.*

The Canterbury Festival

The successful production of *The Coming of Christ* is described in the next chapter. It followed shortly after George Bell had established the organisation The Friends of Canterbury Cathedral for the purpose of maintaining and improving the fabric of the Cathedral. With the remarkable Margaret Babington[25] installed in the Christchurch Gateway as steward and treasurer of the Friends and £800 from the performance of Masefield's play set aside in trust, Bell left for a holiday. He went to Saltzburg to see Max Reinhardt's production of *Jedermann*; Laurence Irving accepted an invitation from Douglas Fairbanks to work for him in Hollywood.

Bell was evidently inspired by what he encountered in Saltzburg, for on his return he determined to establish an annual festival of the arts at Canterbury under the auspices of the Friends.[26] He arranged for Nugent Monck[27] to bring his Maddermarket Players from Norwich to perform *Everyman* and Marlowe's *Dr Faustus*, and for Dr Adrian Boult to conduct the recently formed BBC Orchestra in a series of concerts. Reluctantly, it was admitted that a good deal of Masefield's play had been inaudible[28] and so it was decided that *Everyman* should be performed before the West Door and *Dr Faustus* in the Chapter House. For the next twenty-five years the Chapter House became one of the most unusual play-houses in England.

E. Martin Browne described the building, erected in its present form with money given by the thousands of pilgrims who had sought the shrine of the "holy blessed martyr" Thomas[29] and in which he was to produce *Murder in the Cathedral*, thus:

> This is a rectangular building of the early fourteenth century, with arcading round the walls to provide a range of stalls for the monks and, on the east wall, more imposing ones, raised higher, for the prior and other offices. At the end of the century, the walls were heightened and the roof given a barrel vault of Irish bog oak.[30]

The Chapter House presented enormous difficulties to actors, producers and technicians: the high, long roof and great expanses of stone and glass caused acoustic problems that could only be overcome by careful articulation and projection; entrances and exits were confined to a central aisle, ninety feet long; and electricity supply had to be brought from the Cathedral crypt!

Figure 5: A Laurence Irving design for a Festival poster.

The summer festival of 1929 established the pattern for future festivals at Canterbury and demonstrated the driving energy of both Bell and Margaret Babington. But at this point Bell was called to the Bishopric of Chichester where he immediately showed his continuing concern for drama by appointing E. Martin Browne as Director of Religious Drama for the diocese[31] in the belief that: "Through religious drama, religious truths may be brought home afresh and the imagination stirred and healed."[32] Between them, Bell and Browne, "who has driven more poets to drama than any living man",[33] were to determine largely the development of verse drama in England for the next decade.

Bishop Bell, however, retained his interest in Canterbury and remained a trustee of the fund established by *The Coming of Christ*. He ensured that subsequent deans acted as chairman of the Friends and that the festivals continued to take place each summer. In 1930 Ben Greet,[34] another of the important figures in the revival of medieval drama, produced scenes from Shakespeare's *Henry IV, Part 2* and *Henry V* in the Chapter House but already the absence of both Bell and the professional advice of Laurence Irving were having their effect. The following year saw no drama at all and, in 1932, a production of Tennyson's *Becket* was crudely staged in front of drapes.

The 1932 production was, nevertheless, important for a number of reasons, some of which were not realised at the time. An 'acting edition' of the play was made by the producer, Eileen Thorndike,[35] and published by a Canterbury firm, H. J. Goulden. This was the first of a series of Canterbury plays published over a number of years, a publishing venture that provided a unique encouragement to living playwrights in this respect. By selecting *Becket* the festival management began a tradition of plays connected with the history of Canterbury and, by involving members of the Thorndike and Casson[36] families, formed a link with the professional theatre in general and the Old Vic in particular.

The limitations of staging forced the producer to adopt techniques which looked back to Elizabethan times, or forward to Brecht: "Changes of scene were announced by clearly worded placards giving time and place, and the moving of a few simple properties."[37]

Figure 6: Margaret Babington as Queen Eleanor, Mary Casson as Rosamund with E. Ewbank (Eileen Thorndike's son) as Little Geoffrey in *Becket* (1932).

Lighting was of the most rudimentary kind - a pair of arc floods which could illuminate large areas but were incapable of subtle balance or any illusory effect. These lights were operated for this and every succeeding year by Mr Fairbrass of a local firm of electricians, S. W. Bligh.[38] This involvement of the local community in an event of national significance was an important feature of the Festival. Local family businesses, public schools and private houses which clustered around the city centre and the Cathedral precincts provided services and hospitality, free of charge, to actors, producers and playwrights. It represents, perhaps, the nearest approach in modern times to the community involvement of the medieval festivals;[39] but it also explains why such an event would be impossible today. There was, however, the great danger that an inward-looking, self-congratulatory atmosphere might cause a decline in artistic standards:

> Mary Casson as Rosamund was altogether delightful, and the scene in the bower between the King, little Geoffrey and herself made a charming picture.[40]

It was this lack of perception and the onset of mediocrity that Laurence Irving recognised on his return from America. Taking advantage of a gift of one hundred pounds, he designed a permanent setting for use in the Chapter House and this "the first open stage in England"[41] was seen, together with his magnificent costume designs, in a production of *Becket* in 1933.[42] Irving's stage consisted of moveable screens which echoed the medieval architecture of the Chapter House and provided a variety of entrances, textures and shapes. E. V. Lucas attended a performance of the play, which was again produced by Eileen Thorndike from a further revised acting edition, and gave a vivid account of the impression which the open stage made on him in an age still dominated by the proscenium arch:

> I have that feeling of participation in it all which is the test of good presentation and good acting; and this, I think, though due of course to the sincerity of the production, is due even more to its simplicity, dispensing as it did with footlights, with orchestra, with scenery, with intervals and perhaps above all with the ordinary stage entrances and exits at the wings . . . That inviolate dividing line, the footlights, may

mean an increase of mystery and illusion in the theatre proper, where the two worlds, the real and the unreal, never mingle; but you have but to cause that mingling to occur and . . . new elements of intimacy and realism come in.[43]

The advances made at Canterbury filtered into the commercial theatre, but it was at least another 20 years before the open stage was widely accepted as an alternative to the proscenium arch.

Figure 7: Tennyson's *Becket* (1933). Laurence Irving's permanent setting is used for the first time. Russell Thorndike as Thomas Becket.

E. V. Lucas was acutely aware of the savagery of the cuts made in Tennyson's text. Even some of the most famous passages in which Lucas recalled "Irving's attitude, his tones, the beauty of his face"[44] had disappeared; but he had no hesitation in commending Russell Thorndike's performance as Becket or in suggesting that the production of the same play with Laurence Irving's costume and setting should become an annual event.[45]

Bishop Bell and Laurence Irving were interested in new ideas, however. In the previous October (1932), Bell arranged a conference at Chichester to which he invited Lascelles Abercrombie, Laurence Binyon, Martin and Henzie Browne, Mona Swann (an expert on choral speaking), Geoffrey Whitworth and Charles Williams to discuss the whole question of religious and biblical drama. They agreed that the text of the 'Authorised Version' of *The Bible* was the most suitable basis for the language of religious plays, but that writers should have absolute freedom to express individual ideas. Jasper records that "they regarded the most appropriate form as the masque accompanied by music and ceremonial" but that they "felt that great reserve should be exercised in representing the Deity."[46] Binyon and Abercrombie apparently made a particular impression on Bell and when, shortly, the question of the Canterbury play for 1934 arose, Laurence Binyon was asked if his play, *The Young King*, could be used.

Binyon's play had been performed in November 1923 at John Masefield's Boars Hill theatre,[47] but it was now completely revised for Canterbury where it had the attraction of providing an historical sequel to the events described in *Becket*. Binyon himself attended some rehearsals, directed by Eileen Thorndike, and two performances.[48]

Another feature of the 1934 Festival was a lecture by Dame Sybil Thorndike entitled *The Theatre as a Service to the Community* in which she reminded her audience of some of the developments of which they were, in all probability, entirely unaware. She maintained that:

> The beginning of the downfall or perversion of the theatre was when the Church let it go . . . The theatre had become an excrescence instead of an integral part of religion and life . . . The proscenium was the

beginning of something that made a division, a gulf between actor and spectator and stopped the theatre from becoming the common art.[49]

Figure 8: Design by Laurence Irving for *Becket* (1933) -
The Procession of the French King.

Whatever their contribution in bringing live theatre to the people of Canterbury or to the development of stage techniques, neither *Becket* nor *The Young King* can have satisfied George Bell as having established a relevant, meaningful Christian drama. He decided, therefore, to use the money in trust from *The Coming of Christ* to sponsor new plays which did not simply celebrate history but explored the Christian faith in twentieth century terms. Bell's genius for recognising new talent had already shown itself again in 1930 when he first met T. S. Eliot and introduced him to E. Martin Browne. The result of this meeting had been *The Rock* (1933). Bell now approached Eliot with the request for a Canterbury play, offering him £100 and performance guaranteed! Remember that this was at a time when commercial theatre managements were giving little incentive to the writing of verse plays.

Neither the use of verse nor the subject-matter was stipulated by Bell or anyone else, but successive playwrights maintained the traditions that had been established. How Eliot came to write *Murder in the Cathedral* is exhaustively documented in E. Martin Browne's *The Making of T. S. Eliot's Plays*,[50] which also describes the production itself in great detail. It is important to note, however, that Eliot was acutely aware of the setting of his play, so near to the spot where Becket had been murdered, and of Tennyson's earlier play which had so recently been performed there.[51] The scenes in *Murder in the Cathedral* where the knights enter the Cathedral are a conscious reworking of the final two scenes in Eileen Thorndike's acting edition of *Becket*:

> **Becket:** Prate not of bonds, for never, oh, never again
> Shall the waste voice of the bond-breaking sea
> Divide me from the Mother Church of England,
> My Canterbury . . .
> **Fitzurse:** The King commands you to absolve the bishops
> Whom you have excommunicated.
> **Becket:** They have but to submit . . .
> **The Four Knights:** The King commands you
> We are all king's men
> (Scene Five in Tennyson's *Becket* arr. Eileen Thorndike).

These lines echo very clearly in Eliot's play. The incidents of the knights returning armed and the unbarring of the doors were the same. Eliot's greatest dramatic shock, when the knights suddenly turn and address the audience, was intensified at Canterbury because the audience would have been expecting them to turn and rush out, as they had done in *Becket*. Eliot's *Murder in the Cathedral* brought to Canterbury both E. Martin Browne, as producer, and Robert Speaight as the leading actor.[52] These two men were mainly responsible for the play's subsequent commercial success and Speaight was eventually to give more performances of Thomas Becket than had Sir Henry Irving.

The immediate effect of the 1935 production of *Murder in the Cathedral* was to increase the status of the Canterbury Festival, so that Bell had no hesitation in asking Charles Williams, a notable lay theologian and already a prolific writer of verse, fiction and biography, to write the Festival play for 1936. Williams was already known to Bell and was at that time engaged in helping Bell's massive *Randall Davidson* through the Oxford University Press. He accepted Bell's invitation to visit Canterbury to see the stage and here he met the forthright Margaret Babington who complained bitterly that for the previous four years the plays had ended with the protagonist's body being carried in solemn procession up the aisle. "We want no more of that," she added.[53]

Williams obliged and announced that his play would be *The Masque of Thomas Cranmer of Canterbury* which dealt with the sixty-fourth Archbishop of Canterbury who actually ran to his death! *The Canterbury Cathedral Chronicle* of April 1936, which also announced the death of Kipling (one of the first Friends) and of Holst gave an impressive list of events for the approaching Festival. The Poet Laureate, John Masefield, would speak; Alfred Noyes would lecture on Dickens; the many concerts would include a new work by Arthur Bliss; and:

The play gives us Mr Robert Speaight, whom we are indeed happy to have with us again, a magnificent chance for the creation of character; and there are many good parts, Henry VIII among them. The verse is original and interesting . . . The form of the play, too, is fresh and beautifully adapted to the needs of the Chapter House. It may be reckoned a worthy successor to Mr Eliot's play, and should make exciting entertainment for anyone who enjoys both colour and thought on the stage.[54]

Such was the impression made by Williams's play that *The Times* now felt that the Canterbury Festival had created a new "school" of drama:

If Mr T. S. Eliot may be said to have founded it with *Murder in the Cathedral*, Mr Charles Williams helps to establish its characteristics. This school of drama, written for performance in the Chapter House ... has no tradition to follow. The world has changed too much to allow the early, ecclesiastical Miracles - much less the later, civic Miracles - to stand for precedent; and religious plays written - by Mr Masefield, Mr Boulter and a few others - for performance in church have been too few to create a tradition. The Canterbury Cathedral drama could follow what course it would; and if it continues to be rather mystical than eventful, rather lyrical than dramatic, there is no reason why it should not develop on whatever lines it pleases.[55]

The writer was obviously too close to events to be aware of the various traditions that helped to shape the Canterbury Plays.

What was important for the continuation of the creative activity of the Festival was that those involved felt that they were exploring new approaches. Charles Williams had for some years been discussing his mystical Christianity in a lively correspondence with C. S. Lewis and Dorothy L. Sayers. The trio called themselves "inklings" because they felt that they "all had a glimpse of the meaning of God."[56] Dorothy Sayers was approached to write the next Canterbury play. At first, this seemed a strange choice: her only experience of writing for the theatre had been an adaptation of one of her Peter Wimsey stories at the suggestion of Muriel St Clare Byrne, a contemporary at Somerville College and now, in 1936, a lecturer at the Royal Academy of Dramatic Art. *Busman's Honeymoon*, which opened in Birmingham in 1936, was hardly a promising pedigree for a Canterbury play, but a collection of Dorothy Sayers's verse, *Catholic Tales*, had contained a verse playlet, *The Mocking of Christ*, in which various characters from a contemporary life joined in the mockery of Jesus. The playlet had, at the time of publication in 1918, been considered shocking to read and unthinkable to produce; yet it demonstrated a desire to represent the Christian faith in dramatic terms, which had grown more insistent.

The Times Literary Supplement appreciated both the dilemma that faced Dorothy Sayers and her response to it:

As the years go by, it does not become easier to write a play for performance in the Chapter House. Mr Eliot has written such a play, and taken the great Canterbury subject . . . Mr Laurence Binyon . . . had made such fine dramatic use of other troubles in the life of King Henry II . . . Mr Charles Williams had 'done' Cranmer. Subjects suitable for the Canterbury Festival are not very many; and Mr Eliot's example and influence might well have prescribed . . . a mode which imitation would stereotype and sterilise. But here were the very circumstances fitted to nerve Miss Dorothy Sayers to strike out for herself.[57]

Few playwrights have projected themselves so completely into the production of one of their plays as did Dorothy Sayers. From March 19th 1937, when she gave the first reading of *The Zeal of Thy House*, until June 19th when the cast gathered after the final performance, she took up residence in Canterbury. Here she developed a firm friendship with Margaret Babington and much of their correspondence has survived. She also helped in the sewing of costumes, discussed theology long into the night with Ben Travers, the writer of farce who was staying with Laurence Irving, and attended rehearsals.[58] The Chapter House was filled with the beautifully modulated voice of Harcourt Williams, who had once played Paolo to Dorothea Baird's Francesca in Stephen Phillips's play;[59] and in William of Sens, the architect who rebuilt the Choir of the Cathedral shortly after the murder of Becket, Williams created a memorable rôle.

Dorothy Sayers's enthusiasm even extended to giving signed and inscribed photographs of herself to the cast and stage management[60] and she became so attached to Harcourt Williams and Frank Napier,[61] the joint producers, that she bequeathed them the rights of the play in her will made in 1938. Part of this gratitude was due to the fact that Williams and Napier arranged for the play to be produced at the Westminster Theatre after the Canterbury Festival and thence at the Duke of York's, the Garrick and finally, with virtually the same cast, at the New Theatre, Oxford in May 1939.

For a time it seemed that no play could be found to follow Dorothy Sayers's work, but as the *Canterbury Cathedral Chronicle* remarked:

> It is Mr Laurence Irving . . . who makes our Drama possible. When all seems blank despair he discovers a new Play, he designs the stage sets and the 'Canterbury Pilgrim' Festival poster.[62]

The 'new' play was already written when the Friends started their search for a play in 1938. It was *Christ's Comet* by Christopher Hassall,[63] whose serious work for the stage has been discredited, somewhat unreasonably, because he, like Laurence Irving, had written libretti for Ivor Novello. *Christ's Comet* broke the Canterbury tradition of plays of local interest; it is the story of a fourth wise man, though Hassall was at pains to point out that the play was almost complete before he heard of the existence of Henry Van Dyke's nineteenth century book *The Fourth Wise Man*. The playwright did, however, give his principal character Van Dyke's chosen name of Artaban, and it was to play this part that Robert Speaight returned to Canterbury to work under the distinguished producer Michael MacOwan.[64]

A greater variety of scene location than had previously been the case in Canterbury plays was required in *Christ's Comet*: it had not been written for, nor did it exploit the features of, the Chapter House. This necessitated a skilful adaptation of Laurence Irving's basic setting and employed the slightly greater sophistication of lighting which the replacement of the carbon arcs by mirror spotlights with colour filters permitted. To some extent, therefore, the production of *Christ's Comet* marked a watershed in the Canterbury Plays: the physical setting of the Chapter House or Cathedral ceased to be an integral part of the playwright's original conception of the play.

Two versions of *Christ's Comet* now exist. The second was a thorough revision of the play which Hassall undertook at the instigation of E. Martin Browne for his production at the Marlowe Theatre, Canterbury in 1958. Browne felt that the second version was vastly superior to the original, but whatever we may now think about *Christ's Comet* or twentieth century verse drama in general, at least one critic, writing after the 1938 production, felt differently: "Mr Hassall, in fact, is that rare being, a poet who is a dramatist, one whose poetry is drama, and his drama is poetry."[65]

As a direct result of Christopher Hassall's experience at Canterbury his play, *Out of the Whirlwind*, was written for performance in Westminster Abbey as part of the Coronation celebrations. It did little to enhance Hassall's reputation as a dramatist; but it is of some interest because the play deals with the problems encountered by a playwright, John Protheroe, who has undertaken to write a play for a cathedral; and who is challenged by the Devil to create a drama in which evil is not doomed at the outset! Hassall returned, perhaps more successfully, to the theme of the Nativity in his sacred masque *The Song of Simeon* which, with music by Malcolm Arnold, was produced at Drury Lane in 1960.[66]

The 1938 Festival also included an event which demonstrated the extent to which the Canterbury plays were seen to be a vital feature in the development of twentieth century drama. This was a 'public conversation' between E. Martin Browne and Ashley Dukes, who had managed the series of plays by poets at the Mercury Theatre since Eliot's *Murder in the Cathedral*. Their conversation was concerned with *The Chorus in Drama* and reports suggest that it was one of the most cogent statements ever made. The conversation included examples from W. H. Auden's *The Ascent of F6* and Browne and Dukes

> . . . concluded by suggesting that the difficulty of writing a modern chorus lay in the lack of general assent among the audience which the Greek and medieval dramatists commanded . . . Hence the unique importance of Christian drama, where a measure of assent does exist. This was illustrated by the fact that the Canterbury plays have already made more dramatic history than almost any others written in the twentieth century.[67]

But the prospects for continuing that history were not entirely promising. Margaret Babington reported a disappointing profit of only £189. 14s. 9d for the 1938 Festival and, with George Bell's influence decreasing and vivid recollections of previous pleasant, cloistered summers, the management invited Dorothy Sayers to write another play for 1939.

The result was, *The Devil to Pay*, a re-telling of the Faustus story which made considerable demands in terms of stage design: involving a medieval Hellmouth and an elaborate study. Anxiety over the acoustics of the Chapter House had resulted in the hanging of a velarium over the real wall, which also had the effect of making a blackout possible.[68] Dorothy Sayers's play pressed for spectacle and illusion and she insisted on Harcourt Williams as Dr Faustus, although he was far too old to be suited to the part. In spite of the play's obvious shortcomings when seen in retrospect, the ingenious effects achieved by Frank Napier, the exquisite costume designs of Elizabeth Haffenden[69] and the tireless energy of the playwright left a sense of excitement in the Cathedral. *The Times* found the play:

. . . always fascinating to follow through its ingenious development, always intellectually coherent and always couched in the spiritual idioms of the present.[70]

The wider public, however, were less impressed and when the play opened in July 1939 at His Majesty's Theatre, London, it ran for only one month. Perhaps too few had heard Miss Sayers's lecture, *Our National Attitude to the Theatre*, in which she urged her Canterbury audience to patronise a good play in the first three weeks of its run.[71]

Wartime and Offshoots from Canterbury

Margaret Babington obviously viewed the outbreak of war as a monstrous intrusion upon the Canterbury Festival and went ahead with arrangements for a Festival in 1940, which would include a revival of *The Zeal of Thy House*. Of the seven scheduled performances of the play, with Harcourt Williams again in the leading rôle, one was to be exclusively for members of the forces. But the details of the 13th annual Festival were despatched a few hours after the invasion of the Low Countries and it soon became manifest that arrangements would have to be cancelled.

Dorothy Sayers was invited in 1940 to write a series of radio plays on the life of Christ for *Children's Hour*. Even before the plays were broadcast they sparked off the controversy (which had surrounded Nugent Monck and George Bell) concerning the representation of Christ by an actor. The Lord's Day Observance Society declared in 1942:

> The fall of Singapore to the Japanese forces is surely God's judgement on the British people for allowing the BBC to disseminate this blasphemous outrage.[72]

With her usual blend of single-minded enthusiasm and obstinate self-will, Dorothy Sayers stipulated that Val Gielgud should produce her cycle of plays, *The Man Born to be King*, and refused to make any major cuts in the text. In the tradition of Canterbury, Robert Speaight took the main rôle and the plays became not only compulsive listening for millions of adults and children, but also one of the major drama publishing successes of the century.[73]

Another development greatly influenced by the activities of George Bell at Canterbury was the establishment of the Religious Drama Society. As far back as 1929, Mrs Olive Stevenson, the Secretary of the Women's Guild of the Congregational Union of England and Wales, had drawn attention to the potential of drama as a means of evangelism and the need for professional guidance in its use by the churches. She organised an inter-denominational conference, to which leaders of drama organisations were also invited, and an address on *Religious Drama* was given by Laurence Housman. From this first meeting conferences were arranged and in 1930, with George Bell, Bishop of Chichester as President, the Religious Drama Society was established.[74]

With the backing of the Society and the examples at Canterbury and Chichester, drama began to assume a greater importance in church life, although most of the activity was in the Anglican Church. In 1932, Bishop Bell gave his blessing to a performance of Henzie Raeburn's *Disarm*, which set out "ideals for the Geneva Disarmament Conference of that year",[75] and in the years that followed there were plays in Exeter, Southwark, Truro and Winchester Cathedrals and at St Margaret's, Westminster. T. S. Eliot recognised the particular rôle which cathedrals could play in providing a centre for drama:

> I like to think that at some time in the future every cathedral will have its own permanent company of amateurs and its own cycle of modern

religious plays, and that they will rival each other in perfection of production . . . Under present conditions, the universal craving for drama is imperfectly satisfied.[76]

Shortly before the outbreak of war the Religious Drama Society Limited was formed to finance a tour of *The Zeal of Thy House*. With the cancellation of the Canterbury Festival and the "universal craving for drama" still a reality, the tour of *Zeal* gave a clue to possible wartime activity for those still strongly committed to the cause. At the suggestion of Mrs Allardyce Nicoll, E. Martin Browne and his wife, Henzie Raeburn, founded the Pilgrim Players who, with the support of the Religious Drama Society, toured Britain giving professional performances of religious plays in air-raid shelters, barracks, churches, halls, schools and even on board a destroyer.[77] One of the most popular plays in the repertoire of the Pilgrim Players was James Bridie's *Tobias and the Angel*.

After the war the Religious Drama Society expanded its activities considerably and these are outlined in Kathleen Bainbridge Bell and June Ottaway's historical sketch of the society. Perhaps the most important single event was the First International Conference on Religious Drama held at Lincoln College, Oxford, in July 1955 at Bishop Bell's instigation and with a generous grant from the Rockefeller Foundation. Looking back over the movement which he had done so much to inaugurate, Bishop Bell commented:

I think we can say . . . that there is a new interest and contact between the Church and the Theatre. They are not yet married, but they are shyly 'walking out'.[78]

Until recently, under the name Radius and the chairmanship of Dr E. Martin Browne, the society organised training courses and conferences from its headquarters, George Bell House. Radius now continues this work from new premises and by its publications keeps its international membership aware of developments in religious drama. It also maintains an extensive central library of reference books and play sets, which include the plays of Ionesco, Pinter, Shaffer, Wesker and Wole Soyinka; and offers an advisory service to Christians of all denominations.

Canterbury After the War

Laurence Irving's setting, the dressing-rooms beneath the Cathedral Library and many costumes from past productions were all destroyed in bombing raids on Canterbury - "Only the Devil's tail hung for many weeks from a broken window."[79] But by 1947 another Festival was made possible by the proceeds from two performances of *Murder in the Cathedral* at the Lyric Theatre, London.

Despite persistent ill-health after his return from Burma, Laurie Lee wrote a new play.[80] *Peasants' Priest* was the story of John Balle, the priest involved in Wat Tyler's rebellion of 1381, which had first gathered momentum at Canterbury. With Bernard Miles[81] as John Balle, the play was directed by E. Martin Browne and a simple setting of painted backdrops was devised by Harold Melvill.[82] Written with an awareness of the nature of the stage in the Chapter House and with an economy of language and setting, *Peasants' Priest* was vastly different from Dorothy Sayers's play of 1939; but *Punch* felt that some of the magic of Canterbury had returned:

A perfect setting at Canterbury, where the Chapter House made a marvellous background for *Peasants's Priest* . . . Such an atmosphere made it easy to go back six hundred years.[83]

Yet there were serious problems. Laurence Irving, in an address at the conclusion of the Festival, pointed out that of the local amateur actors who had regularly supplemented the professional casts before the war, only Philip Hollingworth and William Fordyce[84] were available in 1947. The financial position of the Festival had also been precarious and so, with a view to continuing the enterprise, the Arts Council of Great Britain had been approached for a grant. This would ensure that proper fees could be paid to artists who, in the past, had given their services to the Festival; but the situation would be reviewed each year.

The play written for the Festival of 1948 was *Thor With Angels* by Christopher Fry. After the war, especially in the early fifties, Fry became the most successful verse dramatist writing for both the Church and commercial theatre, but he also owed his early inspiration to George Bell. As Bishop of Chichester, Bell had made a special journey in 1937 to the East Sussex parish of Steyning to see the first performance of *The Boy With a Cart*. The obscure playwright, thus encouraged, was introduced to E. Martin Browne and a further performance was arranged in the garden of the Bishop's Palace.[85] When, in 1951, the Religious Drama Society was asked to commission a play to celebrate the Festival of Britain, it was Fry to whom the commission went. His play, *A Sleep of Prisoners*, was performed by an all-professional cast at Oxford and in St Thomas's, Regent Street.[86] Subsequently, Fry was also attracted to the Canterbury theme of Becket and wrote his play, *Curtmantle* in 1961.

Thor With Angels, the story of a Jutish household's conversion to Christianity by St Augustine of Canterbury, concluded two decades of dramatic creativity inspired by the vision of George Bell. By this time, however, the idea of drama in churches and cathedrals had become more widely accepted and the centre of the verse drama movement had shifted to the Mercury Theatre in London. The Canterbury Festival was no longer the unique event it had been and there were increasing problems in securing a new verse play. It was decided, therefore, that the play for 1949 would be a revival of Dorothy Sayers's 1937 play, *The Zeal of Thy House*.

Every effort was made to maintain the standard of production: a distinguished cast included Michael Goodliffe as William of Sens, Jill Balcon (the wife of the poet C. Day Lewis) as Lady Ursula and Joseph O' Conor (who played Prospero in the Welsh Drama Company's 1976 production of *The Tempest*) as the Angel Michael. The play was produced by the playwright Christopher Hassall and an elaborate set was constructed to satisfy a growing pressure group who wanted "real scenery".[87] This was almost certainly an artistic blunder, as one of the best aspects of the pre-war productions was the effectiveness with which they had used the Chapter House setting itself. To construct scenery representing part of a cathedral, when the play is actually being staged in an ecclesiastical setting was to attempt an impossible blend of the real and imaginary, the flat and the three-dimensional. As an added feature to the 1949 production, the Friends published a special edition of the main historical source of the play: Gervase's *Of the Burning and Repair of the Church of Canterbury in the Year 1174*.

The remaining years of the Festival were, unfortunately, a continual struggle against mounting costs. Large-scale hospitality of the sort offered to visiting performers before the war was no longer possible; and family businesses that had supported the Festival in the past were gradually disappearing into larger, impersonal combines. There were also problems in the internal organisation of the Friends. An ambitious headmaster of the King's School, who wielded inordinate influence in the Chapter, had ideas for a festival of his own under the mistaken idea that schoolboy amateur dramatics were of similar stature to the world premières of the plays of Masefield, Eliot or Fry. Laurence Irving detected "apathy and intrigue amongst the clerics",[88] and as the Friends failed to attract new, younger members there was the increasing danger that the Festival would degenerate into an occasion for annual nostalgia for the elderly. Undoubtedly, some of the amateur actors, as Robert Speaight has observed, became increasingly "jealous of their rights in the Festival"[89] and without the very firm handling of a producer like E. Martin Browne, tensions and petty rivalries could soon develop. An entertaining and probably very accurate account of the problems of a cathedral drama festival is in fact provided by Hugh Walpole, who was educated at the King's School, Canterbury, in his novels *The Inquisitor* (1935) and *The Cathedral* (1922) - the latter was made into a three-act play in 1937.

Nevertheless, three new plays were commissioned: Robert Gittings's *The Makers of Violence* (1951), Hugh Ross Williamson's *His Eminence of England* (1953) and Patric Dickinson's *A Durable Fire* (1962), but none of these plays achieved the success or attracted the same attention as the earlier plays. The Festival ceased to be an annual event and relied instead on sporadic outbursts of energy. In 1958, Hassall's *Christ's Comet* was produced by E. Martin Browne at the Marlowe Theatre and both George Bell, the origina-tor, and Margaret Babington, the chief perpetuator of the Festival, died. The loss of these two figures was too much for the weakened fabric of the Festival and it quickly crumbled. In 1960, an amateur production of *Everyman* and *The Deluge* (with Christopher Hassall as the voice of God) directed by Philip Hollingworth were well-received and revived hopes of a regular event in the Chapter House. Laurence Irving made a final effort in 1962 when he persuaded the Friends of Canterbury Cathedral to commission Patric Dickinson's *A Durable Fire*.

As E. Martin Browne reminded readers of *The Canterbury Cathedral Chronicle* at the time of Bishop Bell's death, we have come to accept the various arts festivals associated with cathedrals as part of our cultural life and it is easy to overlook the important pioneering work done at Canterbury.[90]

Nevertheless, the demise of the original Canterbury Festival was, by no means, the end of the energy and theatrical invention to emanate from this small, ancient city. As before, however, developments within the commercial theatre and within the Christian faith itself contributed to a further phase in the history of Church-Stage relations. This is described in Chapter Fourteen.

Notes to Chapter Four

1. G. K. A. Bell, *Randall Davidson: Archbishop of Canterbury* (London 1935).

2/3/4. Ronald C. J. Jasper, *George Bell: Bishop of Chichester* (London 1967), 4, 9.

5. E. Martin Browne, *The Making of T. S. Eliot's Plays* (Cambridge 1969).

6. Jasper, *op. cit.*, 36-38.

7. Dietrich Bonhoeffer, *No Rusty Swords: Letters, Lectures and Notes 1928-1936 from the Collected Works*, ed. Edwin H. Robertson (Lon. 1965), 1, 33.

8. R. Rouse and S. C. Neill, ed., *A History of the Ecumenical Movement* (London 1954), 564.

9. Quoted in Roger Lloyd, *The Church of England* (London 1966), 464.

10/11. Quoted in E. Martin Browne, 'George Kennedy Allen Bell' *Canterbury Cathedral Chronicle LIII* (1958), 10/7-8.

12. G. K. A. Bell, 'Sermon on *The Coming of Christ*' preached at Wittersham Parish Church on Sunday December 13th 1933.

13. John Masefield, *Grace Before Ploughing: Fragments of Autobiography* (London 1966), ch. 27.

14/15/16. L. Irving, *The Precarious Crust* (London 1971), 15, 194, 148.

17. Phyllis Hartnoll, ed, *The Oxford Companion to the Theatre* (London 1967), 480. Also Laurence Irving, TR1, see Bibliography D.

18/19. Thomas Lowinsky, 'Charles Ricketts', The *Dictionary of National Bibliography 1931-1940*, ed., L. G. Wickham-Legg (Oxford 1949).

20. Laurence Irving, TR1, see Bibliography D.

21. Laurence Irving, *The Canterbury Adventure* (Canterbury 1959), 2.

22. Thomas Lowinsky, *loc. cit.*

23. Review of *The Coming of Christ*, *The Times*, December 14th 1953, 11.

24. William V. Spanos, *op. cit.*, 34.

25. See Appendix.

26. Nicoll maintains that Reinhardt's production also inspired the Malvern Festival. See Allardyce Nicoll, *English Drama 1900-1930: The Beginnings of the Malvern Period* (Cambridge 1973), 93.

27. See Appendix.

28. Laurence Irving, TR1, see Bibliography D.

29/30. E. Martin Browne, *The Making of T. S. Eliot's Plays* (Cambridge 1969), 36, 56.

31. The first appointment of its kind in Britain.

32. Kathleen Bainbridge-Bell and June Ottaway, A *Brief Historical Sketch of the Religious Drama Society of Great Britain* (London 1957), 5.

33. Christopher Fry quoted in Bainbridge-Bell & Ottaway, *op. cit.*, 9.

34/35/36. See Appendix.

37. A. Friend, 'Tennyson's *Becket*', *Canterbury Cathedral Chronicle XII* (1932), 9.

38. TR4, see Bibliography D.

39. cp. Herbert Howarth, *Notes on Some Figures Behind T. S. Eliot* (London 1965), 318.

40. A. Friend, *loc cit.*, 9.

41. TR4, see Bibliography D.

42. See Figure 7.

43/44/45. E. V. Lucas, 'Notes on *Becket* at Canterbury', *Canterbury Cathedral Chronicle XV* (1933), 6-7, 7-8, 9.

46. Ronald C. D. Jasper, *op. cit.*, 123-4.

47. See above, p. 64.

48. TR4, see Bibliography D.

49. Sybil Thorndike, 'The Theatre as a Service to the Community', *Canterbury Cathedral Chronicle XXVII* (1934), 15-17.

50. *op. cit.*,

51. *The Oxford Companion to the Theatre*, ed. Phyllis Hartnoll, erroneously states that *Becket* has not been performed since the death of Sir Henry Irving.

52/53/54. E. Martin Browne, '*Cranmer of Canterbury*', *Canterbury Cathedral Chronicle XXIII* (1936), 15.

55. Quoted by Margaret Babington, '*Cranmer of Canterbury*: a Note by the Management', *Canterbury Cathedral Chronicle XXIV* (1936), 11-12.

56. Janet Hitchman, *Such a Strange Lady* (London 1975), 50, 177.

57. Quoted *The Zeal of Thy House*, *Canterbury Cathedral Chronicle XXVII* (1937), 19.

58. TR4, see Bibliography D.

59. Laurence Irving, *The Precarious Crust* (London 1971), 113.

60. She gave a photograph inscribed "To 'Sparks' with all gratitude and kindest remembrances" to the electrician, Mr Fairbrass.

61. See Appendix.

62. 'The Drama', *Canterbury Cathedral Chronicle XXIV* (1938), 8.

63/64. See Appendix.

65. 'The Festival Play', *Canterbury Cathedral Chronicle XXX* (1938),15 cp. Kenneth Muir, 'Verse and Prose', *Stratford-upon-Avon Studies IV: Contemporary Theatre* (London 1962), 115 - "We have not had since the age of Shakespeare a great poet who was also a great dramatist."

66. For a fuller account of *Out of the Whirlwind* see Gerald Weales *op. cit.*, 178-9. The production was repeated in Laurence Irving's local parish church Wittersham. See also I. R. Willison, ed., *The New Cambridge Bibliography of English Literature IV, 1900-1950* (Cambridge 1972), 953.

67. 'Festival Day of the Friends', *Canterbury Cathedral Chroni cle XXX* (1938), 25-26.

68. 'Drama', *Canterbury Cathedral Chronicle CCCII* (1939), 9.

69. See Appendix.

70/71. Quoted 'His Majesty's Theatre, Thursday 20th July. First Performance of *The Devil to Pay'*, *Canterbury Cathedral Chronicle XXXIII*, 17.

72. Quoted in radio programme, *This Blasphemous Outrage*, broadcast Radio 3, October 1974.

73. From 1943-1966 the play ran to 23 editions.

74. Bainbridge-Bell & Ottaway, *op. cit.*

75. Ronald C. D. Jasper, *op. cit.*, 123.

76. Quoted William V. Spanos, *op. cit.*, 18.

77. E. Martin and Henzie Browne, *Pilgrim Story* (London 1946).

78. Quoted *Christian Drama III*, 2 (1955), 53-54.

79. *Festival of Music and Drama: Souvenir Programme*, 1947, 3.

80. 'Address of Mr L. Irving at the Gathering in the Chapter House, 28th June 1947', *Canterbury Cathedral Chronicle XLII* (1947), 18-19.

81/82. See Appendix.

83. Quoted *'Peasants' Priest'*, *Canterbury Cathedral Chronicle XVII* (1947), 14.

84. See Appendix.

85. Ronald C. D. Jasper, *op. cit.*, 126.

86. Bainbridge-Bell & Ottaway, *op. cit.*, 11.

87. TR4, see Bibliography D.

88. Letter to K. W. Pickering, 15th February 1975, see Bibliography C.

89. Robert Speaight, *With Becket in* Murder in the Cathedral. *T. S. Eliot: The Man and His Work* ed. Alen Tate (London 1967), 164.

90. E. Martin Browne, 'George Kennedy Allen Bell', *Canterbury Cathedral Chronicle LIII* (1958), 10.

Part III

The Georgian Plays

5

The Coming of Christ

A headline in *The Daily News* for Monday 29th May 1928, proclaimed an "Historic Event" and the report that followed began:
  Since the murder of Thomas à Becket, Canterbury Cathedral has not
  been the scene of a more startling event than the performance today of
  John Masefield's *The Coming of Christ*.[1]
The Times spoke of "a rare and curious pleasure to be had" at
Canterbury and we can now recreate imaginatively the "memorable pictorial and decorative achievement" in its magnificent and
unusual setting that was, certainly, startling in its impact.[2]

The play was staged on the wide steps which lead from the
Nave to the Quire Screen; after the third, seventh and seventeenth
steps there are landings eight feet deep and these provide three
stages. The middle of the three stages is spanned by a huge arch, a
natural proscenium twenty feet wide, and at this point the steps are
at their narrowest. Steps from the north-east and south-west transepts lead to the middle stage and provide wings for actors waiting
to enter, but the lower and upper stages can only be approached
directly from the Nave or Quire or indirectly from the middle stage.
The Quire Screen forms a background, but in the centre it is pierced
by a small archway "through which, when a curtain is drawn, one
has a glimpse of mysterious Distance Beyond."[3] The effect of
looking through the great arch over the middle stage to the smaller

121

arch in the Quire Screen is of a narrowing perspective and it creates the illusion of great depth. On to the impressive, split-level stages a strange, mottled light falls from the transept windows and, with supplementary floodlights, the full richness of Ricketts's sumptuous costumes creates a superb spectacle: "Splendid and fantastic costumes fill the stage with beauty."[4]

Above the Quire Screen is a gallery, from which Imogen Holst's choir from Morley College sang the music of the *Heavenly Host* which her brother had composed. Trumpeters joined with the organ in a magnificent tapestry of sound and a small chorus of men's voices were accompanied by simple, resonant chords on a piano.[5] The music filled the Cathedral and the varying directions from which it came added to the sense of wonder and movement.

The interest generated by Masefield's play, both before and after the event was enormous:

Long before the Cathedral doors were open, there were huge queues covering more than 200 yards outside Lanfranc's beautiful Cathedral, and when I left after the performance in the early evening other crowds had assembled for the second performance.[6]

Six thousand people saw the play and, like the cast, were fully aware that they were involved in something quite revolutionary.[7] There had, of course, been a few performances of plays in churches before, in St Paul's, Covent Garden for instance, but a play in the Mother Cathedral of the Established Church was more startling and significant, and the Dean had "faced much criticism" on account of it.[8] Nevertheless, the huge audiences watched "with rapt attention"[9] and the play made an indelible impression on many. K. M. Lobb, writing in 1955 and looking back over many plays in churches, maintained: "The one which will longest be remembered . . . is almost certainly *The Coming of Christ.*"[10]

The dinner-jacketed figure of John Masefield seems, now, an unpromising source of revolution but, by 1928, he had made a number of experiments in biblical drama which had been refused a licence for public performance. In responding to George Bell's request to write a nativity play for the Cathedral, however, Masefield faced a particular kind of challenge. There had already been a number of twentieth century attempts at writing a nativity, but

Figure 9: The nave at Canterbury Cathedral. *The Coming of Christ* was staged on the steps. The altar shown here was removed for the performance.

these had all been recognised by discerning critics as little more than a decorative retelling of the Christmas story; and, as *The Times* reported in 1953:

> Mr Masefield was not the man to add to the number of proper but colourless Nativity plays that are content to relate to a new generation the simple incidents of piety.[11]

Both Masefield and Bell had a serious artistic purpose and were aware of the specific dangers of a nativity play. The nativity playwright takes as his starting-point what is probably the best known plot in Western tradition, but his creativity must provide a new approach. There are examples of theatrical conventions in which audiences attend plays knowing precisely the material of the play. Traditional Chinese theatre, for instance, not only adhered rigidly to certain basic storylines but also to fixed gestures and intonations. In such situations, the re-enactment of a familiar story is, to some extent, participatory for the audience and, at times, comes near to ritual and worship. But, however familiar the material of the nativity play, there is the added difficulty that the events seem absurd unless we understand their significance, and in the erosion of belief of which Masefield was aware, there was an added urgency to make the events meaningful.

To some extent Masefield was aided by the fact that his play was to be performed in the Cathedral. Henzie Browne summarised the situation:

> The audience, by coming into church, are prepared to see something connected with the belief and function which the building stands for; they have already made a contribution to the performance before it begins . . . Even though players and audience as individuals may not share the Christian faith, they are agreeing to presume its significance.[12]

The problem, however, was that Masefield may have wished to voice controversial issues and that these may well have been thought to have been out of place in a Cathedral by an audience that expected piety rather than art.

With the dual purpose of both teaching Christian doctrine and celebrating the Truth for believers, Masefield turned to a modern version of a mystery play for his solution. The popularity of the medieval nativities was well established and Masefield's interest in various forms of ritualistic theatre, especially the No plays, provided an added incentive to explore the possibilities of the mystery form.

The suitability of the mystery for Masefield's purpose derived from the nature of the medieval plays which, as Robert Potter has demonstrated, involved both a desire to re-enact an event, as if telling it for the first time, and a wish to confirm the significance of the event, thus strengthening faith in devotion.[13] The play, therefore, becomes an opportunity for learning *and* for offering an act of worship. These two issues were particularly relevant to Masefield as he viewed his play as an opportunity to express a Christian opinion through the re-enactment of a familiar story, but also as an act of worship in which the artists made an offering of their talents to God and the audience joined in the adoration of the incarnate Christ. He saw also in the Cathedral setting, a potential for impressive ritual action.

There were, however, two main difficulties which faced Masefield in his attempt to adapt the mystery form for modern usage. The first of these was the increasing remoteness of ritual from a twentieth century audience. The medieval plays assumed a knowledge of the narrative shape of outstanding stories from *The Bible* and a familiarity with the central symbols from the Liturgy, but Masefield could not afford to make such an assumption. Nor could he assume that the worship of the Anglican Church provided a basis for drama. The average cathedral service of the 1920s lacked dynamism, symbolism and action. Furthermore, a rediscovery of ritual elements of theatre and language was confined to a small élite for whom the experience was probably artificial rather than vital. There had certainly been a revival among Anglo-Catholics of an interest in the Liturgy, but this movement had been limited in its impact and had done little to restore the everyday contact with icon and ritual which the writers of the medieval moralities could assume.

The second major problem was the style of language suitable for a modern mystery play. The events of the Nativity are biblical and, to some extent, the language of the *Authorised Version* would have been familiar to Masefield's audience. Through the singing of

Messiah and of popular carols and readings in church, the various incidents of the Incarnation had become linked with certain words. But the use of biblical language drawn from the *Authorised Version* immediately raises the problem of archaism, and Masefield was anxious to give the historical events modern significance. It would have been a great deal easier for Masefield if a twentieth century version of *The Bible* had achieved widespread popularity; then his characters could have spoken words that were both familiar and modern, biblical yet contemporary. As it was, he was forced to come to the conclusion that the biblical influences in his text should be from the *Authorised Version* with its magnificent rhythms, powerful images and occasional obscurities.

In recent years, playwrights have attempted to give contemporary meaning to the Nativity by modernising the event itself and then providing appropriate modern speech. Stuart Jackman's *The Backyard Miracle* shows Christ born in the garage of an hotel, where the harassed proprietor deals with the arrival of the Magi;[14] and John Arden's *The Business of Good Government* makes Herod into a puppet Arab statesman.[15] Such developments may be said to owe much to Masefield's early work, but he had to handle his material with far greater caution.

Masefield's choice of language depended on the subject-matter and form he had chosen for the play. He belonged to a group of poets who opposed the growth of Naturalism in drama and argued that verse was the appropriate medium where the subject was the Eternal and the action largely symbolic.[16] The choice of a mystery form strengthened Masefield's belief that, like his medieval model, his play should be in verse. Masefield was probably the most widely read poet of his day, but his style was greatly influenced by the pre-war Georgian Movement that he had helped to create. It is true that he never succumbed to the more enervating features of the Georgians and that he had declined to have his verse published in later editions of *Georgian Poetry*. Nevertheless, a good deal of the taste for faded gentility and what Ezra Pound termed "melopeia", which typified conservative conceptions of poetry in the 1920s, influenced Masefield. Among his vast output of verse, Masefield included a number of vigorous ballads which were both direct and almost crude in style and he therefore had certain qualities which would suit an imitation of medieval verse; but, technically, he was unable to use the new developments in verse that had been suggested in the work of Eliot or Ezra Pound.

Masefield's inability to exploit the new developments in poetry which produced the major poets of the thirties was not his only restriction. He was, it must be remembered, writing verse to be spoken in the very difficult acoustic conditions of the Cathedral. The whole play was bound to be taken at an unusually slow pace if it were to be audible.[17] Furthermore, Masefield felt it essential that the argument should be presented clearly and in such a way that it could be followed at first hearing. The verse, therefore, had to be uncomplicated, suitable for slow delivery, yet appropriate to the character and situation.

Masefield tried to blend the biblical, poetic and doctrinal elements with the practical demands of the production in a style of language that owed something to *Everyman*. His language belongs to no particular time, but varies from direct biblical paraphrase to simple conversation; there are passages which resemble Murray's Greek choruses and others that echo Shakespeare. *The Coming of Christ* is, "a work of extreme unconvention"[18] and one in which he made full use of his experience as a producer of verse plays. The script contains detailed and precise stage directions and every moment of the play is conceived in terms of action in the Cathedral.[19]

The Coming of Christ falls naturally into four sections which are linked by the singing of the Chorus. The action is continuous but is affected by the large physical space which had to be traversed before figures could be visible and audible. Like Mabel Dearmer's play, *The Dreamer*, with which it has other superficial similarities,[20] the opening of Masefield's play is announced by the sounding of angelic trumpets and the scene is established out of time in the eternity of Heaven. Four angels, who represent aspects of God's relationship with the world, enter from the Quire and transepts and, taking up positions on the steps above the middle stage, proclaim their identity. The first is The Power: "My hand is on the stars and on the tides" (p.3, l. 2); the second is The Sword: "I bring

God's justice" (p.3, l.5); the third, The Mercy: "In the world's storm I am the central calm" (p.4, l.5); and the fourth is The Light: "I bring the Light of God into dark hearts" (p.4, l.7). The verse consists of simple, four-line stanzas, but it gains momentum as the angels speak chorally, their verse "rich in the vivid, sudden imagery charactistic of Mr Masefield's best work",[21] joining to survey the wretched condition of Mankind.

This prologue to the main action of the play strongly resembles the first words of God in *Everyman* both in style and dramatic purpose. Whereas the God of the medieval play sees Mankind:

> Living without dread in worldly prosperity;
> Of ghostly sight the people be so blind . . . (ll. 24-28)

> They use the seven deadly sins damnable,
> As pride, covetise, wrath and lechery
> Now in the world be made commendable (ll. 36-38)[22]

Masefield's angels present a similar picture:

> We see the world of man seizing and slaying,
> Lusting for wealth, destroying and betraying,
> With neither hope nor peace
> Save greed, between their darkness and decaying. (p.4, ll.11-14)

The group of angels, standing to the right of the great steps, now confront the Anima Christi who enters the middle stage from the left.

> Dressed in the traditional manner of figures of Christ, but with a sceptre and crown . . . a most impressive figure.[23]

> His white robes cunningly designed to increase the natural height of the actor.[24]

The Anima Christi is about to enter Man's life which is represented by the darkness beyond the curtain in the Quire door, but the four angels come to him as tempters and reason with him concerning the folly of His doing. What the tempters have seen of men suggests that Christ's going among them will not change their nature. But to the Anima Christi the idea of covering a "bright spirit with man's body" (p.6, l.11) is not an "act of darkness" but "an act of danger, humbly dared" (p.6, l.12).

The temptation takes the form of questions and threats by the tempters to which the Anima Christi responds, like Christ in the wilderness, by resolve and scriptural assertion. The Anima Christi is prepared to face future "fierce temptations", the suffering which His message may seem to bring to others and even the rejection of His message. His purpose is to take on full manhood, to overcome temptation and to bring comfort. The whole of Christ's life is now stretched out before Him by the angels: the lowly birth, His ministry of "fierce, swift acts and piercing sentences" (p.6, l.11), the unreliability of His disciples and His appalling death. All this for the sake of Mankind who,

> ... is cumbered so with clay
> That the spirit in him is as stars in cloud. (p.7, ll.12-13)

The same Mankind whom the God in *Everyman* saw,

> ... so cumbered with worldly riches
> That needs on them I must do justice. (ll.60-61)

The Anima Christi counters the angels' threat of impending suffering with the words of *Matthew* xxiv,v. 13: "He who endures even to the end is saved" (p.9, l.16 - words familiar from the Oratorio *Elijah*), and argues that, although His humanity may fail Him, God's mercy will not. A more dreadful and subtle form of persuasion is now used: why leave Heaven where there is so much beauty? Man will not change his nature because of an obscure teacher who dies an ignominious death, the ripples on the surface will soon vanish or, worse still, His life and death will inspire:

> Some Creed which will become the apathy
> About Man's brutal heart . . . (p.10, ll.18-20)

Man after all is,

> ... a storm
> Of wind and water troubling the earth's surface. (p.11, ll.3-4)

Christ's compassion for Man, however, overrules the sense of futility in His mission and, accepting that He may pipe and yet no-one may dance for Him (an image from *Matthew* xi, v. 17), he resigns Himself to make the attempt. The angels had already accepted the Anima Christi's response when they first greeted Him as "divine Wisdom" and "Everlasting who has dared all dangers", for outside Time in the eternity of Heaven what is and what will be are one. Now they submit to His supremacy again and address Him as "Master".

Two new spirits appear on the lower stage and, Faustus-like, the Anima Christi asks them their identity. The spirits reveal themselves as the apostles Peter and Paul. Peter, still carrying his fisherman's nets, breaks the stately progress of the verse with a straightforward statement of his life and faith, whilst Paul outlines the tribulations he will suffer and yet has already suffered for Christ's sake in a verse of *II Corinthians* vv, v. 24-28. Inspired by the witness of the apostles who have not failed Him in the end, the Anima Christi speaks new words of confidence. The verse is based on *John* xvl v, 33 and perhaps on Shakespeare's *Macbeth*, but it has a considerable urgency and power in its simplicity:

I shall overcome the world indeed with these.
Therefore O Spirits, I am resolute,
O lay aside my glory and my power
To take up Manhood. (p.14. ll.13-16)

The great debate concluded, the Anima Christi begins to move towards the gate of Time and Mortality. Each of the angels in turn promises to be with Him and, in a moment reminiscent of Everyman's progress to the tomb, the Anima Christi passes through the angels who have grouped at the Quire door and beneath the Heavenly Host, who have appeared above, and on out of sight into the world, saying,

O brother man, I come. (p.18, l.13)

The scene of the Anima Christi and his four tempters is, in many respects, the most striking and original part of the play and, no doubt, suggested to Eliot the possibility of further development in *Murder in the Cathedral*. The uniqueness of the scene is that it approaches the Nativity not from the traditional point of view of the shepherds, the kings or Mary and Joseph, but from the predicament of God the Son.

Masefield's view of the world, as expressed by the angels, is largely pessimistic. He sees Man as having lost faith and spiritual values, and he despairs of the future with Arnoldian nostalgia: the angels' description of the world has strong similarities with the final lines of *Dover Beach*. There are many indications that Masefield's gloom is a product of writing in the aftermath of the First World War, a period in which "ideas, beliefs, philosophies, theologies and simple faith became the casualties",[25] and he presents the world as a wasteland swept by brutality. Man's chief sin appears to be his passion for self-destruction; Mankind is embroiled in an endless Somme and the images are bloody:[26]

> they awaken
> To the blood's storm (p.5, ll.1-2)

> They war in bloody blindness until taken (p.5, l.4)

and finally, when the "shining spirit" of Christ is about to enter the world of men, He stands:

> at the brink
> Of life's red sea which stains and overwhelms (p.5. ll.11-12)

The Coming of Christ shows God's answer to Man's need of salvation as being the Incarnation. This is the crucial moment for Mankind when Eternity enters Time. Masefield sees Man's salvation in the suffering and rejected God which, by the world's standards is a failure and negation of the world's search for wealth and power. The Anima Christi's conversation with the angels is really an Emmaus road for the audience in which He explains His suffering and asks,

> Was not the Messiah bound to suffer this before entering upon His glory? (*Luke* xxiv, v. 27)

His purpose is not to prevent suffering, but by fully entering into Man's life to point a way to God through suffering. Masefield's pessimism leads him to dwell on Man's response to his Saviour, rejecting Him and murdering Him, but he contrasts this with God's love which grows stronger with Man's misery. There is never, however, a suggestion of the final triumph of the Resurrection, for to promise this at the end would be to make the Anima Christi's decision to enter life briefly, far easier; the Anima Christi is promised only,

> The hard road to the stony Hill of Skulls (p.15, l.18)

It is the knowledge of the awful consequences of His Incarnation that make the Anima Christi's acceptance of Manhood more mysterious and wonderful. And it is this that provokes the adoration which is to end the play.

The second main movement of the play contains some elements of a conventional Nativity because it introduces the three kings with their traditional names; Baltazar, Gaspar and Melchior. The kings enter in colourful procession from the transepts and occupy the middle stage, whilst their retinue of men form a small chorus grouped on the lower stage. Masefield's kings, however, are not the familiar, oriental magi; they are morality figures, each representing a facet of Man's activity on earth. Each is acutely aware of the futility of his exploits, of the transient quality of life and of the imminence of death.

The style of the kings' scene has certain characteristics of the No plays which Masefield admired, "essentially a drama of soliloquy and reminiscence,"[27] for although the three figures appear together, they rarely relate to each other and they announce their identity individually. Again, it must be remembered that much of the language of the play involves bold pronouncement to achieve maximum audibility.

Baltazar speaks in staccato, rhymed couplets and immediately establishes himself as a ruler of totalitarian power, one who attempts to solve problems by violence and actually glories in war:

I love the trumpets and the cry
Of the long rank that moves as one (p.21. ll.13-14)

Masefield's hatred of the military mentality is shown with increased intensity as Baltazar recounts how cruelly his sergeants have pressed the young men into service at the front:

To sweat under accoutre-ings
On muddy tracks, up to some line
Where the death-bringing sling bolts whine. (p.22, ll.1-3)

Now, however, Baltazar adapts Christ's parable of the vineyard (*Mark* xii, vv. 1-9) to his own purposes: he says that his subjects have failed to understand his methods and intentions, and have killed his only son. It is typical of his arrogance that he thus identifies himself with God in an ironic foreshadowing of the crucifixion. Baltazar is left, like Shakespeare's Richard III before the battle, dreading the approach of death, whilst all those whose death he has engineered parade before him in dreams. His blustering confidence and the regular beat of the verse slacken as he indicates that, in old age, he seeks the Saviour-King, in the knowledge that his own reign of callousness must end. Baltazar's kingdoms and armed forces are all to be given to the "good King", but we already know that the "shining spirit" will have no use for them.

Gaspar is another of the rulers of this world whose values Christ rejects. He lives by trade and his main concern is the accumulation of wealth and the power that it brings. Gaspar speaks altogether more smoothly and expansively than Baltazar, telling of all the grandiose schemes of Mankind that he has financed and how, through his sponsorship, he even controls the creation of beauty in the arts. His enterprises, however, have fared no better than Baltazar's for they have not brought the desired satisfaction. His speech builds up to a climax of achievement then tilts towards despair on the line:

But the half of my threads are unspun. (p.24, l.9)

and Gaspar realises that, like Everyman, he cannot take his riches with him to death. The search for eternal values has also led Gaspar to seek the new King who will end despair and conquer death itself.

Melchior is a dabbler in the world's philosophies; he is engaged on an endless quest,

To find what IS beyond what seems. (p.25, l.6)

He is convinced that life is part of some eternal purpose, but his own efforts: intellectual search, asceticism, the "wisdoms of the East" and "the madness of the West" have failed to bring him nearer a resolution. But Melchior has seen the star which suggest's God's coming to earth, God seeking out Man rather than Man seeking God. Like the other two kings, Melchior yearns to see the real Truth before he dies.

The formal, presentational style of the action is changed by the mention of the star, for the kings cease to be universal types and become the magi of the Christmas Story. They draw together and discuss how they will thwart Herod who has already sent his killers in search of the baby. Christ's Nativity is now an event in historical time, but Man continues his brutality and the image of blood reappears strongly. The depressing picture that confronted the Anima Christi before Incarnation has already become reality. Aware of their desperate need for a Saviour, the kings reverse their usual rôle of gift-bringers and ponder together as to what gifts they will ask of the infant King. Each hopes to amend his life, Baltazar resolves to ask "that the fierce be kind", Gaspar for an end to injustice and Melchior for an understanding of the Divine purpose.

Man in need of salvation, in the shape of the three kings, follows the star, a symbol of the light that has already come into the world. To conclude their simple but extremely effective scene, the kings leave the middle stage and descend to the lower stage where they are joined by their followers. The procession moves to the north-west transept and as they go into the distance they sing of the erosion of primitive religion and the void they hope to fill. Their voices are heard echoing in the high arches of the Quire long after they have disappeared from view.

From the entry of the three shepherds, Rocky, Sandy and Earthy it is clear that Masefield has taken the inspiration of the third part of his play from the medieval Nativity plays. Rocky's opening words,

> Draw here to a side where the wind will not bite to the bone
> (p.28, l.13)

recall

> Lord, what these weathers are cold,

the opening line of the *Wakefield Second Shepherds' Pageant* from the *Towneley Cycle*. Unlike their medieval counterparts, who complain of their wives and taxes, Masefield's shepherds complain of oppression by wealthy landlords, the owners of the sheep, but the structure of the first part of the scene adheres very closely to the medieval play. Opinions differ widely as to how successful Masefield's adaptation of the *Secunda Pastorum* was: K. M. Lobb found the comparison "not always to Masefield's disadvantage",[28] whereas Herbert Howarth found "a tinsel replica of the Wakefield shepherds."[29] Masefield's intention, however, is quite clear for, as Spanos points out, we look to the shepherds in the medieval tradition to bring the main human interest and topicality to the play.[30] In this respect Masefield was largely successful.

There are elements of lively characterisation in Masefield's shepherds and we become involved in their personal lives. They are recognisable as individuals rather than as types and the action of their scene is accordingly more naturalistic than the rest of the play. They are rather humourless but they are clearly the men whom Baltazar and Gaspar have exploited or relied upon for personal gain.

Rocky, the senior of the three, is God-fearing and content with his condition; both Sandy and Earthy regard him as an old fool, "a hard old sergeant",[31] who frowns on drink and pleasure and prevents their active rebellion. While Rocky goes to a nearby farm for food, Earthy and Sandy voice their discontent; Earthy, superstitious and lacking initiative, nurses a deep grudge against "the rich and great" for having forced him into military service:

And there I stayed among the mud
In beds of lice and deeds of blood,
Until they chose to let it be.
Four years they kept me 'serving' so they said
Ordered like dogs, and Death to all who disobeyed. (p.30, ll.3-7)

Sandy, the more articulate of the discontented shepherds, has decided that the future lies with the workers. He has thought through the implications of his ideas and, as *The Daily News* critic remarked with some amazement, "actually declares that what we want is a good revolution."[32] Sandy goes further and suggests:

It's time the workers should command and have the wealth they make. (p.30, l.8)

It therefore comes as something of a disappointment that, as a first step, they should steal a sheep! Earthy, as if shell-shocked, views everything in relation to his personal experience of the war and invariably brings the conversation back to it, but it is Sandy who pronounces dispassionately

War isn't any glory: it's a crime! (p.33, l.8)

The expression of strong anti-war sentiments and of "Bolshevic opinions"[33] by the shepherds not only achieved topicality, but deeply shocked conservative elements in the Cathedral audience, which included a number of high-ranking officers from the nearby barracks.[34] There were suggestions that such things should not be spoken of in a cathedral, a view that E. H. Baughan in *The Daily News*, dismissed as "absurd".[35] Only the *Isis* critic, Peter Fleming, managed to soothe the indignation of the generals by pointing out that the "sergeant shepherd", when he returns to the scene, rebukes the others for suggesting that their superior officers should be disobeyed.[36] The attack on incompetent officers and pointless suffering is too sustained, however, to be dismissed so easily and it typifies the outspoken opposition to violence with which George Bell became associated.[37]

The re-appearance of Rocky, who has overheard a good deal of the contentious conversation, leads to a heated debate on the existence of God, of whom Rocky claims personal knowledge. The two examples of religious experience which Rocky gives are both unconvincing and cannot shake Sandy's conviction that God is an invention of the ruling class to frighten the populace into submission, nor Earthy's conditioned suspicion of the Establishment. Earthy dismisses Rocky's testimony as "old generals' tales" and Sandy vehemently denies the possibility of there being a God. With miraculous timing, however, it is at this moment that the Angel, Power, appears above them to announce the birth of Christ and, as the shepherds fall to the ground in terror, the whole Host of Heaven, robed in white, is seen on the upper stage, in the gallery and in the clerestory. The Cathedral resonates to the sound of the familiar words "Glory to God in the highest" and an extended chorus follows. At this point the Cathedral comes into its own.

As the angels' singing dies away, the procession of the kings is heard approaching, also singing. A complete change of mode is signified and the play becomes a ceremonial and formalised expression of worship. Singing is an important feature, for when human beings wish to unite in purpose and to reach out to a power beyond themselves, they sing; in western tradition it is the most common form of controlled, shared emotion. The Host of Heaven lead the kings towards the place of Christ's birth and as they near the end of their journey they sing:

> Lo, here we come in the midnight cold
> To a shepherds' inn on the outer wold
> And the guiding star stands still, behold. . .
> Can this be the King's abiding-place? (p.40, ll.5-8)

Man's search, the angels assure us, is over for:

> God is more near in Man's despair
> Than a man has wisdom to be 'ware,

and the challenge is issued to all:

Open your hearts, your King is there;
You shall look at Him face to face. (p.40, ll.9-12)

As the Angel, Light, sings a simple, carol-like verse, the Virgin and Child are revealed, framed in the Quire door and in a formal, canopied structure like a painting by Fra Angelico. *The Times* spoke of the "splendid pageantry of the Nativity scene, the most beautiful picture in the play."[37a] The seekers and the doubters all kneel in turn to present their gifts and the traditional scene of the Adoration is re-enacted. To this simple and moving spectacle Masefield adds a touch of genius - as the shepherds join in the singing with the kings and the angels, they draw the audience into the Adoration by lifting the litter, in which the Virgin is sitting, and by carrying it down the steps and into the Nave. The act of worship is thus extended to everyone present, and the four chief angels remind the congregation of the paradoxes of salvation: "mercy and martyrdom", "darkness and light". With a last reference to Man's warring, bloody nature the play ends with its divine antidote, the Coming of Christ as the Coming of Spring. In lines resembling a medieval carol, Power finally issues an invitation to adore the Christ Child:

Friends, Christ has come within this hall
Bow down and worship one and all
Our Father for this thing. (p.47, ll.7-9)

The shift from dramatic entertainment to liturgical enactment which characterises the final part of *The Coming of Christ* made a deep impression on all who attended. Laurence Irving speaks of its having been "more of a spiritual experience" than a conventional production of a play. George Bell recalled the original impact in 1953 when, at Irving's instigation, the play was revived:

No one, who was there, will ever forget the inspiration or the joy . . . the colour, the movement, the acting, the singing, the music, the bells, the procession, the stir, the wonder, the awe, the concord and the worship within the Cathedral![38]

All Christian worship is both an offering and a strengthening, it is based on the assumption that Masefield makes in the final scene of the play that, as we draw near to Christ, He comes to us. In worship, both words and actions take on more significance than their face value, the combination of movement, sound and colour produces an expression of the transcendent, but it is meaningful only to those who participate. Such celebrations of belief were a cultural necessity in the middle ages, but in an age of increasing unbelief they are baffling to many, difficult to assess as drama and increasingly remote from accepted means of communication. Masefield's play suggests that we must believe what we cannot fully understand or explain, acknowledge the activity of a concerned Deity and respond to an in-built desire to confirm our faith in symbolic acts.

George Bell was obviously delighted by Masefield's play and was unrepentant in the face of criticism. He placed his own interesting interpretation on *The Coming of Christ* and argued its continuing relevance in the years that followed its first production. The most dramatic moment in the play was, he always maintained,

> ... when the Anima Christi, having been warned by the Four Powers of shame and the suffering which await him ... renounces the emblems of divinity with these words:
> 'I lay aside my glory and my power
> To take up Manhood.'

This, said Bell, "presents the very essence of the Christian Religion", which is that "God through sacrifice involves himself with human suffering."[39] But speaking in 1953, Bell surveyed the increasing materialism and looming nuclear threat in the Western world and added:

> The message of Christianity to the rich nations especially today is that they should lay aside their glory and power, and set themselves ... to relieve the suffering of the poorer people and continents ...[40]

Bell was also entirely supportive of the play's opposition to violence and the view that war could, in any sense, be glorious. Other favourable critical reaction included J. C. Trewin's description of the play as "a text of such loveliness"[41]; K. M. Lobb's contention that,

> There were many remarkable things about this lovely play...it told the sacred story so beautifully, so simply, yet with such dramatic effect...[42]

and Gerald Weales's view that *The Coming of Christ* was Masefield's best work for the stage.[43]

But several critics took a contrary view, and perhaps the most trenchant criticism came from T. S. Eliot in his *Criterion* commentary for June 1928:

> We venture to counsel our spiritual pastors, that they should see to it either that they employ artists who are definite in their theology, or else who are really good artists.[44]

Herbert Howarth spoke of the play's "feeble doctrine and feeble poetry"[45] and Murray Roston commented:

> *The Coming of Christ* was an uninspired series of biblical and morality scenes occasionally relieved by sparks of poetry. Characters introducing themselves 'I am a shepherd who keeps fold . . .' could scarcely stimulate an audience bred on Ibsen and Shaw.[46]

None of these three severe critics had, in fact, seen the play and were therefore unable to judge the effectiveness of Masefield's careful use of the Cathedral setting, nor is it possible to obtain from a reading of the text any sense of the spiritual experience of the play in performance. Roston's comment on the words of the shepherd as he kneels at the manger are particularly inept - the conventional, formal Adoration was no more intended as naturalism than were the Renaissance paintings. It is important to know what sort of play is being judged before making such a comment. But there certainly is "feeble poetry" and the language of the shepherds constitutes a major weakness in Masefield's play.At times the verse of the shepherds sinks to the level of Mabel Dearmer:

> But soon the morning comes, O glory,
> I'll make a little cradle for 'ee. (p.43, ll. 13-14)

At other times, it seems as though Masefield has avoided the pitfalls of Housman's *Bethlehem* when the shepherds speak with vigorous modern directness and Earthy's description of the war (already quoted)[47] stands comparison with the work of First World War poets for its pathos and evocation of despair. Masefield, however, can never quite break free from the 'mock rustic' and some of the lines given to Earthy are like a parody of a bad nativity play. Masefield had a profound personal knowledge of rural speech and he may well have produced a more accurate, pastoral language than he has been given credit for, but it is difficult to see how any modern actor could say,

Aroint 'ee, now, Grim-One and hag,
Bless Small Folk and all with good cheer

without acute embarrassment. Such lines merely detract from the interesting debate of the shepherds, they produce an unacceptable blend of styles and add nothing to the characterisation. They seem to confirm E. Martin Browne's impression that Masefield had no real sense of humour[48] and L. A. G. Strong's feeling that he lacked self-criticism.[49]

The verse, as a whole, is of very uneven quality and was affected by the Cathedral setting. However, E. H. Baughan observed after the first performance that it was "easy to speak, concise and rhythmic."[50] The need for simplicity does not ,though, excuse the naïvety and contorted syntax of:

By fools and sages
With death for wages,
Souls leave their cages
And man does deeds. (p.44, ll.9-12)

Some of the most satisfying verse is contained in the sung chorus passages. These are partly a device for providing continuity while characters take up new positions, but they also comment, in a detached way, on the action. The chorus presents a cosmic view of the issues involved and draw images and comparisons from mythology and nature. Man's progress since Creation is described in a retelling of the myth of Prometheus; and Zeus, who continues to punish Prometheus for having stolen the sacred fire, is contrasted with God, who freely gives His Light to men. God's revelation of Himself to the world in Christ is represented by a number of powerful images: the coming of spring to a winter world; the light in the darkness; the song of birds on bare branches; and the warmth melting the snow. There are some sensitive lyric passages:

You who have known the darkness slowly yield,
And in the twilight the first blackbirds cry
Come, with the dripping of the dew new-shaken
From twigs where yellowing leaves and reddening berries lie,
And seen the colour come upon the field,
And heard the cocks crow as the thorps awaken . . .
You know with what a holiness of light

The peace of morning comes . . .

These add richness and colour in contrast to the drabness of some of the dialogue and they increase the sense of God's purpose as being one with creation. Death and Fear are the winter and the darkness which, the chorus constantly reminds us, Christ comes to dispel. Masefield's theology is not dogmatic, the emphasis is on personal response to Christ's coming rather than on definite doctrinal statements.[51]

He tries to show that all sorts of people are Christ's concern however arrogant, cruel, stupid or unbelieving they may be. The fact that the world generally rejects Christ does not, Masefield suggests, prevent His loving the world and Masefield makes each of his characters constantly aware of a power beyond themselves to which they reach out in their need. In some respects, he is more successful in demonstrating the need of salvation than he is in showing how Christ's coming resolves that need. He comments clearly and powerfully on personal and universal evils such as greed, materialism, selfishness, violence and war, but the play ends rather abruptly with the Adoration and the significance of the Incarnation is only explained to the characters of the play in a series of images sung by the Heavenly Host.

The change from disbelief to Adoration is handled formally and in many ways is entirely acceptable, but Masefield has already generated substantial interest in the varying personalities and opinions of the shepherds and we are left wondering how, for example, Christ's coming affects Sandy's socialist views or Earthy's attitude to his former generals. A further reason for a sense of anti-climax in the Adoration is the knowledge that, although the characters of the play are kneeling and the beautifully ordered combination of procession, singing and poetry invite the same response from the audience, we have already seen that Christ will, in fact, be rejected. The Adoration in *The Coming of Christ* therefore provokes a more complicated emotional response than in other Nativity plays, it is a mixture of sorrow and joy and it suggests a theme that Christopher Hassall used in a later Canterbury play: the Cradle and the Cross are one.[52]

Masefield's play never gives the overall impression of quaint-ness or of an unhappy attempt to fit modern thoughts to a medieval form. If he fails, it is because he never fully solves the problem of language: he appears to be either writing verse or dialogue, never both together. The impact of the play is achieved by taking some of the basic ideas of a morality - representational staging, universal figures, a blend of teaching and worship - and fitting them to the eternal truths of Christianity seen in the actual world of 1928.

The Coming of Christ moved and disturbed over six thousand people in four performances and that, by any standard, is a remarkable achievement. As George Bell remarked in 1958:

It might fairly be called a landmark because it was on the one hand the creation of a new work of art by three contemporary artists of the front rank at the invitation of the Church, and on the other hand its production set the seal of the Mother Church of English Christianity on the drama as dedicated to the service of God. At that Whitsuntide 1928, 30 years ago, the poet and the artist re-entered the Church. [53]

Notes to Chapter 5

1. E. H. Baughan, 'Review of *The Coming of Christ', The Daily News* London, May 29th 1928, 7.

2. 'Review of *The Coming of Christ', The Times,* London, May 31st 1928, 14.

3. E. H. Baughan, *loc. cit.*

4. *The Times, loc. cit.,* 14.

5. The full score is still available from the library of Radius.

6. E. H. Baughan, *loc. cit.*

7. Laurence Irving maintains that the cast "felt like students in a demo." TR1., see Bibliography D.

8. E. H. Baughan, *loc. cit.*

9. *Ibid.*

10. K. M. Lobb, *Drama in School and Church* (London 1955), 112.

11. 'Review of *The Coming of Christ* in Wittersham Parish Church', *The Times,* London, December 14th 1953.

12. E. Martin and Henzie Browne, *Pilgrim Story* (London 1946), 76.

13. Robert Potter, *The English Morality Play* (London/Boston 1975), 15-16.

14. Stuart Jackman, *The Backyard Miracle* (London 1970).

15. John Arden, *The Business of Good Government* (London 1963).

16. *cp.* above, pp. 74-7.

17. *cp.* above, p. 93.

18. *The Times* (1953) *loc. cit.*

19. All references to the text are to John Masefield, *The Coming of Christ* (Cathedral Edition, London 1928)

20. *cp.* above, pp. 43-4.

21. *The Times* (1928) *loc. cit.,* 14.

22. A. C. Cawley, ed., *Everyman and Medieval Plays* (London 1956).

23. E. H. Baughan, *loc. cit.,* 7.

24. *The Times* (1928) *loc. cit.,* 14.

25. Norman Goodall, 'Struggle of Faith Since the Twenties', *Reform* (June 1975), 19.

26. Something of Masefield's concern with the 1914-18 war can be obtained by noting his output: *The Old Front Line* (London 1917); *The Battle of the Somme* (London 1919); *St George and the Dragon* (American title); *The War and the Future* (London 1918). Sadly, his own son was killed in action in the Second World War.

27. Phyllis Hartnoll, ed., *The Oxford Companion to the Theatre* (London 1967), 502.

28. K. M. Lobb, *op. cit.,* 113.

29. Herbert Howarth, *Notes on Some Figures Behind T. S. Eliot* (London 1965), 267.

30. William V. Spanos, *op. cit.*, 138.

31. After the initial production Rocky was referred to as the "sergeant shepherd". Although the text gives no clear indication that the first shepherd had actually been a sergeant in the war, it is obvious that Masefield must have explained to the cast that he intended this meaning.

32. E. H. Baughan, *loc. cit.*, He refers to l.10 p.29.

33. E. H. Baughan, *loc. cit.*, 7.

34. Laurence Irving, TR1., see Bibliography D.

35. *loc. cit.*, 7.

36. Laurence Irving, TR1., see Bibliography D.

37. *cp.* above, p. 87.

37a. *The Times* (1928) *loc. cit.*, 14.

38. G. K. A. Bell, 'Sermon on *The Coming of Christ* preached at Wittersham Parish Church on Sunday December 13th 1953' (Local private printing, undated, and un-paginated). Laurence Irving again played the part of Gaspar in his local parish church.

39/40. *Ibid.*

41. J. C. Trewin, *The English Theatre* (London 1948), 56. Trewin is one of the few critics who obviously preferred Masefield's Canterbury play to Eliot's which he des cribes as "Nobly dull, a tiring Canterbury Pilgrimage".

42. K. M. Lobb, *op. cit.*, 112.

43. Gerald Weales, *op. cit.*, 137.

44. Quoted in Herbert Howarth, *op. cit.*, 267.

45. *Ibid.*

46. Murray Roston, *Biblical Drama in England* (London 1968), 290.

47. See above, p. 135.

48. TR2., see Bibliography D.

49. L. A. G. Strong, 'John Masefield', *Writers and their Work* (Lon. 1952), 5.

50. E. H. Baughan, *loc. cit.*, 7.

51. Definite, dogmatic theology is more suited to the sermon than to drama. This, of course, is the solution Eliot employed.

52. See below, pp. 160-1.

53. G. K. A. Bell, Lord Bishop of Chichester, 'Speech on the Church and Religious Drama', *The Chronicle of Convocation: Being a record of the Proceedings of the Convocation of Canterbury, Session of January 14, 15, 16, 1958* (London 1958), 83.

6

The Young King

Laurence Binyon's play for the 1934 Festival, *The Young King*, was the first play by a living dramatist to be produced in the Chapter House at Canterbury. The previous year, Laurence Irving had designed and supervised the construction of a small open stage at one end of the building and this had been used for a performance of Tennyson's *Becket*. Compared to the huge stage for which Masefield had written *The Coming of Christ* the stage in the Chapter House was minute: it was only nine feet in depth; and, as the arcaded wall of the Chapter House formed the background, there was no means of entry to the stage except through the auditorium or from the very small wings provided by the screens that had been designed to blend with the architecture of the walls. The screens added a three-dimensional effect to an otherwise flat setting and could represent buildings and doorways, if lit directly, or simply merge as part of an interior. A fixed central throne in the rear wall of the stage provided a useful property for court scenes.

Movement on the tiny stage was, of course, very restricted, but it was possible to convey a sense of movement by use of the aisle through the auditorium. This practice, which had first been used in modern times by Poel in *Everyman*, was consistently used at Canterbury for processions and effective entrances and exits. *The*

Times of 1934 commented on *The Young King*:

> ... all the characters have to get to the stage by coming up through the audience; but Miss E. Thorndike (the producer) . . . made very clever use of this disability.[1]

The use of a small open stage for *The Young King* was perfectly in keeping with the scale and style of the play as it had originally been written for performance at John Masefield's small Boars Hill theatre a few years earlier. No scenery had been possible in its first production and this was regarded increasingly as an advantage by the Boars Hill dramatists. Bottomley, for example, felt that the failure of Tennyson, Browning and Stephen Phillips was due to their having attempted the verbal richness of Elizabethan plays written for the bare stage in the modern theatre of mechanical illusion.[2] Nevertheless, Binyon and Eileen Thorndike undertook a substantial revision of the play for its performance at Canterbury and Laurence Irving recalls how Binyon reacted to this discipline:

> I remember poor Binyon, on a cold day in the Chapter House, wincing when he saw what had been done to his play; but his play was all the better for it and I think he recognised this.[3]

Eileen Thorndike's main concern was almost certainly to avoid the gentility of the Boars Hill production and to stress the action of the play. The electrician was asked to provide sound effects for the battle scenes and he produced spectacular and ingenious explosions under the stage.[4] A general sense of lively attack characterised the whole production and *The Times* remarked on the unexpected results:

> Those who consider that Mr Binyon's plays are not dramatic might reconsider their opinion after seeing the very spirited way in which the Cathedral Players kept the action going.[5]

In order that the audience could follow this lively action without difficulty, they were provided with an *Argument of the Play* which also provided detailed historical background. This material was, however, so enormously complex that it is doubtful if it achieved its aim. It does, however, show how Binyon and Eileen Thorndike reduced a mass of historical material into a viable stage play. The Acting Edition of the play, which was produced for Canterbury and was available for sale to the audience as well as for use by the cast, certainly gives the impression of a play of energy and freshness. There are lines which actors trained by modern techniques would find almost unspeakable, but this is not entirely a reflection on Binyon's poetic mode. The same sense of embarrassment applies to the contemporary naturalism of R. C. Sheriff's *Journey's End* (1928) or the peasant simplicity of Shaw's *St Joan* (1924), both written in the same decade.

Figure 10: *The Young King* (1934). Vera Coburn Findlay as Queen Eleanor and Ann Casson as Queen Margaret.

Binyon's *The Young King* was chosen for the Canterbury Festival primarily because it formed a sequel to Tennyson's *Becket*. Binyon was obviously impressed by Tennyson's play, for he wrote two plays which continue the story of *Becket* and, in some ways, copy its style. The first of these was *Godstow Nunnery*, a one-act verse play for women that was performed at Boars Hill in 1929, and the second was *The Young King*, a verse history which, in its handling of chronology and language, has many of the marks of an imitation of Shakespeare.

The Young King deals with the events in the reign of Henry II after the death of Becket. At Canterbury the continuity was preserved by having Henry played by Ronald Adam, who had been Henry in the previous year's performance of *Becket*. The troublesome Irish territories and his need to arrange a public absolution for the Archbishop's death with the papal legates, necessitates lengthy absences from court. Accordingly, Henry has his son Harry and his wife Margaret, crowned as titular king and queen; but, in spite of their demands to be given actual dominion over part of the realm, "the Young King" remains king in title only. Encouraged by Henry's wife, Eleanor, and assisted by his brothers, Geoffrey and Richard, and the disloyal lord, Bertrand de Born, the Young King organises a revolt in Anjou. Henry also has other troubles at home:

> . . . all the land is up.
> William the Lion has broken out of Scotland
> And marches southward, harrying and slaughtering.
> Some say he has taken York and left it in flames.
> Leicester flies rebel colours and is gone
> To meet the murdering Scot: and in Thames' mouth
> The Flanders fleet comes crammed with men-at-arms.
> (Scene 1, p.3, ll.9-15)[6]

But the King's public penance in Canterbury (with which Anouilh's later play *Becket* opens) brings the favour of the Almighty: the rebels are defeated at home and Henry is able to confront his son abroad. The argument continues, but Henry consistently refuses to grant his son's requests and, after years of war, the Young King is driven to pillage the Abbey of Rocamadour

148

where he dies of a fever, leaving his father grief-stricken. The funeral procession, which became a feature of the first four years of Chapter House drama at Canterbury, ends the play.

Modern English drama was not in a healthy state in 1934. Out of the 28 plays by living playwrights announced in *The Times* during the week when *The Young King* was playing in the Chapter House, only J. B. Priestley's *Laburnam Grove* would ever be likely to be performed today. Gordon Daviot's *Queen of Scots* was attracting a good deal of attention and proving that there was still an audience for costume drama; and for the only other theatrical event of note, London theatregoers still relied on the apparently tireless Ben Greet with his production of *Twelfth Night* in Regent's Park.

Even against this depressing background, Laurence Binyon was an obscure figure. His last commercial production, *Arthur,* had been seen eleven years earlier and since that time, with public taste turning away from romantic verse drama, he had relied entirely on John Masefield for productions of his plays at Boars Hill. Shaw had not considered Binyon a serious contender to write a *St Joan* and Binyon's output since *Arthur* has never been mentioned by critics or drama historians, though *Godstow Nunnery*, by virtue of its brevity and its all-women cast, has made its way into anthologies of one-act plays.

At Canterbury in 1934, however, the prospect was entirely different. In perfect summer weather the management of the Festival could afford to ignore popular, commercial tastes. The cool Chapter House with its Gothic atmosphere was a perfect setting for Binyon's romantic historical play, *The Young King*. A group of actors, already experienced in verse drama and the particular problems of acting in the Chapter House, surprised their audience with the effectiveness and vitality of the play. Binyon's drama, released from the cloying influence of elaborate scenery and musical wash, was seen to advantage and it was obvious that, unlike many of his nineteenth-century predecessors and his poet-dramatist friends, he could shape his material into a well-constructed, exciting and gripping play. There was the added attraction that *The Young King*, though no part of the action is set in Canterbury, contains constant reminders of Henry II's suffering as a result of the death of Becket. The King walked to his public penance along the very streets by which the audience of Binyon's play would have approached the Chapter House.

It is doubtful that Binyon's decision to write his play in imitation of Shakespeare would have struck many of the audience as unusual or unnatural. As we have already noted, there was still a strong link between poetry-speaking and drama, particularly if the subject was removed from everyday life, and the occasional archaism in Binyon's verse ensured that it was in accord with the popular middle-class conception of what poetry ought to be. Besides, the verse of *The Young King* appears crisp and convincing as dramatic dialogue: it gives the impression of characters talking to each other, rather than of speaking verse to the audience. There are some splendid moments for a powerful actor in Binyon's eminently speakable lines, such as when young Harry defends his decision to plunder the Abbey:

> ... Does God
> Need silver and gold, and a handful of bright gems,
> Who has all the world for His own and a million stars?
> I need them and will have them.   (Scene 5, p.47, ll.20-23)

The verse is not always as colourful as this, but it creates the sense of another age without quaintness and obscurity and, even when the scene is melodramatic, rarely becomes a mere painting of the passions.

Viewed from a distance, we can see how far out of line with the most interesting developments of poetry in the thirties *The Young King* was. But drama presented a special sort of problem: there was a long-standing tradition of iambic blank verse, what Bamber Gascoigne calls "the poetic cobweb which has stifled dramatists for three-hundred years",[7] and by 1934 nobody had yet produced a wholly convincing alternative. Binyon himself was not altogether happy with the situation. Though he had experimented widely in different forms of versification since his early associations with Robert Bridges at Oxford, he had never been able to extend these experiments into drama. Yet he increasingly felt the restrictions of blank verse and, in 1941, two years before his death, he wrote to Gordon Bottomley expressing his loss of confidence:

It may be the infection of the moderns, but I think it is something in the air these troublous times; somehow the traditional movement of blank verse doesn't seem to correspond to one's needs, it is too smooth.[8] This sense of the inappropriateness of pseudo-Shakespearean drama to the world of the 1930s colours all judgements that we can make on *The Young King*. Kenneth Muir, for instance, in a discussion of Binyon's plays, maintains that the playwright had,

the negative virtues that his blank verse is not obviously derivative; it never lapses into romantic tushery and does not call attention to itself.[9]

All this can be said of *The Young King*, but the implication of Muir's comment is that, having elected to write in blank verse, Binyon was unlikely to achieve any positive virtues. The most obvious fault is the lack of variety of cadence, which William Poel considered essential for a verse drama to establish characterisation. Binyon's characters have different behavioural traits, but they speak in a similar manner. Generally, the verse is not strong enough to convey the emotions the playwright intends and the climaxes are in the action rather than in the language. These features suggest that Binyon was at times producing words to a pattern. There are instances when he appears to long to break free from gracefulness and the fixed line.

The choice of Binyon's *The Young King*, both as a verse drama and a religious play, seems a regressive move after the earlier Festival play by a living playwright, *The Coming of Christ*. As a religious play, *The Young King* has little to offer. It certainly provoked no controversy concerning Christian drama, nor did it bring the audience to their knees. The idea of God in *The Young King* is similar to that in Shakespeare's histories. God is an agent of judgement, He exacts a penalty from Henry II for the death of Archbishop Becket by punishing him through his own son. For a while it seems that the act of penance has restored Henry to divine favour but, although the King expresses regret, he never feels real contrition and finally, both Henry and his son blaspheme and challenge God's mercy. The debate as to whether or not God is just, whether He mocks or is merciful continues throughout the play, but it is made clear that the views are held by the historical characters themselves and at no time is the play an expression of faith.

Later Canterbury dramatists rebelled against both the form and intention of *The Young King* for, although it provided a moving historical entertainment, it had no Christian message for the contemporary world and it belonged to an outmoded theatrical tradition. It was George Bell's ideal that the Christian Church with its new association with the arts should, above all, be progressive.

Notes to Chapter 6

1. 'Review of *The Young King*', *The Times*, London July 9th 1934, 9.
2. Gordon Bottomley, *A Stage for Poetry* (Kendal 1948), 3.
3. TR1., see Bibliography D.
4. TR4., see Bibliography D.
5. *The Times, loc. cit.*, 9.
6. All page references are to Laurence Binyon, *The Young King*, (Acting Edition for the Friends of Canterbury Cathedral, Canterbury 1934).
7. Bamber Gascoigne, *Twentieth Century Drama* (London 1962), 59.
8. Laurence Binyon, *The Madness of Merlin* (London 1947). Introduced by Gordon Bottomley, xi.
9. Kenneth Muir, 'Verse and Prose' *Stratford-upon-Avon Studies IV: Contemporary Theatre* (London 1962), 105.

7

Christ's Comet

The play selected for production in the Chapter House for the Canterbury Festival of 1938 was Christopher Hassall's *Christ's Comet*. The choice of Hassall was perhaps surprising as he was only twenty-six years of age and was by no means a well-known author, unlike Masefield or Eliot. In 1937 he was known as an actor who had played Romeo in Gielgud's Oxford University Drama Society production of 1932 and who, after a brief appearance in *Henry III* at the Old Vic, had joined the cast of *Proscenium* as Ivor Novello's understudy.[1] *Christ's Comet* was his first play and, although not specially written for the event and having no particular connection with the history of Canterbury, was chosen by Laurence Irving as a suitable play for the 1938 Festival.

Hassall had written a small amount of verse before and was eventually to become librettist for Ivor Novello, William Walton, Arthur Bliss and Anthony Hopkins. He was, perhaps, the last English poet to draw inspiration from a friendship with Edward Marsh. Indeed, he remained an advocate of the Georgians and his biographies of Marsh (1959) and Rupert Brooke (1962) did something to reverse the attitude of almost unquestioning contempt with which the Georgians had been dismissed from the critical scene ever since the 1930s and '40s. And, as we shall see, many of the weaknesses of *Christ's Comet* derive from Hassall's inability to break free from the Georgian conception of what poetry should be. *Christ's Comet* was in some ways an odd throwback and all the more odd for being written by a relatively young man.

Poetic drama was not in a particularly healthy state in the 1930s and even the success of *Murder in the Cathedral* had not changed the situation in any significant way. In the same year as *Christ's Comet* was written, Lascelles Abercrombie wrote despondently:

> . . . in the theatre today, poetic drama is an alien . . . poetic drama is a medium that has become unnatural; and without a new stage, new actors, and a new audience, must continue to do so . . .[2]

Yet there were some signs of an appreciative audience, if not a new one: Dorothy Sayers's Canterbury play of 1937, *The Zeal of Thy House*, was playing at the Duke of York's and was described as "brilliant entertainment and quite unforgettable."[3] *The Times* greeted *Christ's Comet* with considerable enthusiasm, praising the verse and the ideas of the play and adding,

> . . . the piece appears singularly well suited to an ecclesiastical festival, better suited indeed than its predecessors *Murder in the Cathedral* or *The Zeal of Thy House*.[4]

Nevertheless, despite an encouraging reception in some quarters, the fact remains that *Christ's Comet* was not put on in London after its Canterbury première, nor was it revived until 1958 (in a greatly altered form), although there was a radio version broadcast on Christmas Day 1946.

Although it was not written specifically for the Festival, *Christ's Comet* returned to the theme of the first Canterbury play, the Nativity, and, like *The Coming of Christ*, Hassall's play is concerned with uncomplicated piety. The essential simplicity of its approach is, however, masked by the ornate Georgian style and by Hassall's conception of life in the Near East at the time of Christ's birth, a conception that seems to owe much to Marie Correlli's novel *Barabbas* or Wilson Barrett's play *The Sign of the Cross*. There is, nevertheless, some evidence that he also used the Anglo-Saxon *Dream of the Rood* as a source.

We do not know what kind of production Hassall had envisaged when he wrote the play but, perhaps surprisingly, it seems, within limits, to have worked quite well in the Chapter House. The reviewer for the *Canterbury Cathedral Chronicle* (possibly a partial critic) said that,

Mr Laurence Irving and Mr Michael MacOwan (the producer) showed beyond question that with care and ingenuity, and above all with perception of what was essential and what was not, the Chapter House can take a play of more complexity than has been tried before.[5]

Figure 11 shows how Laurence Irving adapted his original setting to incorporate a central panel which joined the two side screens to form a triptych-like structure. This arrangement included a small balcony which enabled characters to appear high above the stage level and the action of the play, especially in the first act, to alternate between the two levels very effectively. Because of the need to isolate various levels and areas of the stage, a more complex lighting plot than had hitherto been used was evolved.

The electrician's prompt copy shows a considerable number of lighting changes and an increased use of colour. The efficiency of the lighting was greatly enhanced by the introduction of mirror spotlights. These lights were capable of far clearer definition than the crude, carbon-arc floods that had been used previously. Christopher Hassall was insistent that lighting was a most important ingredient and major image in his play. After the 1958 revival of *Christ's Comet* he wrote:

To some plays darkness is essential. Christ's Comet is one of them. The climax of the play is light, both actual and figurative. This cannot be conceived without preceding darkness. The successive lighting effects of late afternoon, storm, twilight and black night, culminating with the brilliant inset piece of the tableau . . . all said practically as much as the spoken word of the text.[6]

Nevertheless, in 1938 there were obvious limitations in the Chapter House: the first scene, for instance, was set in Trebizond, 4 BC and *The Times* critic commented:

Not only were the appropriate scenic and lighting effects beyond the scope of the Chapter House, a picture of the barbaric, pre-Christian eastern world has nothing to gain from a natural setting of Gothic sprung from a flowering period of Christian civilization.[7]

Hassall's handling of time and place in *Christ's Comet* seems to owe a good deal to the kind of historical costume play that had enjoyed considerable popularity throughout the previous hundred years or so and that derives, in part at least, from Shakespeare's historical plays. The settings range from Trebizond to Jerusalem and involve specific locations like "A street alongside the Royal Palace in Pontus" or "The Crest of Golgotha". The action of the play extends over a period of at least thirty years and, indeed, the play is subtitled "*The Story of a Thirty Years' Journey that Began and Ended on the Same Day*". Again, Hassall is quite specific as to the exact time-lapse between various scenes and these range from "A few minutes" to "Thirty years".

Christ's Comet is a three-act play, Act I contains four scenes, Act II, three scenes and Act III, three scenes. For the Festival the usual Friends' Acting Edition was prepared, but this was simply a reprint of the edition published by Heinemann and, probably for copyright reasons, contained no alterations for Canterbury. This Acting Edition was found to be unsatisfactory by the producer, Michael MacOwan,[8] and the prompt copy, on which my account of the play will be based, shows that for the performance the whole of Act I, Scene 3 and Herod's speeches about his son (p.21), beauty (p.29) and wine (p.30) were cut. Substantial cuts were also made in the Robber's speeches in Act III, Scenes 1 (p.40) and 2 (p.48).

For the revival of the play in 1958 the producer was E. Martin Browne and he advised Christopher Hassall to undertake a major revision of the play. The edition published in 1958 has only two acts and several of the minor characters omitted. Another difference between the two versions is that the second version contains far less music. Christopher Hassall was a considerable musician and not only did he compose a substantial amount of music for the 1938 performance, he also played it himself on an organ specially installed in the Chapter House for the Festival.

The main features of the action in the 1938 edition of Christ's Comet can be summarised fairly briefly. Act I is set in Pontus where the King, Artaban, awaits the visit of three other monarchs. The four kings have sworn to meet at Artaban's court every year in the month of comets:

Figure 11: *Christ's Comet* (1938). Strabo (Philip Hollingworth) explains the route to the Kings. Setting adapted by Laurence Irving.

When it is prophesied, and so our hearts
Believe, a fire-ball shall be lifted up
Among the trivial lustres of our darkness
To signify the birthplace of a second
More glorious Alexander.   (Act I, sc.2, 1.4-8, p.3) [9]

They intend to offer their allegiance to this second Alexander who, it is prophesied, "shall uncrown the Roman eagle". Various omens have suggested to Artaban that in this, the seventh of their annual meetings, their patience will be rewarded:

The year is like a pyramid that slopes
Up to this minute.   (Act I, sc.2, ll.11-12, p.4)

The climax of Act I is reached when the royal Astronomer, Strabo, tells the assembled kings that the comet is visible and they kneel together as they see the star. A great feast is held, and then the kings prepare for their journey.

In Act II the four kings, Artaban, Balthazar, Melchior and Gaspar come to Jerusalem some weeks after setting out from Trebizond. In Jerusalem they visit Herod, who is related to Melchior and there is a vivid picture of the tyrant's court. In a long interview with Herod and his advisers, the kings discover that there has been a rumour amongst the common people of a miraculous virgin-birth and Artaban finds that this "Awakes a haunting echo" in his mind. He gradually realises that he has misunderstood the nature of the king he seeks and that he is not yet fit to offer his allegiance to him. Renouncing his worldly kingdom and with only his Mule-teer for company, Artaban leaves the other three kings to continue their journey to Bethlehem and embarks on a life of humility, poverty and charity.

Act III shows Artaban thirty years later, old and blind, still searching to find the full significance of the Nativity. In a chance meeting with Barabbas, who has just been released, Artaban learns of the Crucifixion and is led to Golgotha. Here, an angel explains the meaning of Christ's death and Artaban dies at the foot of the Cross. In a final tableau, however, he comes at last to join the other magi, kneeling at the manger.

The simple story moves from the elaborate, colourful court of Artaban to the grim starkness of Golgotha - changes in mood and setting are suggested by the qualities of light. At the opening of the play the sun is shining and there is speculation about the appearance of the star; yet the first character to comment on the bright sun and the feast of the star is an Old Blind Man who is a symbol of pagan blindness:

Urgent white figures speak as they move. The words are strong, enticing, absorbing. Here is a searching world, artistic and cruel, set in a golden light and surrounded by panic and darkness.[10]

The image continues as three of the kings survey the heavens from the balcony and confess the mystic imaginings concerning other worlds and the gods but see no real answer, while Strabo,

> . . . sits wakeful in his tower,
> Mapping the heavens as a general
> Might figure out a battle. (Act I, sc. 2, ll..22-24, p.5)

As if to add to the sense of mental blindness, the heavens cloud over and there is a strange disturbance in the city. But then, the contrasts between exotic and spiritual darkness are continued in the resolution of the kings' hopes and anxieties. Strabo bursts into their presence to announce that the long-awaited comet will shortly shine out and dispel the darkness of their uncertainty. Assuring the kings that he recognises a new and significant star in the heavens as surely as a careful gardener knows the plants in his rockery, Strabo gives a picturesque description of having first noticed the comet reflected in the waters of a fountain as he looked down from his tower, and then explains that the disturbance in the city which followed his wonderful vision was, in fact, the dramatic arrival of King Gaspar with elephants, white in the moonlight, jugglers, dancers, spice and peacocks (reminiscent of Masefield's *Cargoes*). As the riders in the exotic caravan noticed the comet they had all, said Strabo, raised their heads and shouted with exultation until it seemed to him that "the ground blossomed with faces" and only the mules and camels demonstrated total unconcern. Artaban's reaction is equally colourful:

> Bring out the heaped-up tables, weigh them down
> With cups of Jade, and jars of terracotta
> Standing akimbo in rotund array.
> We'll fortify our hearts in the open air

Tonight, that the great gods may see us dine
With all the stars reflected in our wine.   (Act I, sc. 2, ll.34-39, p. 9)

The star, as a symbol of God's light entering the world, affects the action in a simple and effective way. When it appears to the kings there are very few words, for the image of light makes the statement:

Strabo: Look! Over there!
Balthazar: The Comet!
Artaban: The world reborn!   (Act I, Sc. 2, ll.1-3, p.10)

They all look offstage. One kneels, another shields his eyes and their faces are bathed in an orange glow. The prompt copy adds: "Music".

The idea of bringing Artaban to Golgotha was not entirely original. As we have seen in Chapter Two, Mabel Dearmer's *The Soul of the World* ends with the shepherds and the magi at Calvary and Henry Van Dyke's novel *The Fourth Wise Man* also ends in this way. Hassall, nevertheless, has handled the final movements of the play with considerable skill. We are not shown any of Artaban's inter-vening years, but the details are supplied in the conversation between Artaban and the Muleteer as they enter Jerusalem. The events of Artaban's life described by Hassall follow quite closely those given in Van Dyke's novel[11]: he has lived a life of severe hard-ship, sleeping rough, clothing the needy, comforting the dying, befriending the outcast; but, even though he feels no bitterness for the suffering he has endured, he still feels that he has yet to achieve his aim. All he has done,

. . . is such a little, with life so full
Of scope for him who concentrates on mercy.

                                        (Act III, sc. 1, ll.17-18, p.42)

Artaban dies in the knowledge that the sin of Adam has been forgiven:

O Eden, fatal bower of cinnamon!
A friend has paid the wicked gardener's ransom;
Wither in peace, your ghosts need walk no more.

                                        (Act III, sc. 3, ll.24-26, p54)

The reappearance of the Angel after the total darkness signifies a complete change of mode, for he speaks directly to the audience,

160

like the Angel at the end of *Everyman*, inviting them to share the experience of the central character. A spectator at the 1938 production of *Christ's Comet* wrote:

> To bring back the Angel with a new assurance of the oneness of Beginning and End was the perfect way of translating us from the death of the body to the life of the spirit. It was here too that the visual beauty of the performance reached its highest. The Angel, the Holy Family, the aged frame of Artaban passing from the shadow into the light, made up a scene which those who saw it will be very loth to forget.[12]

The only appropriate response to these final moments is, like Granville-Barker's reaction to *Everyman*, to kneel.[13] The choir sings a carol proclaiming the reign of Peace and the incarnation of Christ - an event that will outlive the words and action of the play, for,

> Poetry must bloom and die,
> But Christ was born to live for aye,   (Act III, sc. 3, ll.16-17, p.57)

and as Artaban kneels at the Manger and opens his arms "in a gesture of oblation" he offers the worship of the audience to the Christ-child,

> Whose blessings fall on everyman
> That treads the path of Artaban.   (Act III, sc. 3, ll.18-19, p.57)

The play, therefore, ends like *The Coming of Christ* with a resolution of the doubts, searching and suffering of its characters in an act of faith and worship.

Although Artaban's journey is the main theme of the play, Hassall has created a number of contrasting characters who contribute substantially to the action. By far the most colourful of these is King Herod. As with the medieval plays about the coming of the kings, in Hassall's play Herod dominates the action. Nor is he any less terrifying, absurd or self-centred than his medieval counterpart: he alternates rant, self-glorification and smooth duplicity with alarming speed. "Mr George Woodbridge", said *The Times* in 1938, "gave genuine animation to the fiercely painted lineaments of Herod."[14]

Once the kings have left his court, Herod's fear and malice explode into the horrific determination to exterminate all Jewish children; no pleas for pity can move his final, icy resolution. Few people in the Canterbury audience can have realised how near the world was approaching to another Herod's court in 1938. There is no more harrowing moment in English drama than the massacre of the innocents and Hassall adds a note of ghastly bestiality with Herod's refusal to listen to pleas for mercy and his last words:

Tomorrow we'll go hear the nightingale.   (Act II, sc. 2, l.19, p.36)

The Muleteer and Strabo the Astronomer are, by contrast, rather tedious characters. In a programme note Hassall says of the Muleteer, that he is,

. . . descended from the Shakespearian Fool, and his prose dialogue aims at no positive virtue in itself, but rather at bringing relief to the studied verse by the contrast of its complete inconsequence.[15]

The Muleteer claims to be a poet, in spite of his usually prosaic language, and his songs and wit are a foil to Artaban's grave seriousness, but both the Muleteer and Strabo are provided with excessive dialogue in proportion to their importance in the plot.

The language of *Christ's Comet* is based on an Elizabethan model and Hassall was probably the last English verse dramatist to write unashamedly in this mode. In his *Notes on the Verse Drama* (1948), Hassall singles out three particular features of Elizabethan drama which we can see imitated in *Christ's Comet* and which were, incidentally, appropriate to a performance in the Chapter House at Canterbury. The first was the iambic which he believed was still capable of providing the basis of verse drama and to be perfectly adaptable to modern speech:

Mr Ivor Brown has provided two good examples in a recent lecture: "Just pop along and get a loaf of bread", and "I'm going to take my cutie to the flicks", which as iambic pentameters are unexceptionable. Contemporary speech must shorten the periods in blank verse . . . but apart from that pentameter line seems to me as natural to the language as it ever was.[16]

In *Christ's Comet* Hassall was determined to avoid "bogus Eliotese or Audenese"[17] and claimed that the blank verse "is often little more than present day conversation, coaxed, almost imperceptibly into iambics."[18]

Secondly, Hassall was concerned to reproduce the Elizabethan ability to create verbal scenery, ". . . our scripts are impoverished because the pictorial function of dialogue has been usurped by the designer."[19] This modern tendency Hassall contrasted with conditions in the Elizabethan theatre:

The outward eye, noting the positions of the actors, and the ear gathering hints from the dialogue at every turn, were continually combining to fetch and carry food for the ravenous imagination.[20]

There are many examples of such verbal scenery in *Christ's Comet*. Many of the images of light and darkness are created in this way and the astronomer Strabo provides rich material for the imagination in his description of the arrival of Gaspar and the appearance of the star. In the final scene, the Muleteer creates the environment on a bare stage:

There is a high wind carrying the clouds
That scud for life, like a despairing army.
The crosses over there seem to be falling,
Leaning and falling, nearer to the ground,
Because of the black wreckage of a sky
Fountaining up behind them into space,
And whirling overhead.   (Act III, sc.3, ll.20-26)

Complex scenic and lighting effects would, indeed, have been inappropriate with such verse to do their work.

Hassall looked back to the style of Elizabethan dramatic verse which, he said, was dictated by the difficult acoustics of Elizabethan playhouses. The Elizabethans had written: "The kind of verse that can be slung about in a big echoing space . . ."[21] and therefore,

Dramatic verse, and that sort of verse only, must use the big vocal gesture, and only sound right and natural when projected into an auditorium."[22]

Hassall considered that the move to indoor theatres and then to naturalistic settings had caused the art of verse-speaking to die out. This was particularly serious because, "Dramatic verse is a pattern of instructions for the human voice speaking in public."[23]

The Georgian poets were especially anxious to revive the art of verse-speaking and Christopher Hassall, their disciple, was no exception. He was a fine speaker and reader of verse[24] and in *Christ's Comet* provided what Laurence Irving described to me as "some lovely lines"[25] to be slung about in the big echoing space of the Chapter House. The Muleteer, for example, speaks to the Roman soldier in these words:

Hard Roman, do not think I envy you
Your seven statue-covered mounds, nor all
Your sunlit porches giving on the Tiber
Hewn out of solid light, and the clear water
Flows fathom deep between contented meadows,
And it is only one small hill away
From earth . . .   (Act III, sc.3,ll.12-19, p.55)

In the hands of the experienced speakers of dramatic verse who acted at Canterbury, such lines made a considerable impression. *The Times* spoke of "verse that is traditional and eloquent, yet unrhetorical and alive"[26] and of "the assurance of beauty which is everywhere implicit in the verse and in the drawing of characters."[27] *The Canterbury Cathedral Chronicle* was moved, like *The Times* to mention Robert Speaight's handling of the verse: "the grave beauty of the speech and acting",[28] and maintained that:

> There is no display or strain in Mr Hassall's verse; but no less in its simplest moments than in such a speech as Artaban's address to the Spirit of Beauty, it enfolds the very essence of the truth, emotional or spiritual, which he means to convey. Mr Hassall, in fact, is that rare being, a poet who is a dramatist, one whose poetry is drama, and his drama poetry.[29]

Taking Beddoes as his example, Hassall reproduced a number of other Elizabethan features in *Christ's Comet*. Beddoes's *Death's Jest Book* (1850) only became available in its full text in 1935. Both Hassall and Dorothy Sayers admired it greatly and Hassall felt it to be a perfect example of the adaptation of an Elizabethan model to modern usage. It is evident that in *Christ's Comet* he hoped to produce something similar. The three acts are divided into scenes, six of which end with rhyming couplets. The effect of the couplets is to provide a memorable idea to be carried into the action of the next scenes, but they also contort the language into archaism:

Man: We must obey them, be they fool or wise.
They are the merchants, we the merchandise.
                                                 (Act I, sc. 3, ll.15-16, p.11)

or

Artaban: Set on. United we begin our quest,
And with one hope. Let fate decide the rest.
                                                (Act I, sc. 3, ll.13-14, p. 15)
Shakespearean echoes are created by such lines as:
  . . . let the trumpeter
  Talk to the citizens with brassy lip,
  Proclaiming our alliance.   (Act I, sc.3, ll.24-26, p.14)
and by the mixture of verse, prose and song, direct dialogue and soliloquy.

There are, however, obvious Georgian influences. Hassall was an admirer of Bottomley's *King Lear's Wife*, and *Christ's Comet* contains strong reminders of Lascelles Abercrombie's descriptions of Baghdad in *The Sale of Saint Thomas*; of Walter de la Mare's *Arabia*; of the oriental poems and plays of James Elory Flecker;[30] and of John Drinkwater's *Moonlit Apples*. Unfortunately, these influences combine to produce an over-decorative and self-indulgent style which fails to advance the action or provide information. Melchior provides two striking examples of verbal decoration for its own sake. To Artaban's enquiry about the disturbance in the city as the kings watch from the balcony, he replies:
  I only hear the sea
  Looking for mermaids in her weedy caverns.
                                                (Act I, sc.2, ll.10-11, p.6)
And, a little later, as Balthazar remarks on the approaching dark, Melchior observes:
  The big black animal has closed her eyes
  Let fall the lids over her clots of fire.   (Act I, sc.2, ll.17-18, p.7)
Not only are the images weak but the words hold back the development of the main idea.

This is further exemplified in the four speeches which follow, where the apparently naturalistic action is slowed down by Artaban's poetic cadenza,
  Balthazar: Someone is running up the spiral stairway.
  Artaban: That soldier has been quick.
  Melchior: What could have happened?
  The noise was of a discontented city.
  Artaban: How fearful is the dead language of a footstep!
  It taps a message out, but good or bad,

165

What listener can perceive? *(Enter Strabo.)*
Why, Strabo!   (Act I, sc.2, ll.19-26, p.7)

The four speeches here move from the ordinary rhythm and construction of everyday speech (in the first three lines), to the elaborate artificiality of verse based on an iambic line (the remaining four lines), with their more complex structure and vocabulary. There are times when the language moves from prose to verse without apparent justification, Laila and the Blind Man, for instance, converse in prose in Act I, Scene 1, but in verse two scenes later. The Muleteer, whose "inconsequential prose" is supposed to provide a marked contrast to the verse spoken by other characters, speaks some of the finest verse of the play in Act III. This cannot be entirely explained by the change in his character wrought over the thirty years of his journey with Artaban, though the transcendent matters with which Act III deals are, the Georgians would argue, more suited to verse.

Notes to Chapter 7

1. J. Wakeman, ed., *World Authors: 1950-1970* (New York 1975), 619-20.
2. L. Abercrombie, 'John Drinkwater', *English II*, 5 (1937), 387.
3. *The Evening News* quoted in *The Times,* Monday June 27th 1938, 12.
4. 'Review of *Christ's Comet'*, *The Times,* Monday June 27th 1938, 12.
5. 'The Festival Play', *Canterbury Cathedral Chronicle* XXX (1938), 14.
6. Christopher Hassall, '*Christ's Comet* in Retrospect', *Canterbury Cathedral Chronicle LIII* (1958), 14.
7. *The Times, loc. cit.,* 12.
8. See Appendix.
9. References are to: C. Hassall, *Christ's Comet: The Story of a Thirty Years Journey that Began and Ended on the Same Day,* Acting Edition for the Friends of Canterbury Cathedral, (Canterbury 1938).
10. '*Christ's Comet* from the Point of View of a Member of the Audience', *Canterbury Cathedral Chronicle LIII* (1958), 16.
11/12. cp. the description of Artaban's life in Henry Van Dyke's novel, quoted in: 'The Festival Play', *Canterbury Cathedral Chronicle XXIX* (1938), 12, 15.
13. See above, p. 39.
14. *The Times, loc. cit.,* 12.
15. Quoted in 'The Festival Play', *loc. cit.,* 15.
16. Christopher Hassall, *Notes on the Verse Drama* (London 1948), 26
17. *Ibid.,* 25.
18. Christopher Hassall, *Christ's Comet,* preface to first edition (London 1938), 9.
19/20/21/22/23. Christopher Hassall, *Notes on the Verse Drama* (London 1948), 23, 18, 6.
24. Christopher Hassall was the "voice of God" in the 1960 production of *Everyman* at Canterbury.
25. TR1.., see Bibliography D.
26/27. *The Times, loc. cit.,* 12.
28/29. 'The Festival Play', *loc. cit.,* 15.
30. See Christopher Hassall, '*Christ's Comet* in Retrospect', *Canterbury Cathedral Chronicle LIII* (1958), 14. "The remainder is as much an ordinary play for the conventional stage as *Juno and the Paycock* or *Hassan.*"

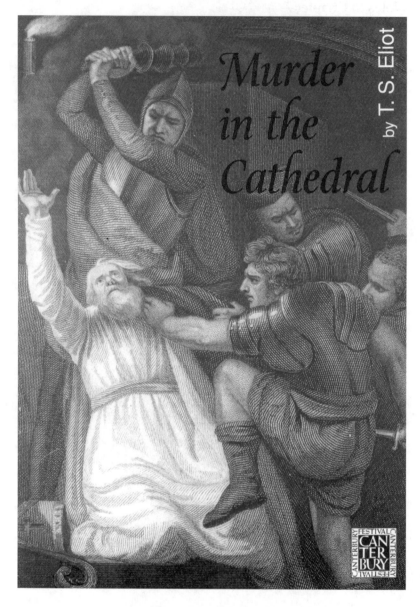

Fig.12: The programme cover for the 1998 Canterbury Festival
production of *Murder in the Cathedral*.

Interlude

Murder in the Cathedral

Murder in the Cathedral by T. S. Eliot was first performed in the Chapter House at Canterbury on 15th June 1935. Since that time, the play has received thousands of amateur and professional productions in churches, colleges, halls and theatres of all sizes throughout the English-speaking world and has been performed in French and Italian. In 1951, the play was adapted by its author into a film with Eliot himself speaking the part of the Fourth Tempter. The play has been recorded, broadcast, televised and recently some words from the play were included in their album *Canterbury* by the rock group Diamond Head. *Murder in the Cathedral* has also received considerable critical attention in the years since its first performance: so much has been written about the play and its author that in 1975 Laurence Irving remarked "In all that has been written about him we cannot discern the man we knew."[1] The play continues to be studied at school and university level: a college and a series of lectures have been established in the University of Kent at Canterbury in the playwright's honour and *Murder in the Cathedral* has achieved the dubious distinction of being a set text for school examinations.

Had Eliot written no other play, his reputation as a dramatist would have been established and had the Canterbury Festival produced no further commissions after 1935 it would still be entitled to claim its part in a revolution in the English theatre. Like the first productions of *Waiting for Godot* or *Look Back in Anger* a single theatrical event created a watershed for the modern stage.

Murder in the Cathedral was the first new play to be written especially for the open stage which Laurence Irving had designed for the Chapter House:

> The introduction of Eliot was the beginning of the phase . . . Bell asked Eliot down to Chichester, liked him very much, then wrote to me (Laurence Irving) and asked me to negotiate with Eliot to write a play for Canterbury. We had a mutual friend, Frank Morley with whom I'd done a book on the Thames a few years before, and Morley invited us both to lunch. Eliot was very diffident - awfully quiet, friendly chap ... and then he came down to stay with us. I spent the next morning taking him all over the Cathedral and showed him the stage. Then we went and had lunch somewhere and I remember my dismay when I said to him 'Has this given you any ideas for a play?' And he said, 'Oh yes, I shall write a play about Thomas à Becket!' We thought we'd had enough of Thomas à Becket - but of course he was quite right - it was entirely new.[2]

Eliot had agreed to undertake the play provided that E. Martin Browne (who had "dragged *The Rock* out of him"[3]) produced it. This was a condition which he also stipulated for every subsequent play he wrote. The fruitful partnership between Eliot and Browne ensured that "the poet really learned what performance meant"[4] and is described in great detail not only in Browne's *The Making of T. S. Eliot's Plays* (1969) but also in the posthumously published book he wrote with his wife, Henzie Raeburn, *Two in One* (1981). It was Henzie who, half-jokingly, suggested to Eliot, a devotee of Sherlock Holmes, that *Murder in the Cathedral* would make a better title for the play, which was originally to have been called *Fear in the Way*. Eliot was greatly taken by the contemporary ring of the new title as it swept away the fustian associated with so many religious plays. The hospitality which the Brownes showed Eliot at their home in Sussex during late 1934 may also have helped the playwright to fix the form of his Canterbury play, for they visited both a performance of Choral Speaking (directed by Mona Swann, a major authority on the subject) in a local school and a production of some mystery plays in the village church.

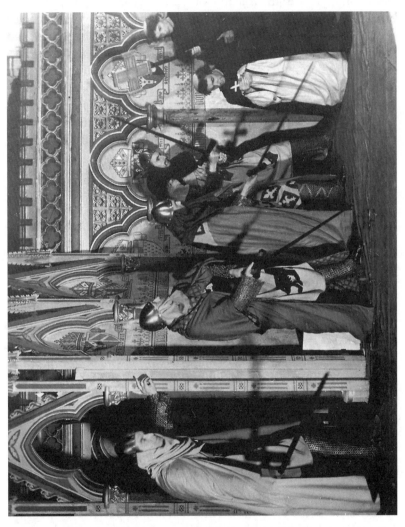

Figure 13: The first performance of T. S. Eliot's *Murder in the Cathedral* in 1935. Robert Speaight as Becket.

The production at Canterbury was to last one and a half hours with no interval and was to be undertaken by the now familiar mix of professionals and amateurs. Robert Speaight, a devout Catholic, was engaged from London to play Becket and such was his fascination with the rôle that only three years later he published a biography of the Saint.[5] Speaight was a particularly good choice because of his deep interest in the ideas of open staging advocated by Poel, of whom he also wrote a biography,[6] and because of his expertise in handling verse. He was also familiar with the liturgical elements of the play and one critic "felt a great sincerity"[7] in his presentation. Co-operation with the amateur actors was not always easy for Speaight and his subsequent accounts of the play reveal a sense of relief when he moved on to an all-professional production in London.

The amateurs were, however, contending with a technically advanced play which has since taxed far more experienced performers and their achievement was remarkable. Their appetite for the play was first whetted in a piece which E. Martin Browne wrote for the *Canterbury Cathedral Chronicle* in April 1935:

> Some members of the *Cathedral Players* have very big chances this year. The four Knights' parts, for instance, are in their hands. The styles of speech in these range from exalted poetry to colloquial prose, for Mr Eliot has given the Knights the chance to justify themselves in the eyes of posterity - as represented by the Canterbury audiences - for their deed.[8]

This was reinforced by Browne's reading of the play to all interested amateurs who were willing to rehearse during April, May and early June. Thirty-four years later Browne still recalled the gasp which went round the room when he read the transition from the Chorus to the Knights' address to the audience.

Such variations in style were only one of the problems facing both cast and producer. Another was Eliot's introduction of a chorus of women which demanded an expertly trained and orchestrated group of performers. These were to be drawn from students at Elsie Fogerty's Central School of Speech Training and Dramatic Art and would only arrive in Canterbury for the dress rehearsal.

Elsie Fogerty had established herself as the leading authority on choral speaking. Basing her voice-production work on scientific principles she had pioneered a style of apparently effortless, resonant speech which enabled her students to be easily recognised in the very influential positions in the theatre and education which they came to occupy before and after the Second World War. The distinctive sound produced by Central School students was to be enhanced by the acoustic qualities of the Chapter House, but the very small stage available and the lack of wing space meant that the Chorus of eleven women would have to remain on stage and be relatively static throughout the performance.

Irving's permanent setting was to be complemented by costume designs by Stella Mary Pearce, a friend of Eliot's who had also designed for *The Rock*. These were particularly bold and striking designs: those for the Tempters incorporated aspects of their characters, giving them a contemporary feel and the Chorus costumes provided a subtle blend of individuality and unity.

From the outset, the conditions of rehearsal and performance placed many constraints on playwright and producer but the use of the Chapter House instead of the Cathedral Nave gave Eliot freedom from ecclesiastical censorship and the working relationship he had established with Browne enabled the play to be partially shaped in rehearsal. The text of the play itself underwent many revisions from the first drafts of sections sent to the producer to the version which was fixed at the time of Eliot's death. "When we first read it", wrote Canon J. M. Crum, "it was at once very clear that you, Gentlemen and Ladies (the cast), had had great courage."[9] Such preliminary reading was made possible by the printing of 750 copies of an Acting Edition permitted by Eliot's own publishing house of Faber and Faber on payment of thirty guineas and on condition that any unsold copies be destroyed. In the event, all copies were sold and a few, including the electrician's prompt copy on which this chapter relies, survive today.

Almost simultaneously with the printing of the Acting Edition, Eliot was guiding a longer version of the play through the press at Faber and Faber. This version, some three hundred lines longer, was later to incorporate changes made during rehearsal and performance at Canterbury. There are substantial differences be-tween the edition published in 1968 and the Acting Edition. To some extent these simply reflect the physical conditions of the first performance compared with subsequent productions in the com-mercial theatre. All the entrances and exits marked in the Acting Edition refer to the fact that the only approach to the stage was from a central aisle so that, for example, "*Enter the four Tempters, cloaked, to below the stage*" (p.8) in that edition reveals the necessity to have one major entrance of characters, with a further stage direction, "*First Tempter uncovers himself*" (p.8). In the Faber editions, how-ever, this episode presupposes that each of the tempters can enter in turn from the wings and the stage direction reads "*Enter First Tempter*" (p.24). A similar contrast in the use of entrances occurs at Becket's first appearance in the play: whereas the Acting Edition uses the long entrance up the aisle - "*Thomas has entered during this speech*" (p.6) - later versions state "*Enter Thomas*" (p.21). The Acting Edition shows a far greater degree of specificity as to how the play was to be staged. The opening of the play has these directions:

PartOne

In the Precincts of the Cathedral
Enter a band of the Women of Canterbury who form the chorus. (p.2)
but by 1968, after countless productions, this has become:

The scene is in the Archbishop's Hall, on December 2nd, 1170
Chorus. (p.11)

Reading the Acting Edition one certainly does have the impres-sion that "Mr Eliot has devised the play with a knowledge of the conditions of the production in the Chapter House",[10] neverthe-less, a further one hundred lines are shown as cut by the producer in the course of rehearsal and it is interesting to note that the first performance of this great play omitted what have become some of its most famous lines.

Other differences between the Acting Edition and the 1968 version are of three kinds. Firstly there are instances where lines have been re-distributed amongst characters, particularly the Priests and the Knights. These are largely the results of moments in rehearsal where the producer felt that some verbal reaction from each character was necessary or of Browne's intention that the

176

actors playing the Tempters should double those playing the Knights. This led to his seeking some continuity between the characters of the Fourth Tempter and the Fourth Knight.

Secondly, in later versions we find additional or modified lines designed to strengthen dramatic moments in the play. One of the best examples is where the rather weak exit line of the Knights in the Canterbury version:

We come for the King's justice, we come again. (p.27)

becomes

We come for the King's justice, we come with swords. (p.72)

but there were also changes to many of the Priests' lines, to Becket's sermon and to the final speeches of the Knights.

Thirdly, there are numerous minor changes in single words and phrases which are clearly the result of the playwright having seen and heard the performances and of his discussion with the producer and his cast. A number of these changes were also made for historical accuracy. All the major changes to the text are examined in great detail by Browne in *The Making of T. S. Eliot's Plays* and the precise nature of all these changes is shown in the tables below.

In addition to the variations listed below, the speeches of the four Knights were considerably expanded after Canterbury and, because of the casting in the subsequent professional production, the Third Knight was introduced as the "eldest" instead of the "youngest" member.

Page	Lines	Page	Lines	Page	Lines	Page	Lines
12	8-24	29	5-11	48	1-8	75	1
15	6-12	30	1-2	57	1-18	75	8-9
17	3-14	33	10-21	58	1-9	79	9-22
17	19-21	37	9	63	2-5	83	7-21
18	2-3	38	3-16	69	15-16	86	10-14
19	20-25	44	4-9	70	6-7	88	1-18
20	7	44	21	71	11	89	3-5
24	6-10	45	1-11	73	7-16	89	9-17
25	2-16	47	7-24	74	18-22		

NB. 'Lines' are taken to begin with capital letters in verse sections.

Table 1: Material in the 1968 version omitted at Canterbury

DRAMA IN THE CATHEDRAL

Page in 1968	Line	Faber version	Acting Edition
11	L.10	*. . . and the land became brown*	. . . and the land is brown
11	L.12	*While the labourer*	When the labourer
12	L.1	*Remembered the martyrs*	And remembered
13	L.11	*But only to wait and to witness*	But only to wait and to witness. Let us listen.
20	L.4	*We have been afflicted with taxes.*	We have sometimes been afflicted with taxes.
22	L.2	*They know and do not know, that action is suffering And suffering is action. Neither does the agent suffer.*	They know and do not know that acting is suffering And suffering is action. Neither does the actor suffer.
22	L.17	*Have better prepared our hearts*	Have better directed . . .
23	L.9	*. . . Sandwich*	Dover (changed to Sandwich in rehearsal).
24	L.21	*Mirth and sportfulness*	Wit and sportfulness
26	L.4	*. . . that roars most loud.*	that roars too loud.
27	L.12	*You, master of policy.*	The master of policy.
27	L.17	*. . . still may be regained*	. . . still may be set right
27	L.18	*Power obtained*	Power possessed.
30	L.4	*Yes! Or bravery*	Yes! Bravery
37	L.4	*And with me . . .*	But with me . . .
42	L.12	*For such a vision of eternal grandeur*	For such a vision of spiritual pride
43	L.6	*. . . that action is suffering*	. . . that acting is suffering
43	L.7	*Neither does the agent suffer*	Neither does the actor suffer
46	L.17	*The forms. . .*	Its forms . . .
51	L.1	*to men of good will*	good will towards men
51	L.4	*For whenever Mass is said, we re-enact the Passion and Death of Our Lord . . .*	For at the moment when we celebrate the Birth of our Lord we shall be re-enacting His Passion and Death.

178

Page Line in 1968		*Faber version*	Acting Edition
54	L.8	*I would have you keep in your hearts these words that I say, and think of them at another time.*	I would have you ponder no longer on these things now, but at a later time.
58	L.10	*. . . St Stephen, First Martyr*	St Stephen the martyr
59	L.2	*That which was from . . .*	What was from . . .
59	L.5	*Declare we unto you. In the midst . . .*	Declare we unto you. There went this saying abroad yet Jesus said not unto him: He shall not die. In the midst.
59	L.8	*Out of the mouth of very babes, O God.*	Out of the mouth of many babes, O God, and of sucklings hast Thou.
64	L.2	*. . . to carry out his command*	to enforce his command
67	L.2	*Now and here!*	Now.
70	L.16	*And there is higher . . . It is not I . . .*	But those who would have him more than King. For there is higher than I or the King I am no traitor, no enemy of the State; The King is his own enemy, the State the State's. The Law of God is above the law of man. It is...
72	L.1	*. . . justice, we come with swords*	justice, we come again
75	L.4	*To the altar, to the altar.*	To the altar, to the altar. They are here already. To the sanctuary. They are breaking in.
76	L.11	*To vespers! Hurry.*	To vespers! Take his feet! Up with him. Hurry!

Page Line in 1968		Faber version	Acting Edition
78	L.9	We are safe. We are safe. They dare not break in . . .	We are safe, we are safe. The enemy may rage outside, he will tire in vain. They cannot break in. They dare not.
80	L.2	And have conquered	And have conquered the beast
80	L.3	Now, by suffering. This is the easier victory.	Now, by suffering, not by resisting: now is the easier . . .
80	L.4	Now is the triumph of the Cross . . .	Now is the triumph of the Cross, now and al- ways. Through suffering, persecution, our victory
		. . . OPEN	comes . . . OPEN
80	L.6	Up the stair.	Up the stairs
82	L.4	Traitor! traitor! traitor!	Traitor! traitor! traitor! traitor!

Table 2: Textual changes to the 1935 Acting Edition
in the 1968 Faber Edition.

Eliot seems to have drawn ideas for the form of his play from a great variety of sources. We have already noted his debt to Tennyson and to some extent he capitalised on the continuing popularity of the historical costume drama. In spite of his disparaging remarks about both Masefield and Gilbert Murray as dramatists, he used the same models as they had done. His play had the liturgical basis of a Morality play and he aimed for a neutral verse form similar to that in Everyman. Like Masefield, he introduced four Tempters and relied on huge banners for scenic devices. It is doubtful, too, whether he would have conceived the idea of a Chorus speaking in the mode of Greek choric odes had he not seen Murray's adaptation in production. Such was his use of the Greek tragic form that he originally called the 'Messenger' a 'Herald' in the manner of Euripides.

Like a medieval morality, Eliot's play was to be both celebration of an event and a dwelling on its significance; like a Greek tragedy it recounted an event which had become myth on the sacred site. The historical was to have contemporary meaning. For the penultimate and most controversial scene of the play, Eliot clearly derived something from the epilogue of Shaw's *St Joan*, although in my estimation he was more successful. Indeed, the most remarkable feature of *Murder in the Cathedral* is that while it is possible to see it as the culmination of many strands of influence, many of which we have traced in earlier chapters, it is nevertheless a work of astonishing innovation and originality.

Perhaps the best introduction to *Murder in the Cathedral* was written by E. Martin Browne to the play's patrons, the Friends of Canterbury Cathedral in their *Chronicle* for April 1935:

... Naturally he (Eliot) was attracted to St Thomas as a subject, but the problem he wished to investigate was how the saint's mind came to be attuned to Christian martyrdom.

Believing that the Church and the thousands who thronged to Canterbury for centuries to visit the shrine did not without justification reckon Thomas a saint, he seeks to discover the reason.

The play is not, therefore, a biography of the saint nor a drama of English history at the time, but simply a study of the martyrdom. It begins on the day of Thomas's return to Canterbury:

"He comes in pride and sorrow, affirming all his claims,
Assured beyond doubt, of the devotion of the people,
Who receive him with scenes of frenzied enthusiasm."

His faithful priests try to rejoice; but everyone is fearful and nervous of the future. He comes, very simply; and the rest of the act, "Is shadows and the strife of shadow". He has to wrestle with temptations; visitants come to him, not realistic acquaintances from the past but figures representing the various phases of life which he has set aside to become God's servant and, last but not least, his own spiritual pride:

"But think, Thomas, think, of glory after death.
When king is dead, there's another kind,
And one more king is another reign.

King is forgotten, when another shall come:
Saint and Martyr rule from the tomb."

The treatment of the happenings on Tuesday December 29th is not realistic. The interest is in the opposing characters and points of view; and there is a body of people who throughout the play act as a balance between them - the Chorus. These are eleven women of Canterbury, ordinary women - "the scrubbers and sweepers" they call themselves. But they have the women's power of foresight and intuition of good and evil; they are right where the male characters in the struggle are wrong; they know beforehand both the full horror of the murder and the full glory of the saint. It is safe to assert that no finer verse for such a body of speakers has been written in our time than some passages in this play.[11]

Murder in the Cathedral falls naturally into seven sections: the first deals with the preparations for and the actual return of Thomas from France on December 2nd 1170, the characters involved being Priests and the Herald; the second is the temptation of Thomas by the four Tempters; the third section consists of a sermon preached on Christmas Day by Thomas directly addressing the audience; the fourth is a symbolic representation of the passage of time using the appropriate liturgical Introits which establishes the day as 29th December and we see Thomas's first confrontation with the four Knights - they leave uttering threats. Thomas is taken by his Priests to Vespers and the door is barred. The fifth section shows Thomas ordering the door to be unbarred although his Priests plead with him. The Knights, now drunk, return to insult Thomas and then murder him. In the penultimate section, the Knights turn and address the audience, justifying their actions and tempting us, the spectators, just as Thomas had been tempted, to waver in our judgement by the apparent reasonableness of their case. The final section is a celebration of the new saint through ritual, and the body of Thomas is borne out as it had been in Tennyson's *Becket*.

Each section of the play is punctuated by the speaking of the Chorus, reacting, foretelling, commenting - sometimes addressing Thomas and at other times talking amongst themselves, always present but never participating in the physical action of the main scenes. The historical events comprising these scenes are presented with accuracy insofar as Eliot has used some of Becket's recorded words and has followed contemporary accounts of the activity of the Knights. The ritual murder of Becket was devised at Canterbury to resemble the famous wall painting of the event and Eliot was sufficiently concerned with the historical background of his play to recommend everyone who had read or seen it to read Speaight's biography of Becket when it appeared in 1938.

The production at Canterbury opened with the striking of a bell and the entry of the Chorus. It is increasingly difficult for modern readers to appreciate the impact of those first moments unless they have experience of the intensity and orchestration of that kind of choral speaking which has now, sadly, become unfashionable. Choral speaking is not to be confused with chanting or the ecclesiastical voice - its modulations and cadences produced, and can still produce, a great emotional response from audiences:

... It was team work: whether you spoke together or took up in turn your own characteristic phrases in your musical voices. You helped us. Your music haunts us. We float on your supporting sentences, from mood to mood, always imagining - which is perhaps not what we do most easily in this time and country.[12]

wrote J. Crum and his enthusiastic response to the rôle and style of the Chorus was reinforced by the reporter from the *Kentish Gazette*:

... their perfectly delivered prophecies and lamentations given on a somewhat mournful note - gradually build up an atmosphere of horror which cannot but thrill all who are present. The choral verse is spoken with singular beauty.[13]

From the outset, the Chorus introduce the play's recurrent theme: birth, death and regeneration. This is represented first by the seasons of the natural year; then by the birth and death of hope in waiting and the passage of time; then in the paradox of the celebration of Mass at Christmas; then the cycle of the Church's year; and finally in the glorious emergence of a saint in martyrdom. The theme is reinforced in the recurrent image of the turning wheel. Each group of characters contributes to the theme, but whereas the Priests, the Tempters and Knights argue from expediency and the temporal, the Chorus and the protagonist see the significance of events as out of time.

Figure 14: The Chorus of *Murder in the Cathedral* (1935).

From Becket's first entrance it is obvious that he is aware of a
Divine Will to which he must submit, whereas his Priests throughout are concerned for their lack of a spiritual pastor. Speaight's
performance in the leading rôle was "magnificent ... full of a dignity
and saintliness which covers the restrained fire of the normal
nature"[14] and he elected to sit throughout the difficult scene of
temptation. The First Tempter reminds Becket of carnal pleasure,
the second of secular power, the third of the political possibilities in
his current situation. Of these, the most terrible is surely the third
who claims to be "a rough, straightforward Englishman" (p.11) -
so utterly devious and full of self-interest. The Tempters each
uncloaked themselves in turn at Canterbury and the unexpected
revelation of the fourth raised the level of tension. This wrestling
with his own spiritual pride is the most prolonged and agonising
and it is only after dealing successfully with it that Becket sees his
future course clearly.

The temptation scene is the most taxing scene to sustain in
performance, largely on account of its inherently static nature and
of the obscurity of some of the dialogue. Canon Crum may well
have had this scene in mind when he wrote to the cast:

And you got us through our voyage, a little bewildered at moments,
and giving you credit for meaning at times something, although we
didn't quite understand.[15]

Whereas much of the remainder of the play consists of various
forms of monologue in which a complex argument can be presented with clarity, the cut and thrust of debate between characters
in the temptation demands greater clarity if the audience is to
follow at speed. *The Times* reviewer identified this problem in the
first production,

Occasionally - as when Becket is confronted with the Fourth Tempter
. . . the argument becomes too subtle to be readily apprehended under
the conditions of the stage.[16]

This is a serious weakness and was a flaw in Eliot's attempt to
discover a new form of dramatic dialogue, but we must remember
that at Canterbury there was an established tradition of reading the
play before seeing the performance. Martin Browne undertook the
exacting rôle of the Fourth Tempter and by all accounts did so

Figure 15: Robert Speaight as Becket in *Murder in the Cathedral* (1935)

brilliantly: "Oh, you Fourth Tempter were great"[17] wrote J. M. C. Crum. It is an indication of the difficulty of the part that Eliot himself insisted on playing it in the film. Another highly praised performance at Canterbury was that of Norman Chidgey as Third Tempter and Knight, bringing considerable humour into the rôle as the plain Englishman, believing in his country and fair play. Like Browne, Norman Chidgey went on to give other notable performances at later Festivals.

Becket's sermon on Christmas Day, described as an 'Interlude' in the play, stands as one of the most effective direct addresses to the audience in the modern theatre. Apart from *The Coming of Christ* none of the previous Canterbury productions can be truly said to have broken out from the all-pervasive dominance of the proscenium arch in spite of their open stage setting. But Eliot went much further than Masefield in his assault upon the minds and emotions of his audience - demanding their attention *and* their response. On the level of theatre language the sermon is spellbinding in its simplicity, restrained emotion and timing. As an exposition of the paradoxes of the Christian faith and the meaning of martyrdom it is unsurpassed. It contrasts events in time and views of the world with Eternal purpose, examining the concept of the peace of God as opposed to the worldly idea of peace as the absence of war. The sermon prepares the audience for what is to come, making it inevitable as an historical event yet giving it significance and permanence. The speech, of course, gained something from being given from a pulpit (which was brought on for the purpose) in an ecclesiastical setting. But, as is so often forgotten, the Chapter House is *not* a Church and the sermon can be just as effective in the theatre. At Canterbury a further pair of arc lights were brought on for the sermon so that Thomas could actually see the 'congregation' to whom he was speaking.

Following the sermon, Eliot weaves the Liturgy into the fabric of the play. A group of singers from St Augustine's Theological College were positioned in a gallery erected at the rear of the Chapter House and their plainsong mingled with the action on stage. When the Knights arrive, the Priests become like the disciples in Gethsemane, terrified, uncomprehending and amazed at the calm sense of purpose with which their Master meets his enemies. The confrontation with the Knights is the most naturalistic section of the action, but at their first exit the Chorus freeze the action with their great evocation of corruption and the approach of doom. Thomas speaks to the Chorus directly before his Priests hurry him away. A memorable moment followed in the Canterbury production when the Chorus "spoke the words starkly descriptive of Hell - to alternate with the singing of the Dies Irae."[18]

An even more powerful moment was to come: "I'll remember only the moment when you have given new meaning to that unbarring of the door. How triumphant that was."[19] The sound and action must have threatened to engulf the audience as the Knights re-entered. Slightly tipsy, they now speak in a parody of Vachel Lindsay's *Daniel Jazz* which, together with *The Congo*, was a popular choral speaking piece in the 1930s: it is therefore a cruel parody on the Chorus itself and, indeed, of the Liturgy.

As the Knights kill Becket the great Chorus "Clear the air!" is spoken. Superbly suited to the resonant acoustics of the Chapter House, this Chorus with its unforgettable image of "a curtain of falling blood" is one of the great examples of modern ritual theatre. Then, "with startling abruptness",[20] the Knights address the audience in colloquial prose. We can never entirely reproduce the shock of that transition in the first performances and yet it is still among the most disconcerting and uncomfortable of theatrical experiences. Seen by some critics as a weakness, this incident has a terrifying modernity. The way in which the Knights explain away their actions and the final order to the audience to "disperse quietly" to their homes are reproduced daily by politicians and repressive regimes. In 1959 Eliot claimed to have written *Murder in the Cathedral* as anti-Nazi propaganda[21] and we can see at this point in the play his presentation of the rival secular ideologies by which he felt the Church to be threatened in the 1930s. The audience, shocked out of its complacency, would act, Eliot hoped, and in this he shows a very similar technique to Brecht whose staging methods moved on the same lines.

The final Chorus enables the audience to identify with the sin of the world and to seek forgiveness. Like a medieval morality this becomes an act of worship once the teaching has been acted out, and for non-believers this is the most difficult aspect of the play.

Much of the initial reaction to Eliot's play has been lost with the dwindling numbers of people who recall the performance in 1935. But all the evidence suggests that men were aware that *Murder in the Cathedral* had qualities that would ensure its survival. The reporter for the *Kentish Gazette* wrote:

> My own opinion is that it is the best play on the subject which has yet been presented at the Festivals and I am not alone in thinking that - the play is more thrilling than any biography of Becket or any historical dramatisation.[22]

This, however, was a parochial view, although the use of the word "thrilling" is interesting in the light of the somewhat sombre tones in which Eliot's work is often described. It was Samuel Jeake, Junior in the 'London Letter' of the *New Yorker* who placed the importance of the play in a wider perspective:

> . . . a poetic play was staged in the Chapter House which may well mark a turning point in English drama . . . One hadn't listened five minutes before one felt that one was witnessing a play which had the quality of greatness . . .[23]

This was a response to a performance by an assorted cast of amateurs and professionals brought together at the last moment in primitive theatrical conditions!

Evaluation of the play today is complicated by much that has been written, not least by Eliot himself. Most studies of Eliot as a dramatist approach the plays through the playwright's published and well-publicised views on Poetic Drama and Theology, seeing *Murder in the Cathedral* as an experiment which was abandoned in an attempt to write a more obviously commercial play. This is done excellently by David Jones in *The Plays of T. S. Eliot* (1960) and, perhaps most impressively of all, by Carol H. Smith in her *T. S. Eliot's Dramatic Theory and Practice* (1963). Both these writers provide insights into Eliot's technique in discovering an acceptable form of dramatic dialogue in *Murder in the Cathedral*, quoting frequently from the playwright's highly developed views, particularly those expressed in a broadcast made in 1936. Eliot's announcement of his conversion to Anglo-Catholicism in 1927, together with his *Dialogue on Dramatic Poetry* (1928) have both led critics to explain *Murder in the Cathedral* in terms of ritual, the sacrifice of the Mass and the parallel Temptation, Passion and Resurrection of Christ. And Eliot's own judgement of his play as a one-off has certainly coloured critical opinion.

In a recent television documentary, Dario Fo, the Italian playwright, said that he thought the ancient Greek dramatists never intended their plays to survive, they were intended for a particular time, a particular audience and a specific festival. The same might easily be said of the Canterbury plays. They seem to have served their original purpose admirably and some would think that they should now be left undisturbed. Eliot's attitude was ambivalent. Even as he was preparing a text for Canterbury, he was publishing a longer version with an eye to London presentations. Yet subsequently, when he felt the need to take a new direction in playwriting, he reverted to a more defensive position resembling Dario Fo's. But some of the great Greek plays and *Murder in the Cathedral* have not only survived, but continue to reward exploration in performance. It is therefore clear that Eliot's play was *more* than a breaking of new ground, *more* than an exciting experiment - it *is* a theatrical work of permanent validity.

Initially, the production of *Murder in the Cathedral* achieved three things: it revitalised theatre language, which had become moribund; it created a genuine theatre ritual; and it restored the impact of the open, non-representational stage. These achievements were necessary reforms of the English theatre in the 1930s. Other experiments in each area had been made, but they were too esoteric to have an impact.

Eliot's language in *Murder in the Cathedral* avoids archaism and, in spite of its wide variety, always seems apt. Although it was recognised as entirely new when it was first heard, it in no way seems dated fifty years later. In contrast with the reviews quoted in this chapter, the words of the play strike us as incisive and timeless.

Eliot's ritual theatre was far more than a blend of liturgy and non-realistic action. Heightened language, choric movement and sound, universal themes and direct confrontation drew the spectator into the significance of the happenings. The performance worked on many levels, from the naturalistic to the allegorical, thus the stage became liberated from the mundane and local. Striking as were all these features in 1935, however, there are others which have ensured the play a place in the classic repertoire.

The perennial fascination of the subject matter itself must be included in the play's appeal. Tennyson and Anouilh both concentrated on the rift between Henry II and Becket and their plays have been successful in performance, but Eliot focused entirely upon the central struggle between the will of Man and the will of God, producing a series of intriguing tensions. The continuing conflict between those who see the Church and politics as distinct and those who press for a social and political gospel is represented in the figure of Becket. Such tensions are conveyed in the rhythms of the play, which alternately suspend and move the action forward. There are moments of gradually built climax and others of sudden shock, but the play has a relentless momentum.

In performance, the play engages both the emotions and intellects of the audience. It arouses pity and fear; the sense of horror is shared with the Chorus; but the "subdued chuckles" recorded at the first performance[24] indicate another kind of emotion. *Murder in the Cathedral* makes constant demands on the spectator:

And we, remembering what was said to us a year ago by Dame Sybil Thorndike about the co-operation of spectators in a drama, knew that we had got something on our part, to do.[25]

The mental effort involved in following the arguments, responding to the challenges and identifying with the conflicts produces a profound experience in the theatre. Some aspects of this can be achieved by reading the play, but its full power is only released in performance.

Balancing the play's ability to present universal and eternal themes is its quality of encapsulating simple human experience in memorable language. Fundamental problems of living are understood and expressed in such lines as:

However certain our expectation
The moment foreseen may be unexpected

When it arrives. It comes when we are
Engrossed with matters of other urgency. (p.63)

which were added after Canterbury. The play clearly acknowledges human weakness, the weakness which allows murder. We admire Thomas à Becket the single-minded martyr, but we sympathise with the Priests and the Chorus in their frailty. We pray with them "Lord have mercy" and yet this is not an act of piety so much as a realisation of our common humanity.

By January 1936 the Friends of Canterbury Cathedral were able to announce in their Ninth Annual Report that:

> Mr T. S. Eliot's play *Murder in the Cathedral* . . . is at this moment enjoying so successful a run at the Mercury Theatre that additional matinées will be put on after Christmas. The Managing Director, Mr Ashley Dukes, generously desires that the proceeds of every tenth performance shall be given to the Friends of the Cathedral. The theatre hopes by this means to undertake a Cloister Bay.[26]

and the play has continued to demonstrate how well it can work away from its original setting.

In 1970, however, E. Martin Browne was invited to direct the play once again at Canterbury to celebrate the eight hundredth anniversary of Becket's martyrdom. With the possibility of using sophisticated sound equipment and of designing a special stage to extend towards the audience, it was decided to perform the play in the Cathedral itself, using the steps on which *The Coming of Christ* had been presented as the rear of the stage. Thus *Murder in the Cathedral* came to be acted within a few feet of the actual spot of Becket's murder.

Although Browne writes movingly in *Two in One* of the effect of the performance of the play on the participants and of his intentions in the production, it was not an entirely successful venture. The acoustic problems were never fully overcome and Henzie Browne, who led the Chorus, was by this time frail and forgetful. New production ideas were needed to suit the presentation to changing tastes.

Evidence from recent theatre developments suggests that we have probably yet to see the best productions of *Murder in the Cathedral*. The experience of The National Theatre's production of

The Passion in the shared space of the Cottesloe Theatre demonstrated that a Christian play demanding the spirit of meditation and worship from its spectators can move and fascinate a largely agnostic audience. On the other hand, modern experiments with Chorus work in Greek drama have moved away from the refinement of ensemble speaking towards greater physicality in performance and more inventive uses of vocalisation indicating new possibilities for the exploration of Eliot's great play.

Notes to Interlude

1/2/3/4. TR1.

5. See Bibliography.

6. See Bibliography.

7. J. M. C. Crum, 'Mr T. S. Eliot's Play', *Canterbury Cathedral Chronicle XXI* (1945), 22-24.

8/9/10/11. E. Martin Browne, 'The Festival Play', *Canterbury Cathedral Chronicle XX* (1935)

12. Crum, *loc. cit.*

13/14/15. 'Impressive New Play', *The Kentish Gazette*, June 22nd, 1935.

16/17. *The Times*, (London) 2nd November, 1935.

18. *The Kentish Gazette, loc. cit.*

19. Crum, *loc. cit.*

20. *The Kentish Gazette, loc. cit.*

21/22. Carol. H. Smith, *T. S. Eliot's Dramatic Theory and Practice* (Princetown 1963), 24.

23. Samuel Jeake, Junior, 'London Letter', *New Yorker*, July 3rd, 1935.

24. *The Kentish Gazette, loc. cit.*

25. Crum, *loc. cit.*

26. *Ninth Annual Report of the Friends of Canterbury Cathedral*, 1936, 30.

Part IV

Plays by "The Inklings"

8

Thomas Cranmer of Canterbury

Charles Williams's new play, *Thomas Cranmer of Canterbury*, received its first and only production in the Chapter House at Canterbury in June 1936. Both E. Martin Browne, who produced the play, and Laurence Irving maintained that this play was, after Eliot's, the most interesting and memorable of all the Festival plays and deserves revival.[1] An anonymous contributor to *The Canterbury Cathedral Chronicle* was equally enthusiastic: "There was no appraising to be done, the play silenced both approval and censure into acknowledged greatness."[2] The criticism of both Weales and Spanos supports the view that *Thomas Cranmer of Canterbury* is a work of considerable literary merit that deserves careful attention.[3]

But others were, and continue to be, uneasy about the play. Philip Hollingworth, whose performance as Henry VIII was highly praised, felt the play to have been "obscure and pretentious"[4]; a local vicar denounced the play as "blasphemous" in his parish magazine after seeing the performance in the Chapter House[5]; and Archbishop Cosmo Lang hinted at his unease in his address to the young people who had just attended a special performance "for youth":

I will not say whether I personally agree altogether with the rendering you have seen, but it is a most powerful one. You have been taken through a very perplexing time in our history and into the inside of my predecessors in whom the fierce currents of that time moved with terrible confusion.[6]

Lang thanked the audience for their "patience and quietness" and added that they must have been almost as perplexed as the man's heart and mind into which they had just been taken.[7]

This view was certainly shared by the reporter from *The Kent Messenger*:

Cranmer of Canterbury is, to be quite frank, an unsatisfactory play. Its form is hard to follow; its language though often beautiful, is obstruse, its action is slow in the extreme, and it develops, really, into an exhibition, albeit brilliant, of elocution by two men . . .

Cranmer of Canterbury . . . is a *tour de force* for Mr Speaight and Mr Browne but somewhat beyond the grasp of the ordinary man or woman.[8]

Press reaction to the performance followed a consistent pattern: warm praise for the acting of Robert Speaight, E. Martin Browne (who also produced the play) and Philip Hollingworth; but a sense of bewilderment with the unusual form of the action, the difficulties of the language and the exact function and purpose of the character of the Skeleton. Though few critics went as far as Janet Adam-Smith who, in her *Criterion* review, suggested that the play "is merely a drama of words which cannot succeed on the ordinary stage",[9] there was a sense in which it became clear that the play, as presented in the Chapter House, made demands on its audience to which few were equal.

Judgement of *Thomas Cranmer of Canterbury* is now complicated by a number of factors that distinguish this play from those already discussed. It was written by a considerable lay theologian with a developed view of both Christian doctrine and worship that inevitably affected his writing; it was also written to follow *Murder in the Cathedral* which had shattered the existing Canterbury tradition of romantic productions and opened the way to new kinds of experiment. Williams went further than Eliot in theatrical terms, his play being highly original and anticipating many post-war developments. Evaluation of his achievement is further complicated by three surviving layers of text.

Charles Williams took his general theological position from Charles Gore, the Anglo-Catholic theologian who, in 1889, edited *Lux Mundi*, a series of studies in the "Religion of the Incarnation".[10] The Incarnation, which William Temple described as the supreme instance of "the immanence of the transcendent",[11] came to acquire new significance for theologians in the nineteen-twenties and thirties because it gave meaning to time and history, and to a passion for social justice. Among Anglo-Catholic theologians there was a shift in emphasis from the redemptive sacrifice of Christ on the Cross to the involvement of God in human material experience through the Incarnation. Williams himself developed a view that the Creation and Incarnation were one, that the Incarnation would have taken place without being made necessary by the Fall, for it was God's decision to assume mortality that,

> was the decree that brought mankind into being. It was His will to make creatures of such a kind that they should share in that particular joy of His existence in flesh.[12]

Man therefore becomes the Image of God; man's body, in an unique sense, contains the spirit of God and cannot be an object of contempt.

Williams, following the writings of Dionysius Areopagite, maintained that the soul may come to God through the 'Affirmative Way'. Recognising God as immanent, as well as transcendent, the way of Affirmation accepts that the material world is an imperfect image of God and that through love, suffering and involvement, the soul may eventually find Him. However, man is not left to search unnourished, for the correlate of the Incarnation, as Horton Davies observes, is "the sacramental principle".[13] Mankind is able to constantly renew his spiritual life through the sacraments aided by the Liturgy. To theologians like Charles Williams, therefore, the experience of Christ's continuing presence in the sacraments was the central concern of the Church.

The extent of Williams's theological writing was very considerable and, additionally, at the same time as he was writing *Cranmer* he was engaged in editing Kierkegaard's *Philosophical Fragments*, the first work by this influential theologian to be published in England.[14] It is tempting, therefore, to read into *Cranmer* many of Williams's known theological views. Spanos, for example, relies heavily on material from Williams's *He Came Down from Heaven* for his interpretation of *Cranmer*.[15] This approach, however, greatly complicates the process of evaluating the play, which essentially has to stand by its effectiveness in performance and its ability to communicate in what is, after all, a public art form. There are, on the other hand, a number of theological issues that have a direct relevance to *Cranmer* for the protagonist, Thomas Cranmer himself, eventually finds God through the Affirmative Way.

The Incarnation and its significance for man's flesh form the basis for Cranmer's search for the Way. From the beginning of the play he puzzles over the implication of the Word becoming Flesh and only at the very end does he accept physical suffering as necessary. For Cranmer, body, mind and spirit are separate; he asks "how can the flesh absorb spirituality?", but the Skeleton replies with a statement that suggests Williams's incarnational viewpoint:

Ah, you do not quite know, incredulous Thomas
what the flesh can do when it is put to it.

And he continues later:

O my people, have you forgotten,
the moment when flesh and spirit are one,
- are they ever separate, but by a mode?

Prompted by the Skeleton, Cranmer finally brings about "the moment" by running eagerly to his physical death. Williams uses Cranmer as an example of the "necessary love" which he believed was implied by the Incarnation. This is total love for all things created because they are images of Christ. Cranmer himself has sought Christ in images all his life and his creative energy has been spent in trying to produce images. But he fails to see the reality beyond the image. Williams's view of man's life is, however, that his acts in history are important in themselves because the Incarnation has reconciled Time and Eternity.

Another important issue which Williams introduces in *Cranmer* is the nature of the Eucharist. Williams himself made no direct statements as to his precise interpretation of the Eucharist, but he believed in its function as the chief agent of spiritual nourishment for Christians. His Anglo-Catholic position was in itself a compromise between Catholic and Protestant approaches to the sacraments and, in a number of ways, Cranmer is presented as holding a similar position. The premise on which the doctrinal disputes of the play are based is that the Eucharist is essential as a means of grace and should therefore be both frequently celebrated and undertaken with appropriate ritual and solemnity. Williams then contrasts the Catholic and the Protestant interpretation of the Eucharist, taking the ideas of 'adoration' and 'communion' to symbolise the main difference. This is an extremely complex historical issue to convey in dramatic terms, particularly as there was no absolute agreement among sixteenth-century Protestant Reformers as to the nature of the Eucharist, and Catholic views ranged from the lucid to the superstitious. Generally, however, Williams uses the Lutheran and Tridentine standpoints and demonstrates how, at a popular level, these become trivialised.

The Catholic view of man's redemption was established by the authority of the Church. Christ, the Passover Lamb, was sacrificed for the sins of the world. The vicarious suffering of Christ ensured an original pardon for man's sins but, in order to receive the benefit and grace of God, mankind had to co-operate with the Divine by participating in the sacraments. To some extent, it is misleading to refer to a 'Catholic view' of the Eucharist, but a large proportion of the doctrinal work of the Council of Trent was given over to a strong restatement of the centrality and nature of the Mass, and an increasing emphasis on the sacrificial element and the frequent celebration of the Mass characterised the Catholic spiritual renewal, sometimes referred to as the Counter Reformation. The essential beliefs concerning the Eucharist, restated in the Tridentine decrees, were that at the Eucharist the elements of bread and wine are miraculously transubstantiated into the body and blood of Christ which contain His soul and divinity. It is therefore proper that adoration and praise should be offered in the Eucharist and that, as Christ continues His priesthood by a constant visible sacrifice in the Mass, the celebration should take the form of solemn festivals and public rites.[16]

Protestants relied entirely on the authority of scripture for their interpretation of the Eucharist. Inevitably there were many variations of response, but most reformers accepted Luther's basic contention that Christ had made atonement for man's sins and that his justified punishment was cancelled. Now, by faith alone, man must accept God's redeeming work. There was, therefore, no continuing sacrifice by Christ, for that had been made once and for all. The interpretation of the Lord's Supper is accordingly hinged on the precise meaning of Christ's words at its institution:

"this is my body which is broken for you; this do in remembrance of me."[17]

Luther insisted that, while transubstantiation was impossible, the words of Christ must be taken literally and that, in some mysterious sense, Christ was present in the elements of bread and wine. By faith, man was therefore able to communicate with Christ in the Eucharist and, while Luther introduced a service in the vernacular, he nevertheless retained a liturgy and the holding aloft of the elements to show his sense of solemnity at the Real Presence of Christ. Other reformers began to interpret the Eucharist as a service of remembrance and advocated greater simplicity in the celebration. For these reformers the elements became symbols of Christ's body and blood and by meditation on Christ's death and resurrection they claimed to communicate with Him in a special way.

These, then, are the issues as they affect the play. Thomas Cranmer is a Protestant who insists on scriptural authority for all doctrine and is therefore concerned that the Word of God should be available freely for all to read. During his years at Cambridge he also debated the significance of Christ's statement:

This is my body; take eat:
Drink this; this is my blood.

He has become convinced that God's favour is communicated to man through the Eucharist. Yet he finds the Catholic way unacceptable because, instead of Christ Himself being adored in the Mass, there is an obsession with rite and ceremonies. At one point, he is prompted by the sight of a vested priest with his acolytes and incense, to lament that "man's new fall" is his failure to take advantage of God's means of grace by blind adoration of the means only; and he likens man to Adam admiring himself in the Euphrates, with "false awe and false delight", having lost the way to salvation.

Cranmer is determined to restore reverence for the Eucharist which he feels has been "quenched" by adoration, but his great feeling for words and his conviction of the vital importance of the Eucharist leads him to evolve his own Protestant liturgy. For Catholics, Cranmer's service is inadequate because it denies the miraculous aspect of the Mass and is over-simple; for the extreme Protestants it does not go far enough, there is too much ritual and it suggests kneeling, which could be interpreted as adoration rather than remembrance. Cranmer personally rejects the idea of the Real Presence but he insists that both Catholics, who have lapsed in regularity of the celebration of Mass, and Protestants, who desire an infrequent, simple service of remembrance, are denying people access to Christ. He defends his liturgy on the grounds that words are like

... muscles and veins to Christ's Spirit bringing communion,

and claims to have created his ritual for the good of the land.

A further consideration affecting *Cranmer* is the rôle of the king in relation to the Church. It is a special feature of the play, as E. Martin Browne pointed out, that:

the throne with the crown suspended above it remains, whether occupied or not, the symbol of that which is too often in conflict with, though it should be the complement of, the Kingdom of God.[18]

Williams uses the words of Psalm 72, *Give the King Thy Judgements, O God*, to establish the idea of the king as God's supreme agent on earth. The peace and justice that the king creates in his earthly kingdom, says the Psalm, are to reflect the Kingdom of Heaven, for the king is to defend the poor and weak, and to exercise judgement on God's behalf. Furthermore, it is the king who should ensure that his subjects fear the Lord and live in righteousness. Cranmer believes that God's Word should be both proclaimed and imposed by the power of the crown, that the state should, in fact, be responsible for correct doctrine. This, of course, is only possible if the monarch is head of the Church and Cranmer tells King Henry:

"within Christ's law there is none above the King", and later dares to say to the Catholic Queen Mary:

> . . . your Grace, by God's grace, is the head of all the people of England, therefore the head of the Church they are: one folk, one Church, one head.

This view excludes the Pope, it is the loophole that King Henry has sought in his attempt to acquire a divorce, but Henry is very conscious of his position; "My soul", he says, "is the power of God over this land." Cranmer provides Henry with reassurance that service to God is service to the king and that Henry can therefore rely on his loyalty. Williams's main theological position in *Cranmer* appears to be support for the centrality of the Eucharist and for the idea of an established Church. This derives from his developed view of the Incarnation.

Williams's play is also notable for its dramaturgic experimentation. Superficially, *Cranmer of Canterbury* reflects the influence of *Murder in the Cathedral*, it is unconventional in form, experimental in language and makes interesting use of the liturgy. Both plays are, to some extent, non-realistic in action and both have choric movements and involve the mental struggle and martyrdom of the protagonist. Whereas, however, the Women of Canterbury in Eliot's play can at times be thought of as actual characters in the drama, the Singers in *Cranmer* have a different function. Only once is there any interplay between Cranmer and the Singers, and that only in the highly formalised nature of versicles and responses. Otherwise, the Singers represent both the Celestial Church[19] and an extension of Cranmer's mind, commenting on the dilemmas facing him by quotation from the scripture and in his own words from collects and offices in *The Book of Common Prayer*. The Singers also set the historical events of the play in the larger framework of God's providence and, by using familiar words from Anglican worship, they invite the audience to worship and pray during the performance itself.

The entrance through the cloisters of a group of singers was the first striking moment of Charles Williams's technically advanced play. The Canterbury audience, accustomed to plays set in the twelfth century, were now taken into Tudor England:

In the silence the voices began to intone the prayer which opened the play - again perfection demonstrated itself, startling because one does not hear a chosen group of Cathedral voices every day in that other, lesser life. "The Priest and the Preacher run on", and the play was loosed. An hour and a half later the perfect voices of the singers declared "world without end. Amen", as though nothing had happened, and one rose unsteadily and went out . . . one remembered horrors and delights: trumpets pealing over one's head from the Cloisters behind; processions moving up the aisle . . . heavy in Tudor magnificence . . . black gowned and masked Executioners with flames flickering in their hands . . .[20]

The play was shaped entirely to fit the demands of the Chapter House and its open stage. The only essential 'prop' was the fixed central throne; otherwise, very little scenery was needed.

The events of the play are presented in a series of short episodes but, although these scenes are indicated in the text by a title and date, the action proceeds without a break. At Canterbury, the division of the play into two parts was also ignored, so the problem of presenting the passage of time was even more difficult for the producer. The action of the play is rarely directly representational of historical events nor is it usually localised. The method is impressionistic - ideas and historical movements being given some form of dramatic expression. The action is extremely economic, one dramatic event being used to represent or suggest far more of the history than is actually presented. For example, the doctrinal conflicts of the Reformation are suggested by the intermittent arguments of the Priest and the Preacher, whereas aspects of Cranmer's mental conflict are represented by 'Figura Rerum', a Skeleton, who, at one point in the play, feigns blindness and gropes around the stage asking to be shown the way.

Some of the action is very clearly ordered by the stage directions; for instance, at the climax of the incident in which Cranmer comes under attack from the Lords and Commons for his religious reforms, the stage directions read:

The Lords come between the King and Cranmer, back to back, with outspread arms. The first Lord advances, driving Cranmer back before him, the second stands over the Throne.

Figure 16: The Commons are driven back by the Lords. *Thomas Cranmer of Canterbury* (1936)

The Skeleton then freezes the action. Telling the audience directly that he will intervene to save Cranmer the convenience of an early death, he prompts the king. Other moments in the play are conceived in dance-like movements which are accompanied by carefully orchestrated vocal rhythms in the text.

This impressionistic technique makes an attempt to approach the play entirely through the study of the characters (i.e. of the way they act and react), misleading because the majority of them embody an idea and act as mouthpieces rather than developing individual characteristics. They are representing forces operating on Cranmer and even King Henry is never realised in entirely naturalistic terms.

Williams's use of short scenes, each with its headline title, may be said to anticipate the adoption of Brechtian techniques on the English stage by some twenty years. In the original production, E. Martin Browne conveyed this essential information - for example, *"Cranmer in Cambridge 1528"* and *"The Fall of Anne Boleyn"* - by setting up a huge book at the side of the stage, the pages being turned at appropriate moments by a child in purple and green Tudor dress. Our experience of the projections and placards of Brechtian productions or the terse announcements of Osborne's *Luther* make this kind of dramatic approach familiar to us, but one wonders what the reaction of the audience would have been in 1936. One report, at least, suggests some bewilderment:

> The method of presentation was a combination of the Shakespearean and the ultra-modern. There was no interval, no scenery, no curtain - chronology was sacrificed to dramatic demands, and except in the final scenes of recantation, there was little attempt at climax.[21]

The combination of simple action representing great events with occasional moments of more realistic action; the use of authentic words of an historical figure; the symbolic rôle of the Skeleton; the continuity and comment provided by the singers; and the use of direct address to the audience have now become a recognised part of the technique of documentary theatre. In the late 1960s, for instance, the Royal Shakespeare Company devised a play, *Us*, which, at one point, involved a scene of groping blindness in which a group of Vietnamese peasants asked to be shown the way; this was reminiscent of 'Figura Rerum' and his feigned blindness in *Cranmer*.

One major difficulty in *Cranmer* is Williams's treatment of history, which compresses the events of twenty-eight years into an hour and a half and, as E. Martin Browne observed, "sometimes takes too much knowledge in the audience for granted."[22] Major historical issues like the disputes surrounding Cranmer and the King or the actual events themselves are conveyed with great simplicity.

The King first enters to the sound of a trumpet and takes his place on the throne, while the Lords and Commons, whose reactions to the behaviour of Cranmer become a vital feature of the action, go to the places assigned to them. After Cranmer has been created Archbishop (the Skeleton gives the crozier to the King, who hands it to Cranmer), the Commons erupts in noisy dispute:

Adoration! Communion!
Adoration!
Communion!

Cranmer is the target as the charges and counter-charges are hurled:

Shibboleth! [Author's note: the test of identity used in an obscure story in *Judges*]
Shibboleth!
Abracadabra!

Verbal claims to know "the way" are energetically joined by the Priest, the Preacher, the King, the Lords and Cranmer himself, until the Skeleton over-tops them all, crying to the audience:

Yet O my people - can you believe it?
blessed and chosen are they who receive it -
there is a way; I am the way,
I the division, the derision, where
the bones dance in the darkening air.

The figures dance strangely until the Skeleton stops the action and tells us that the king has married Anne Boleyn. The Lords approach the throne with an antiphonal chorus of complaint against the monasteries (substantially cut at Canterbury) and then the scene becomes more naturalistic as the King speaks with Cranmer.

The death of King Henry is handled symbolically; the Skeleton touches the King and leads him away, saying ironically "Give the King thy judgement, O Lord!" The Skeleton returns and leaves the crown on the empty throne, and the Lords quickly move to perch on the arms of the throne announcing that they have the infant

Edward VI in their "guard". The action of the play continues to involve a combination of movement, dance and sound and it is significant that Williams originally intended to entitle the play *The Masque of Thomas Cranmer of Canterbury.*

Such writing required a style of ensemble acting technique and an attitude on the part of the audience that would certainly have been unfamiliar in 1936. The actors not only lacked experience but they also lacked the rehearsal time that Williams's play demanded and, coming on top of other difficulties, this accounts for the play's very mixed reception and the fact that it did not become a popular success.

A key figure throughout the action of the play is the Skeleton, an aspect of the drama that perplexed a number of the original audience. The concept of a skeleton may well have been derived from Poel's revival of *Everyman* in which Death appeared as a skeleton, an idea which had persisted in subsequent productions of the medieval play. Elizabeth Haffenden's design for the costume of the Skeleton in many ways resembled that of Death in Poel's *Everyman* but in the coloured head-dress, a wreath of green ivy leaves and golden corn, there was an attempt to suggest the promise of life through death (see Figure16). The Skeleton's appearance disturbed the *Kent Messenger* reporter who described it as "a grotesque figure":

Alternatively severe and clown-like, speaking in sepulchral tones yet with a caustic humour that grated on the sensibilities . . . its pantomime appearance discounted any dramatic effect it might have had.[23]

The part of the Skeleton was played at Canterbury by the producer and the report added: "Mr Browne's interpretation of the part was remarkable and his diction was at all times perfect."[24] Another report spoke of the Skeleton "Weaving a spectral and mysterious pattern" and continued:

Mr E. Martin Browne, whose colourful and dramatic production has earned many congratulations, himself plays this grisly part with much force and sense of drama. At times forbidding, at others sarcastic and biting, he leavens the innate horror of the rôle with Puck-like skips and jumps.[25]

As these reports suggest, the Skeleton had some of the qualities of a medieval Vice, and a closer examination of his rôle in the play confirms this.

Figure 17: The death of Henry VIII. Robert Speaight as Cranmer, Philip Hollingsworth as Henry, E. Martin Browne as the Skeleton. *Thomas Cranmer of Canterbury* (1936)

From his first appearance in the play the Skeleton is something of an enigma. He is heralded by the Singers with the words "Blessed is He that cometh in the name of the Lord", but Cranmer seems unaware of his presence and continues in prayer. The Skeleton and Cranmer only achieve a relationship with each other towards the end of the play, when Cranmer hears and sees the Skeleton for the first time. But at his first entrance the Skeleton establishes direct contact with the audience and he remains on stage throughout the rest of the play, apparently controlling the action and explaining its significance. At one point, for example, he behaves like the hand of destiny, touching Cranmer on the shoulder and leading him to kneel before the King and, as a result, Cranmer receives the Archbishopric. At appropriate moments, the Skeleton also symbolises physical death and he has the ability to freeze and release the action at will. The true identity of the Skeleton provoked considerable debate in the original production and it was a product of Williams's extraordinary originality.

Charles Williams also displayed considerable powers of invention in the dramatic verse of the play. The choice of an appropriate style of language was, no doubt, complicated by the fact that the subject of the play, Thomas Cranmer, was himself an artist in words. Cranmer's superb prose from the *Book of Common Prayer* is an integral part of the play and Williams had to devise a form of dramatic speech that would blend easily with the Tudor English. Williams, rather like Cranmer, gives the impression that he "vaults on language"; his verse is strongly alliterative; irregularly rhymed - often internally; and is generally based on a five-stress line. The influence of Hopkins, whom Williams admired enormously, is evident:

O that the King, O that God's glory's gust
from heaven would drive the dust of the land,
smite his people with might of doctrine.[26]

Williams is at his best when he is dealing with Cranmer's own delight in language, the Archbishop's desire to create in the *Book of Common Prayer* "a strong order, a diagram clear, a ladder runged and tongued". In the scene when Cranmer presents *The Bible* in English to the King the language is direct, simple and magnificent:

O but speech
never found reach of wing or vision more
than soars here! . . .

O now
our common English, whereto we were born, left
forlorn of this health, yet having and meant to have
wealth so great of words, language of power,
this hour receives its consummate miracle;

The reporter from the *Kentish Gazette* responded favourably to such lines:

> By far the most pleasant part of the play was the poetry used by Mr Williams, which had a striking cadence and, at times, a memorable beauty.[27]

and there are many moments in the play when it is possible to share Cranmer's enthusiasm for "the blessed beauty of the shaped syllables".

There are three main reasons why *Thomas Cranmer of Canterbury* failed to achieve wide popularity in 1936. The first was the general difficulty and occasional inadequacy of the language; a later Canterbury playwright, Christopher Hassall, might well have been discussing Williams's play when he wrote:

> . . . a line of dialogue is a matter of seconds, and a play as a whole must be good there and then, or never. *Trial of a Judge* . . . by Stephen Spender . . . suffered in this respect . . . The onlookers' intelligence was often lagging behind his eye, delayed by the meaning of one line while his sight took in the action which accompanied the next.[28]

It was this problem, precisely, that applied to *Cranmer* and coupled with the second reason for failure, the inability of the cast as a whole to appreciate and achieve the appropriate acting style, it made impossible demands on the audience.

The third factor was the rôle of the Skeleton. Any consideration of the original nature of the play and the sense of bewilderment experienced by the original audience must, inevitably, return to this, the most enigmatic and fascinating figure in the action. The confusion over the nature of the Skeleton, which E. Martin Browne described as "one of Williams's finest creations"[29], is certainly understandable for, during the course of the play, the Skeleton offers at least thirty definitions of himself or his function! The Skeleton, however, is unable to make a single, all-embracing definition for, in dramatic terms, he represents the totally new concept of embodying on stage multiple forces in a single figure, thus enacting the spectator's fusing action. This multiple function is seen clearly in *"The Protestant Ascendancy"* in which the Skeleton comments on Cranmer's predicament and then invites the Lords to ensnare the protagonist by throwing them an imaginary rope.

More recently, the Common Man in Robert Bolt's *A Man For All Seasons* served a similar dramatic purpose. He is, therefore, a macabre dancer, a playful Vice who is also Death, Chorus to historical events and apparent foe who reveals himself as a friend to the protagonist. Finally, he is an extension of Cranmer's own personality, the non-rational part of Cranmer's being which Cranmer rejects. The Skeleton is thus by nature indefinable and Cranmer only finally recognises him

> when the pure intellectual jurisdiction
> commits direct suicide.

It is therefore extremely important not to see the Skeleton as simply another character, either real, as in the case of the King, or representative, as with the Priest or the Preacher.

He cannot be equated with other characters in the play because he is visible only to the audience, presumably to the Singers, whom he refers to as "my Singers", and, later in the play, to Cranmer. This suggests powerfully that, although the play appears to concern Cranmer's struggle with the historical and personal forces which constitute the events of the action, it is really about his conflict with inner spiritual forces (represented by the Skeleton) of which he only gradually becomes aware.

One of the major weaknesses of the Canterbury production was that the moment at which Cranmer acknowledged the presence of the Skeleton was not clearly defined. In certain respects this was appropriate because Cranmer had no sudden insights, but in the full text of the play Williams makes the point far more dramatically. The incident occurs at the conclusion of the scene in which Cranmer has been seen writing the *Book of Common Prayer*. The Skeleton addresses Cranmer, "My Lord!", and for the first time

Cranmer sees him. Dimly imagining that they have met before, Cranmer is nevertheless unable to recognise the stranger; his eyes are tired with study, his blindness to the truth of things is what the Skeleton has come to heal.

Obstinately refusing to give a more explicit answer as to his identity, the Skeleton describes himself as a figure of things that are - Figura Rerum, who has come "to gather you into that nothing". Cranmer, he darkly hints, resists the initiative of God's love, takes refuge in his work and fails in total obedience to God's will. Revealing, for the first time, the fierceness of Divine Love, the Skeleton challenges Cranmer to run to him, to seek God in utter poverty of spirit, to open himself to grace. Cranmer, yet again, escapes to his work, so the Skeleton, now no longer content to be at the crossroads, but to pursue Cranmer until he finds the way of the Cross, becomes a more dominant figure: "How I speed, how heedfully I speed!"; dancing and determined he terrifies the Commons; names the Singers as his own and allows them to sing ironically Cranmer's own words which emphasise the sacrifice which their author has yet to make:

Here we offer and present unto thee, O Lord
ourselves, our souls and bodies, to be a reasonable
holy and lively sacrifice . . .

The omission of the whole exchange between Cranmer and the Skeleton at this point in the Canterbury version not only weakened the action and impact of the play but also left the expression "Figura Rerum", which appears in the cast list, without any explanation.

Another omission from the Canterbury text provides, indirectly, a further clue to the real identity of the Skeleton. From the scene entitled "The English Bible 1537" Williams excised a substantial number of lines referring to the King's relationship with Anne Boleyn, they include perhaps the most obscure and difficult lines in the play, but Spanos has provided an illuminating commentary on these, as yet, unperformed lines:

What is only a vague uneasiness in Cranmer's mind is made explicit
by the Skeleton. At the bottom of his actions, he says, lies 'the grand
hydroptic desire of humane learning' which Christ spurned but which

Cranmer thinks 'good and better than Anne!' The allusion is to Walton's famous statement in *The Life of Dr John Donne*, about Donne's intellectual pride; he was 'diverted by leaving that (study of law) and embracing the worst voluptuousness, a hydroptic immoderate desire of humane learning and languages'.

The Skeleton, putting Cranmer's exclusive concern for words in to the same category as Anne's false image of the crown and the King's false image of Anne, warns Cranmer that words as such are no wiser nor safer than these, and goes on to hint darkly at the unauthentic nature of an image of the Christian life grounded in the love of verbal systems . . .[30]

While the lines discussed here are examples of Williams's failure to construct a consistent dramatic poetry, they illustrate that the Skeleton is concerned with Cranmer's refusal to respond with his whole being to the challenge of Divine love.

As a Vice-figure guiding the audience through the complexities of the action and offering the sudden challenge to conscience, the Skeleton shows some of the impishness of his medieval counterparts. Given to bizarre singing, such as in his song *Ohé, the King is Dead*, the Skeleton becomes a street-singer whose words terrify Cranmer with thoughts of martyrdom; and later, almost gleefully, the Skeleton announces:

My hour is nearer; I will show myself again.
The way he treads is turning into a rope
under my hands; he pauses, I pick it by a trick
from under his feet . . .
. . . I am his match
to delay and dismay. Catch my children, catch!
He makes a motion of throwing a rope to the Lords.

As Chorus, the Skeleton not only controls the action of the play but provides necessary information; his rôle as Chorus and Vice relating the action to the audience is best illustrated by the moment when Henry expresses dissatisfaction with Anne Boleyn:

Skeleton: But what, in the interval, is this? the King had his desire: does he run so soon after heaven to be rid of his desire?
Cranmer re-enters. Anne falls at the King's feet.
The King: Thomas, Thomas, Anne is not what I thought.

The Skeleton *(speaking to the audience)*: A remark few of you die without making *(over his shoulder to* **Cranmer***)*, nor shall you die without making.

This is an attempt to universalise the significance of the action of the play which would otherwise consist of a series of historical events involving Thomas Cranmer.

The gradual revelation throughout the play of the true meaning of the Skeleton, as opposed to his dramatic function, is achieved mainly by his continuing descriptions of himself. Some of his nature derives directly from his skeletal form: Cranmer, for instance, the supreme artist in words, has constantly created images of his faith, but the Skeleton is, in E. Martin Browne's phrase,

the bare bone of fact eternally behind all the ideas and words of men.

"I", says the Skeleton, "am the broken image"; "I set the images free"; "I, a moment's geometrical formation of fate, am the delator of all things to their truth." He frequently refers to his bony structure, his lack of flesh is what marks him as different because he represents the decay of physical life. He speaks of "the jangling bones that make up me"; the bones which "dance in the darkening air"; a "jangling of my bones"; "the Jawbone of an ass"; "points and joints in me"; "the bones of the image"; "the perfect end in the diagram of bones"; "life shivers between their bones"; and "the thing that lives in the midst of the bones". And he mentions "the tomb of the earth" where he died.

The Skeleton embodies a series of paradoxes; as the jawbone of the ass on which Christ rode into Jerusalem he demands the same blend of strength and humility which that represents. He stands "at the cross-ways", but is "the voice of the one way"; he has died in the "tomb of the earth" and now demands the death of things temporal, if we are to find the eternal. There is always a choice:

Till on the hangman's day
and along the hangman's way,
we all three run level
mind, soul, and God or the Devil.

In order to reach God, Cranmer must cut through a faith of words and find the essential, which in the end is revealed as "necessary Love where necessity is not". To bring him to this point,

216

it is sometimes necessary for the Skeleton's way to be inscrutable, to be, in fact, "Christ's back". Thus he is "Anything, everything - fellow, friend, cheat, traitor", "the Judas who betrays men to God."

As an agent of God's grace he is, therefore, active. He is "a functioning spectrum of analysed eternity" who both waits for what he is working and is "sent to gather you into that nothing." For the Christian idea of losing one's life only to find it, supports much of the imagery of the Skeleton's function. "Lose yourself, there is only I", says the Skeleton, but this is no paltry promise because, although "I only am the pit where Gehenna is sprung", "I am the way . . . to hell, to salvation." The Skeleton is the promise of "life in death, death in life." He reminds us of the means of grace when he becomes a figure of the crucifixion and it is only when Cranmer discovers the way of the Cross that he enters into the peace which he had prayed for all his life, but never fully discovered.

Notes to Chapter 8

1. TR1 & 2, see Bibliography D.
2. 'The Performance of *Cranmer of Canterbury* in the Cloisters of Canterbury Cathedral.'
3. William V. Spanos, *op. cit.*, 104-24. Gerald Weales, *op. cit.*, 110.
4. TR3, see Bibliography D.
5. A. C. H., 'Perplexing Play Brings Some Criticisms', *Kent Messenger*, June 6th 1936, 6.
6/7/8. *Ibid.*
9. Janet Adam-Smith, 'Review of Thomas Cranmer of Canterbury', *Criterion XVI* 62, (1936), 141.
10/11. Horton Davies, *Worship and Theology in England: The Ecumenical Century 1900-1965* (Princeton 1965), 150.
12. Charles Williams, 'Natural Goodness', *The Image of the City and Other Essays*, ed. Anne Ridler.
13. Horton Davies, *op. cit.*, 450.
14. Soren Kierkegaard, *Philosophical Fragments*, ed. Charles Williams(1936).
15. Charles Williams, *He Came Down From Heaven* (London 1938).
16. Francis Clark, *The Catholic Reformation* (Bletchley 1972), 44-46.
17. These words of "institution" are taken from St Paul's discourse on the Last Supper in *I Corinthians* ii, 24-34.
18. E. Martin Browne, Introduction to *Four Modern Verse Plays* (Harmondsworth 1957), 13.
19. E. Martin Browne, 'Producer's Note to the Play', Festival Programme.
20. 'The Performance of *Cranmer of Canterbury* in the Cloisters of Canterbury Cathedral.'
21. A. C. H., 'Perplexing Play Brings Some Criticism', *loc. cit.*, 6.
22. E. Martin Browne, Introduction, *op. cit.*, 12.
23/24. A. C. H., *loc. cit.*, 6. Although the design of the Skeleton was attributed in the programme to Elizabeth Haffenden, it was based on a drawing by Laurence Irving which was used for the dust cover of the published version of the play.
25. E. H. O., 'Cranmer of Canterbury', *Kent Herald*, June 26th 1936, 7.
26. In 1930 Williams provided a critical introduction to an edition of Hopkins's verse.
27. 'Cranmer of Canterbury', *Kentish Gazette*, June 26th 1936, 7.
28. Christopher Hassall, *Notes on the Verse Drama* (London 1949), 11.
29. E. Martin Browne, Introduction, *op. cit.*, 12.
30. William V. Spanos *op. cit.*, 109 and 355.

9

The Zeal of Thy House

The Zeal of Thy House by Dorothy L. Sayers was chosen for the Canterbury Festival of 1937. This became one of the most popular of the Canterbury plays, achieving a substantial run in London and the provinces immediately after its performance in the Chapter House and being widely read, reprinted and anthologised. When the play was revived for the 1949 Festival it became the only Canterbury play to have achieved two separate productions in the Chapter House and it has continued to receive spasmodic performances. In 1987, I directed a special fiftieth anniversary production of the play in the Quire of the Cathedral on behalf of the Dorothy L. Sayers Society.

Much of the original success of the play was, no doubt, due to the choice of subject and the suitability of the setting. *The Times Literary Supplement* insisted that judgement of the play must be based on an experience of the play in its setting, although the critic writes in a most extraordinary way and one wonders whether he has his tongue in his cheek:

> To have seen a performance of the play and to have read this review is to have reached the very heart of its meaning and beauty. Adverse criticism could only come from those who have missed both.[1]

Unfortunately, I was not present at the original production and must rely on photographs, reviews, prompt copies and the reminiscences of some who were there to substantiate my views. Nevertheless, it is clear that a major factor in determining the success of the play was its immediate appeal to the Friends.

For their 1937 Festival the Friends of the Cathedral had proposed the theme of 'Arts and Crafts' and Dorothy Sayers accordingly chose as the hero of her play William of Sens, the architect who had rebuilt the Great Choir of the Cathedral after a disastrous fire in 1174. This subject was particularly appropriate to the work of the Friends since their principal concern was the upkeep and restoration of the Cathedral fabric. As her source, Dorothy Sayers used a chronicle written by Gervase, a monk of the Priory of Christ Church, Canterbury, who had been ordained by Archbishop Thomas Becket and had been an inmate of the monastery during the years of struggle between Becket and Henry II.

In his chronicle entitled *Of the Burning and Repair of the Church of Canterbury in the Year 1174*,[2] Gervase describes the fire and then tells how the monks assembled architects from England and France to submit their suggested plans for the rebuilding. The architects disagreed on the best procedure, some recommending repair of the ruins, while others suggested complete demolition and a fresh start. Gervase reports:

> Among the architects was one, William of Sens, a man of great abilities, and a most curious workman in wood and stone. Neglecting the rest, him they chose for the undertaking.[3]

The building, Gervase records, went well for four years, but at the beginning of the fifth year William of Sens, who had shown great care in the choice of materials and invention with the use of machines, made the ascent to fix the keystone at the crown of the upper arch. The scaffold suddenly gave way and he fell fifty feet to the stone floor below:

> No one but himself received the least hurt. Either the vengeance of God or the envy of the Devil, wreaked itself on him alone.[4]

Miraculously William survived and, crippled for life, he continued to direct operations from his bed, whilst entrusting the oversight of the work to a monk who had been in charge of the masons, a move which "occasioned him much envy and ill-will."[5] As if to suggest further some form of Divine or devilish intervention,

Gervase mentions that in the fourth year there had been an eclipse of the sun a few months before the accident and that eventually William, "finding no benefit from the skill and attention of his surgeons",[6] returned to France, having passed on the responsibility to the diminutive William the Englishman.

The Chapter House setting was obviously ideal for the play drawn from this dramatic story and Dorothy Sayers included a scene of the Chapter meeting which fitted perfectly into its surroundings. The theme of all-consuming love for God's house and the inclusion of elements of Anglican cathedral worship made the play eminently applicable to a Cathedral Festival and it is hardly surprising that the play was given a second production at the Canterbury Festival of 1949.

Dorothy Sayers, like Charles Williams, was a lively, Anglo-Catholic apologist who made a number of interesting statements on religion, art and their relationship. *The Zeal of Thy House*, although it was not so technically advanced as *Cranmer*, did have certain very distinctive features in production and in both form and language was unusual and varied.

Dorothy Sayers held an orthodox, Anglo-Catholic theological viewpoint and was particularly conscious that she was one of a group of Christian writers who were under attack from both radical Christians and agnostic critics. She wrote:

> The indignation is reserved for a small group of Anglicans, such as Charles Williams, C. S. Lewis (the special 'Cambridge' issue of *The Twentieth Century* was a monument to the irritant properties of Christian intellectualism at that university) and, of course, T. S. Eliot, whose so-called 'retreat into Anglicanism' has exposed him to critical savagery which sometimes oversteps the limits not only of charity but of decency.[7]

Adopting a very defensive position concerning her orthodoxy she added:

> It is true that every effort is made to represent Christian affirmations as a mere attempt to reimpose the cold, dead hand of the past. Phrases like 'dogmatic','scholastic','medieval', 'unscientific', 'mystical obscurantism', 'return to the Dark Ages', 'conventional orthodoxy', 'taboo', 'authoritarianism' and so on are bandied about freely in a pejorative sense.[8]

But Sayers remained adamant that Christianity involved the acceptance of a number of basic beliefs and that to contradict them was, indeed, heresy. To a criticism that one of her plays made unoriginal theological statements she retorted: "... it is scarcely the business of Christian writers to introduce novelties into the fundamental Christian doctrines"[9] which was typical of the blunt style with which she asserted her views.

The majority of Dorothy Sayers's published statements on theology and literature were made after the writing of *The Zeal of Thy House* and it is possible to see some of her ideas being worked out in the play. From the play and her later writings, it is obvious that one of her major concerns was the Fall of Man and the doctrine of original sin. Her emphasis on original sin was a response to the growth of socialism in twentieth century Britain. Since the turn of the century there had been a gradual erosion of the concept of man as innately wicked and in need of redemption, in favour of the belief that man is a product of his social conditions which only need to improve for him to progress. This denial of the orthodox Christian view of man's depraved nature led Anglo-Catholic apologists like Sayers to re-examine the myth of the Fall and to restate the reasons for man's original fall from Grace with renewed emphasis.

Both *The Zeal of Thy House* and her later Canterbury play, *The Devil to Pay* (a retelling of the Faust legend), deal with the sin of "aspiring pride and insolence" which caused the Fall of Lucifer and of man. When Lady Ursula first meets the arrogant architect, William of Sens, he claims to share God's experience in Creation: he speaks of

... the craftsman's dream
The Power and the Glory, the Kingdom of God and man.

Ursula reminds William of the Tree of Knowledge and together they re-enact the Fall. Michael, the Angel, becomes the Angel who drove Adam and Eve from Eden and the fatal flaw in the rope, which causes William's fall from the archway, is the flaw in his character. William only recognises it when he is finally forced to consider how Christ accepted pain and apparent defeat with humility:

William: O, I have sinned. The eldest sin of all,
Pride, that struck down the morning star from Heaven
Hath struck down me from where I sat and shone
Smiling on my new-world. (p.57) [10]

The fall of William, reminiscent of Solness's fall in Ibsen's *The Master Builder*, is the result of his equating himself with God by implication and he is saved in the end only by the redeeming blood of the second Adam.

Dorothy Sayers's use of images in *The Zeal of Thy House* was partly due to her interest in the idea of the image being the only way by which certain aspects of God's activity can be recognised. She was later to develop her peculiar usage of the word image in a full-length book, *The Mind of the Maker*,[11] but in her first Canterbury play she gives a speech to the angels which sets out her thinking as it applies to the act of Creation, in which man comes nearest to being an image of God. The angel Michael speaks to the audience at the end of the play:

Praise Him that He hath made man in His own image, a maker and craftsman like Himself, a little mirror of His triune majesty.

The angel goes on to explain that every work of creation is three-fold, either on the heavenly or earthly level: the Creative idea, an image of the Father; the Creative energy, image of the Word; and the Creative power, the image of the Spirit. The Cathedral, built by this three-fold creative process, is thus a symbol of the Trinity.

The suggestion in Sayers's play is that William of Sens's greatest manifestation of vanity is a failure to distinguish between the work of human imagination, with its dependence on pre-existent elements, and the infinite power of God - *creatio ex nihilo*. William's blunder is also a logical one, for in acknowledging God as Creator he is acknowledging that all he has and is derives from God. He can never, therefore, be on a level with his Creator: the concept of God as Creator implies continuing dependence. Both the question of God as Creator and the implications for Man were of interest to theologians in the nineteen-thirties who were tending to discuss these matters under the title of 'Philosophy of Religion' and Dorothy Sayers, though not trained as a philosopher, was keen to involve herself in their debate. The result was, at times, very unsatisfactory, for she tended to write ambiguously and to blur the dramatic outlines of her plays with pseudo-philosophical statements.

It was probably fortunate that the production of *The Zeal of Thy House* was not directed by the young theologian E. Martin Browne, who had produced *Cranmer* and *Murder in the Cathedral*. Skilled producer as he was, he may have been tempted to allow the theological statements to remain in the text. *The Zeal of Thy House* was produced instead by the distinguished producer and romantic actor from the Old Vic, E. Harcourt Williams.[12] A devout high-churchman who shared many of Sayers's beliefs, Williams was, nevertheless, primarily a man of the theatre who quickly recognised the need for cuts in the play to make it stage-worthy. In addition to producing the play, Harcourt Williams also played the part of William of Sens, finding some of the expansive speeches ideal material for his rich voice and impressive acting style. Although Williams had acted many successful rôles since his early appearances with Sir Frank Benson, his playing of William of Sens, both at Canterbury and in commercial productions, was generally recognised as one of his finest achievements.

As with *Cranmer*, Dorothy Sayers's *The Zeal of Thy House* was staged very simply in the Chapter House using Laurence Irving's permanent setting. The opening scene takes place in the Chapter House itself and the remaining scenes in the Choir. The transition was effected by moving a number of items of furniture and the use of appropriate properties; the arch in one of the screens represented the door to an office or store-room; and the niche in the rear wall containing the throne was used for sudden appearances of an angel. The lighting plot for the original production shows a greater sense of theatre than had previously been the case. Although the equipment was still rudimentary, there was more attempt to isolate and light individual areas of the stage, including the small niche, and to achieve dramatic effects by fast and slow fades.

The play was presented without interval and ran for about one hour and forty minutes. Originally *The Zeal of Thy House* was published in an acting edition for Canterbury and from this Harcourt Williams made his cuts. I shall base my further discussion of the play on the prompt copy used at Canterbury. There is, however, a slightly longer edition of the play which was used for the commercial productions; provision was made for the traditional interval and some expansion of the text became necessary. This version, with a preface by Laurence Irving, was published by Gollancz in 1937 and has since been reprinted several times.[13]

Harcourt Williams's cuts and adaptations to the acting edition were of three kinds: lengthy theological statements; unnecessary detail which contributed nothing to the action; and redistribution of speeches for effective entrances and exits (necessary because of Dorothy Sayers's inexperience of stagecraft). The best example of the first kind was the concluding speech to the audience, in which the angel explains the three-fold Creative process. The whole of this speech was omitted in performance and the words reappeared some years later as part of an essay by Dorothy Sayers. The speech was, however, reinstated by Christopher Hassall when he produced the play in the Chapter House in 1949.

As an example of cutting superfluous verbiage, we can take an incident from the second scene of the play. In Scene Two, William, Gervase and Hubert are discussing the problems caused by a load of sub-standard lime, which has been provided by a trader whose estimates were lower than those of the usual source of supply. The problem is that the Father Treasurer always goes for the lowest estimates without regard for quality. The main ideas of this part of the scene are: a) that William insists on the highest quality materials; b) he is prepared to use devious means to obtain them. Here is the dialogue, the words in parentheses were cut in performance:

Gervase: But is it honest?

Hubert: All I know is, this lime here ain't honest. (Prior Wibert, him as built the Water-Tower, wouldn't never have asked his masons to put up with cheap rubbish like this here.)[14]

William: No, of course it's not honest. And it's not exactly safe. That is, it's liable to misconstruction, if proclaimed upon the house-tops. But the Lord commended the unjust steward.

Hubert: You can't make bricks without straw, nor yet mortar without lime. (And if Prior Wibert, rest his soul, was alive, he'd say the same).

Williams then cut all subsequent references to Prior Wibert who makes no contribution to the progress of the play.

VISITING-TIME AT THE CATHEDRAL

The Lady Ursula de Warbois . Miss Marie Ney
William of Sens . . . . Mr. Harcourt Williams
Hubert . . . . Mr. Bartlett Mullins

Figure 18: Cartoon from *Punch,* 6 April 1938

The skill and experience of Harcourt Williams also enabled him to remedy the faulty structure of scenes. For example, in Scene Four William of Sens lies on his bed and Father Theodatus enters to announce the arrival of Lady Ursula. The action, as Dorothy Sayers intended it, was as follows: 1) Theodatus enters with Ursula. 2) Theodatus exits. 3) Dialogue between William and Ursula. 4) Ursula exits. 5) William calls Theodatus. 6) Theodatus looks in and William asks him to fetch the Prior. 7) Theodatus exits. 8) A Psalm is sung. 9) Prior enters. Williams transposed speeches and cut various lines to produce a scene which resulted in: 1) Theodatus enters with Ursula but, before he goes, William asks him to fetch the Prior. 2) Theodatus exits. 3) Dialogue between William and Ursula. 4) Ursula exits. 5) Prior enters. Such economy was partly the result of the difficulty of entrances and exits on the Chapter House stage, but it imposed a salutary discipline on the writing.

The play as produced at Canterbury consists of four scenes, each of which contains three distinct elements: there are the historical events presented in a naturalistic way and adhering closely to the record contained in Gervase's chronicle; there are the activities of the angels; and there is a strong liturgical element. At times these three levels on which the play operates are entirely separate whereas, at other times, they interact. *The Zeal of Thy House*, therefore, has certain similarities with John Masefield's *The Coming of Christ*, as it is really a morality in form.

The naturalistic style of the historical events begins with a meeting of the Chapter to decide who should be given the task of rebuilding the Choir of the Cathedral. The scene has been set and the necessary background information given by the angels; the monks enter in procession, singing - a typical Canterbury entrance. Characterisation of the various members of the Chapter is colourful and clear. In a scene of lively and, at times, amusing parochial debate the Chapter reveal their various concerns: Theodatus piously reminds the Prior that the choice must be made under God's guidance; Stephen, the Treasurer, with a constant eye on his budget; Ambrose, the Choirmaster, obsessed with acoustics. There are nice touches of contemporary reference: Paul dislikes "this trivial modern stuff they are putting up all over the place, with its pointed arcading and flourishing capitals"; and Martin, who is "ashamed to hear sacred words so howled", uses an almost direct quotation from Gervases's chronicle - "where they howled rather than sang . . .".[15] There are constant reminders of the recent death of Becket; indeed, Theodatus suggests that the fire was Divine judgement for the late Archbishop's murder. The motivating force for rebuilding on a lavish scale is the need for a magnificent place of pilgrimage to house the shrine of Saint Thomas.

Three architects, Henry of York, John of Kent and William of Sens, present their rival plans to the Chapter. Dorothy Sayers gives each a distinctive character in keeping with the type of plan they offer. Henry - prepared to patch up the existing fabric, conservative in his estimate, compromising and accommodating in nature; John - determined to build "the wonder of the realm", uncompromising in demands for high expenses and detailed in his plans; and

William - relaxed in handling the Chapter and bringing no detailed plans or estimates but presenting a series of drawings of his fine work elsewhere.

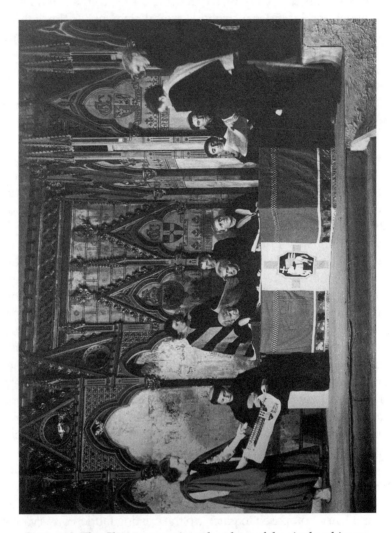

Figure 19: The Chapter examines the plans of the rival architects.
William of Sens (Harcourt Williams) extreme left.
The Zeal of Thy House (1937).

The interviews with the various architects and the sharp contrasts in approach are handled with great skill by the playwright; the outcome is never predictable and the vote of the Chapter is extremely close. It is only when the doddering Father Ernulphus, who has apparently been asleep throughout the meeting, wakes and makes his casting vote for William of Sens that the tension is resolved. Dorothy Sayers includes Gervase himself as a character in the play: he is portrayed as an earnest, young monk who becomes William's private secretary. When William's rivals explode in jealous anger they accuse the successful architect of deception and duplicity and Gervase anxiously enquires of his new master if they have some justification. William hints at his true character and a theme of the play in his reply:

> Listen to me, young man. At my age one learns that sometimes one
> has to damn one's soul for the sake of the work.   (p.14)

The architect and Gervase then leave the stage whilst it is rearranged to represent the site of the Choir.

The second scene in the play continues the naturalistic events two years after the first scene, the stage being frequently crowded with busy workmen and their materials. During this scene, the dialogue moves from colloquial prose to verse as William and Lady Ursula discuss the respective creative powers of men and women. The action remains apparently naturalistic, for the extended speeches occur when there are only two characters on stage. William does however become transported by his vision of another Eden and he speaks in an expansive, poetic cadenza:

> **Ursula:** My simple Adam,
> It is too late to scare women with risks
> And perils - women, that for one splendid risk
> Changed the security of Paradise,
> Broke up the loom and pattern of creation,
> Let in man's dream on the world, and snatched the truth
> Of knowledge from the jealous hand of God
> So that the fire runs in man's blood for ever.
> **William** *(carried away)*: So that she runs like fire in a man's blood
> For ever! Take what thou wilt - the risk, the sorrow,
> The Fire, the dream - and in the dream's end, death.   (p.25)

As William begins to fulfil the promise of his own damnation, hinted at in the previous scene, he prefigures his physical fall by re-enacting the Fall of Man. At this point the action of the play is an image and is interrupted at its climax by the angels. A sudden lighting change after the word "death" introduces the angels and the action resumes on a mundane level after their interjection, with the homely prose of Hubert calling his master, telling him that a stone arch is ready for the final touch of genius.

A further two years elapse between Scenes Two and Three, but the opening of the third scene takes up the theme of the previous one - the building of an archway. Final preparations are under way to enable William to ascend to the top of the great arch to fit the keystone, the climax of his achievement. Before the moment of this spectacular demonstration of William's skill, Theodatus and the Prior are seen disputing the relationship between William's sup-posedly scandalous conduct with the Lady Ursula and his rôle as Cathedral architect. Theodatus, uncharitable and censorious,

> would rather have
> A worse-built church with a more virtuous builder,

but the Prior, always prepared to believe the best of people, is content to leave such judgements to God. He points out that William's workmanship cannot be faulted and that the Cathedral is therefore an offering to God of the finest quality that man can achieve. Theodatus is, however, not convinced and when William enters and asks him to assist a young workman to check the rope for the rigging of the travelling cradle, tension begins to mount and disaster seems inevitable.

While Theodatus and Simon examine the rope for flaws, the Prior gently suggests to William that the scandal he is creating cannot be helpful to the morale of the workmen. William's retort is wholly predictable: the Church can have no complaint about his workmanship and his private amusements are his own affair. The Prior leaves William momentarily shaken by his final comment:

> If you choose to be damned, you must; if you prefer to make a death-bed repentance, you may; but if an idle workman does an unsound job now, no repentance of yours will prevent it from bringing down the church some day or other. (p.33)

The Prior's clear condemnation of William comes as a surprise after he has urged Theodatus to curb his tongue and adopt a more compassionate attitude. The rebuke to William is, however, delivered in the spirit of love and the Prior emerges as one of the most dignified and finely-drawn characters in the play.

In contrast to the humility of the Prior, William's pride assumes even greater proportions as he prepares to ascend the arch. Ursula, the temptress from the previous scene, enters to share his moment of triumph, but as Theodatus averts his eyes in disgust and prays incessantly, a flaw in the rope passes undetected through his fingers. The audience are made aware of this by the angels and this adds great irony to William's arrogant speeches:

> We are the master craftsmen, God and I -
> We understand one another; None, as I can,
> Can creep under the ribs of God, and feel
> His heart beat through those Six Days of Creation; (p.35)

As his presumption reaches new heights, even Ursula is terrified by his blasphemy:

> **William:** This church is mine
> And none but I, not even God, can build it . . .
> **Ursula:** Hush! God will hear you . . .
> Tempt Him not
> Lest He should smite and slay.
> **William:** He will not dare;
> He knows that I am indispensable . . . (p.36)

William's exit is superb, as he leaves the stage to enter the travelling cradle he remarks:

> Like God
> I must be doing in my little world,
> Lest, lacking me, the moon and stars should fail. (p.37)

and the angels gather to watch the event.

Suddenly, the stage is filled with a crowd of people all gazing upward, and we see the ascent through their eyes. The description is distributed among the various speakers in the crowd, but only a small boy claims to see an angel with a sword at the moment when everyone else sees the rope break and William falls fifty feet to the ground.

The remainder of the scene is full of gloom and contrition. Theodatus, who is as guilty as William of making himself equal with God, is condemned by the Prior for seeing himself as the instrument of Divine vengeance and is ordered to care for the stricken architect. But the Prior also assures Ursula and the workman who had been checking the rope with Theodatus, that the mercy of God is infinite.

Figure 20: Theodatus (Frank Napier) kneels in contrition to the Prior (Philip Hollingworth). *The Zeal of Thy House* (1937).

The final scene, which continues the story six months after the architect's fall, shows William as a pathetic figure. Carefully tended by the humbled Theodatus and the other monks, William attempts to direct operations from his bed. Although he obstinately refuses to admit that he is dispensable, it is obvious that William can no longer cope with the task and various craftsmen among the monks are beginning to make important decisions without consulting him. A moving moment occurs when William, in a last attempt to find peace and establish control over his project, has his couch brought to the site of the Choir itself, but just when he appears to be solving a major problem that has arisen from the plans he is overcome by exhaustion and sinks despondently down.

Desperate to feel peace of mind and still unable to recognise the sin which caused his fall, William sends for the Prior. There is a very powerful scene in which William confesses his fleshly sins and the Prior urges him to search his soul more deeply to discover his greater sin. But even the Prior cannot cure William's spiritual blindness and insists that William must discover the truth for himself. Granting him absolution from those sins he has confessed, the Prior leaves William to sleep. This is an awesome moment, for the audience is left with the same sense of dissatisfaction as William.

At this point the action ceases to be naturalistic: William is convinced of his sin of pride in a remarkable dream and the ordinary events are only resumed briefly when he wakes and tells Gervase and Hubert that he has decided to resign and recommends that William the Englishman should be appointed. He has a last realised that he is not unique:

I am not
The only architect in the world - there are others
Will do the work as well . . . (p. 59)

Surprisingly he asks to be taken to Ursula's lodgings to "make amends". This is an unsatisfactory resolution, for it is never fully explained what William intends and why Ursula has not yet entered the convent. It is also disappointing that the Prior is not reintroduced in the final moments of the play as he has played an important part in William's final enlightenment. Nevertheless, the action of the play as I have described it constitutes a lively, moving and accurate account of the building of the Choir and of the "destruction of the artist by vanity."[16] It would be possible to extract the action of the play on this level and perform it as an effective short play on its own.

Dorothy Sayers's intentions, however, were not primarily the documentation of an historic event. She wished to demonstrate that the ordinary events described were really under the control of God's Providence. This has always provided dramatists with a major problem and Dorothy Sayers, by her use of the angels, seems to have been influenced by Marlowe's method in *Dr Faustus*. The second, and clearly the most unsatisfactory element of his play is the introduction of the angels Michael, Raphael (with his Thurifer), Gabriel and the recorder Cassiel. Their main function is to demonstrate that the apparent accidents, and even the supreme achievements of man's imagination are, in fact, part of the Divine Plan.

At first it must have seemed to the Canterbury audience that Masefield's angels had taken flight and landed in the opening movement of Dorothy Sayers's play. Their stunning costumes (they could hardly not intrude on the action) and their first words were remarkably similar:

> **Michael:** I am God's servant Michael the Archangel;
> I walk in the world of men invisible,
> Bearing the sword that Christ bequeathed His Church
> To sunder and to save. (p.2)

On three occasions the angels apparently affect the action of the play, though in the first two instances there are also rational explanations of what happens. Gabriel whispers to the slumbering Father Ernulphus in the Chapter Meeting, thus ensuring his vote for William of Sens, although it appears that Ernulphus simply wakes and repeats the last name mentioned. Michael, having announced at the opening of the play that he is invisible, is seen to cut the rope with his sword and cause William's fall; and it is in dialogue with the angels that William is finally convinced of his sin of pride.

Much of the effectiveness of the angels is destroyed by Dorothy Sayers's faulty sense of humour.[17] She clearly wished both to instruct and amuse, but she succeeded only in trivialising the angels. Although the angels find men "very amusing", "very pathetic" and "very perverse", they themselves seem to be a good deal less intelligent and articulate than mortals and their actions seem almost capricious. Michael claims to have been responsible for the fire which destroyed the old Cathedral, his account is accurate according to Gervase's *Chronicle*, but when Raphael enquires: "Was it done to avenge the murder of the Archbishop?" Michael simply replies, "I do not know. I am a soldier. I take my orders." (p.4). Again when the young cherub enquires why God created two sexes and thus caused so much trouble, "the Angels are inexpressibly shocked" (a stage direction) and retort:

Raphael: Hush! you mustn't ask why.
Michael: Angels never ask why.
Gabriel: Only men ask Why. (p.27)

This is hardly an effective method of presenting the inscrutable ways of God nor of engendering much faith in the manner of His intervention in the affairs of men!

The angels' other functions in the play are doctrinal comment, as an occasional chorus providing background information and, lastly, as the agents of enlightenment for the egocentric William. In the frenzy of his dream, William hears the angels' insistent reminders of Christ's redeeming suffering and it is Michael who addresses the audience at the end of the play.

The Zeal of Thy House is structured around a liturgical framework: the action is punctuated by singing and antiphonal speech until, in the last scene, the heightened language of the liturgy becomes an integral part of the action. The liturgical material consists of five latin hymns; versicles and responses of scriptural verses; five psalms in the Prayer Book version - including part of *Psalm LXIX* from which the title of the play is taken; a section of the *Dies Irae* and *Quid Sum Miser* from the *Requiem Mass*; and a number of direct quotations from scripture which are included in the dialogue itself. In selecting the material, Dorothy Sayers has used the approach of an oratorio librettist, taking passages of scripture out of one context to illuminate another. In fact, the first versicle and response:

Versicle: He maketh His angels spirits
Response: And His ministers a flaming fire   (*Psalm* civ.4) (p.2.)
had already served this purpose in Mendelssohn's *Elijah* and the
second:

V: Their sound is gone forth into all lands
R: And their words unto the end of the world (*Romans* x.18) (p.3.)
in Handel's *Messiah*. The influence of the oratorio, the popular form
of Protestant music-drama, is very pronounced in the play. There
was a good deal of music in the first performance, settings were
specially composed by the Cathedral organist, Gerald Knight. At
an obvious level, the music helped to establish that the action was
taking place in a monastery, but Dorothy Sayers's selection of
appropriate meditations on the action produced a universalising
effect and a devotional quality. Her choice was extremely wide
ranging and skilled. For example, as the monks leave the Chapter
House after their first meeting, we hear - Versicle, *Haggai* ii.4,
Response, *Luke* ix. 62; and Versicle, *Eccllesiastics* iii. 22, Response,
Deuteronomy xxxii. 3. All of these verses have some bearing on the
subsequent action of the play.

Towards the end of the play, in the dream sequence, the angels
and William alternate in their expression of the need for salvation;
the play begins to acquire the full rhythm of liturgy and rational
debate is replaced by a sense of ecstatic worship:

William: O send Thy spirit
To blow apart the sundering flames, that I
After a thousand years of hell, may catch
One glimpse, one only, of the Church of Christ,
The perfect work, finished, though not by me
Versicle: Save me from the Lion's mouth; Thou has heard me also
from among the horns of the unicorns.
Response: For why? Thou shall not leave my soul in hell, neither
shalt Thou suffer Thine holy one to see corruption -
Trumpet.
Cassiel: Sheathe thy sword, Michael, the fight is won.
Raphael: Close the book, Cassiel; the score is paid.
Gabriel: Give glory Raphael; the race is run.
Michael: Lead homeward, Gabriel, the sheep that strayed.

All: Eloi, Eloi, Eloi
Glory to God in the highest; Holy is He!
Michael: How hardly shall the rich man enter in
to the Kingdom of Heaven.   (pp. 57-58.)

This is no longer a drama of action, it is nearer to Elgar's *Dream of Gerontius* in which the narrative becomes an act of verbal worship. The events of the play, the angels and the liturgical elements come together to express the transcendent.

The critic of *The Times Literary Supplement* was particularly impressed by the language at this point:

It is in this scene that the dramatic dialogue reaches its highest merit; but all through the play Miss Sayers's prose is rhythmical and alive, and her blank verse so flexible and natural as to show once more that in good hands this ancient form of English dramatic speech can never wither.[18]

Dorothy Sayers's view of the function of verse received its most interesting exposition in her lecture *The Poetry of Search and the Poetry of Statement*.[19] This was her contribution to a controversy initiated partly by Denis Donoghue, who was shortly to produce *The Third Voice*,which has been inaccurately described as the post-mortem on verse-drama.[20] Discerning two main species of poetry, Dorothy Sayers maintained that it was still possible to write poetry of "statement" even though it may be necessary to "show the workings in the margin" before the point of affirmation was reached. Dante was, for her, the supreme example of the poet who had moved from a poetry of "search" (and she did not deny the existence of great poetry of this kind) to the rejoicing verse of statement in *The Divine Comedy*, but she also demonstrated the same development in T. S. Eliot, strongly resisting any suggestion that it was retrogressive.

The verse of *The Zeal of Thy House* is pure statement; the influences are mainly Miltonic and biblical, but the major problem is that the verse has to sustain too many statements. Inevitably, the theological ideas never break out of their liturgical or biblical imagery and when a straightforward concept requires expression, it is choked with the paraphernalia of a second-rate *Paradise Lost*. The dramatic verse thus has no character of its own and, although the voice of Harcourt Williams must have deceived many into thinking they were listening to sublime language, there is an indulgence in the writing which serves no dramatic purpose. The language of *The Zeal of Thy House* confirms T. S. Eliot's observation that:

> The tendency, at any rate, of prose drama is to emphasise the ephemeral and superficial; if we want to get at the permanent and universal we tend to express ourselves in verse.[21]

Both the angelic and human characters use verse, prose and the specialised language of liturgy and their movement from one mode of expression to another indicates a shift from the transcendent to the temporal. This movement is one of the main reasons for the sense of unease and incompatibility which most critics have discerned. The changes are frequently too extreme to be convincing:

> **Workman:** Master Hubert says, is that rope ready?
> **Simon:** Here you are, mate.
> **Ursula:** Do we presume too much upon God's mercy?
> **William:** We are the master-craftsmen, God and I -   (p.35.)

Such variation is even more perplexing when it occurs within a single character and is at its worst in the treatment of the angels who alternate between formal verse statements, scriptural quotation and chat.

The Zeal of Thy House provided a moving act of meditation and an interesting, historical episode for the Canterbury audience. It gained enormously from its performance in the Chapter House and, with judicious cutting, could still be performed today. Dorothy Sayers probably attempted too much, she left nothing to implication. The visual image of the Fall was, for instance, sufficient to make the point without the intervention of the angels. There are too many modes within a single play, so that it is impossible to evolve a production style that can do entire justice to the playwright's intention. No doubt, however, after the intellectual difficulties and obscurities of Eliot's and Williams's plays, *The Zeal of Thy House* was eagerly welcomed by its first audiences.

Notes to Chapter Nine

1. 'Review of *The Zeal of Thy House*', *The Times Literary Supplement*, June 3rd, 1937. Reprinted in *The Canterbury Cathedral Chronicle XXVII* (1937), 19-22.

2/3/4/5/6. Charles Cotton, ed., *Of the Burning and Repair of the Church in 1174. From the Latin of Gervase, a Monk of the Priory of Christ Church Canterbury* (Canterbury 1930), 9, 11.

7/8. Dorothy L. Sayers, 'Charles Williams: A Poet's Critic', *The Poetry of Search and the Poetry of Statement* (London 1963), 70.

9. Dorothy L. Sayers ' The Faust Legend', *The Poetry of Search and the Poetry of Statement* (London 1963), 229.

10. All page references in this Chapter are to Dorothy L. Sayers, *The Zeal of Thy House* (Acting Edition for the Friends of Canterbury Cathedral, Canterbury 1937).

11. Dorothy L. Sayers, *The Mind of the Maker* (New York 1956).

12. See Appendix.

13. The first cheap edition published by Gollancz was reprinted fifteen times between 1937 and 1947.

14. Dorothy Sayers was, no doubt, anxious to mention Wibert since, in 1937, the Friends had recently been responsible for the restoration of Wibert's Water Tower in the cloisters.

15. See 'Gervase of Canterbury', Elizabeth Holt (ed.) *A Documentary History of Art*, Anchor Books (New York 1957), 52

16. Laurence Irving, TR1, see Bibliography D.

17. See also a fuller discussion of Miss Sayers's humour in Chapter 10.

18. Quoted in *The Canterbury Cathedral Chronicle XXVII* (1937), 22.

19. D. L. Sayers, *The Poetry of Search and the Poetry of Statement, op. cit.*

20. Arnold Hinchliffe, 'Verse Drama', *British Theatre 1950-1970* (Oxford 1974), 34.

21. T. S. Eliot, 'A Dialogue on Dramatic Poetry', *Selected Essays* (London 1951), 46.

10

The Devil to Pay

The Zeal of Thy House was so popular with the Canterbury audiences that the committee of the Friends invited Dorothy L. Sayers to write another play for the Festival of 1939. The playwright accepted the invitation on the understanding that Harcourt Williams should once again produce her play and take the leading part. Williams agreed although, arguably, he was too old for the part and, as with *The Zeal of Thy House*, he was assisted in the production by a colleague from the Old Vic, Frank Napier. The new play, *The Devil to Pay*, was the last to be performed in the Chapter House before the outbreak of war interrupted the Canterbury Festival for several years. Recently discovered correspondence between Sayers and Margaret Babington reveals that Sayers was asked to write a third play after the war but was too busy to undertake it.

The setting for *The Devil to Pay* was by far the most elaborate that had been attempted in the Chapter House. Dorothy Sayers insisted that Laurence Irving's gothic screens be replaced by an imitation of a medieval setting (see Figure 20). Detailed directions for the use of various parts of the stage were included in the text and, unlike previous productions that had relied on extreme simplicity of staging, there was also a considerable list of stage properties and special sound effects.

E. Martin Browne attended a performance and described the staging of *The Devil to Pay*:

There is no more exciting moment in the theatregoer's year than that in which he waits for the Festival Play to begin in the Chapter House at Canterbury. Every year this stage has shown some advance in the dramatic presentation of Christianity: and this year is no exception. Before the actors appear, the stage suggests that we are to see a revival of medieval drama, for here is Heaven raised high on our right, and Hell-mouth on our left, with 'mansions' for the terrestrial scenes in between, according to the method of the old mystery plays.[1]

The use of mansions was, in one respect, entirely appropriate, for *The Devil to Pay* was a reworking of Marlowe's *Dr Faustus* (performed at the 1929 Festival) which itself looked back to medieval drama. The Hell-mouth was used for a number of impressive moments in the play and was a constant reminder of Faustus's precarious position. The Canterbury stage was, however, too small for the mansions to be used effectively and instead of their providing a location for the action, they appear to have served simply as entrances and exits.

Dorothy Sayers's recollection of Marlowe and Goethe in *The Devil to Pay* was quite deliberate and the strongest influence was undoubtedly Marlowe. By 1939, Dorothy Sayers had developed a passion for medieval allegory, and a particular interest in the Faust legend, and in a number of essays she defended her apparent presumption in writing another play on the legend. She acknowledged the common ground that her play shared with previous plays concerning Faust:

. . . certain episodes are reproduced in some form or another in practically all treatments of the subject: Faustus's raising Mephistopheles; his 'disputations' with him concerning the nature of God; his twenty-four years bond to Hell; his journey to Rome, where he plays tricks on the Pope, and to the court of Charles V, where he assists the Imperial armies to achieve their victories in Italy; his having Helen of Troy for his paramour; and the final scene in which the Devil comes to claim his own.[2]

To this base, Dorothy Sayers added three important characters: Wagner is developed from Marlowe's rather colourless character of the same name to be Faustus's devoted and talkative servant;

Lisa, a simple serving-maid, loves Faustus and retains her homely concern for him throughout his exotic adventures; and Azrael becomes one of Dorothy Sayers's chatty angels who cares for the souls of the dead.

The play consists of four scenes, the first three of which contain the incidents listed above. The fourth scene is an entirely original addition in which the dispute over the soul of Faustus is taken to the celestial court. In preparing an Acting Edition for use at Canterbury, Dorothy Sayers indicated certain sections of the text which might be cut in performance.[3]

As in Marlowe's play, Mephistopheles appears in an unacceptable form and Faustus charges him to return in a more pleasing shape. Mephistopheles "takes off his lion's head and tosses it negligently into Hell-mouth" and, at once, Faustus begins to question him concerning his creation and nature. Faustus appears satisfied by his answers and reveals to Mephistopheles that he is sickened by the world's suffering and seeks power to deal with it. Mephistopheles, however, diverts his thoughts by an entertainment of devils and by showing Faustus his own image as a young man, suggesting that this is how he could have been had he not

> meddled
> With virtue and the dismal knowledge of God.[4]

The second scene contains the best moments of drama in the play; the tension in Faustus's soul is reflected in the shifting sympathy of the crowd and the delicate balance of his loyalty. Rome (represented by Mansion Three) is already alive with talk of Faustus when Lisa and Wagner arrive. The Priest, who is overheard by the two servants as he talks to the Cardinal, prepares the ground for the ensuing action:

> He (Faustus) distributes gold to all and sundry, heals the sick, raises the dead, and corrupts the minds of the poor . . . The churches are deserted . . . the people throng to the lectures of Dr Faustus. (p.19)

In a tradition which runs from Marlowe to John Osborne, Dorothy Sayers shows the prelates as hypocritical, self-seeking and concerned only with fear and suffering as a means to salvation:

> No sin, no sermon; no cross, no cardinal; no pain, no Pope! (p.20)

When the Priest first addresses the crowd he almost succeeds in turning them against Faustus and his efforts to relieve suffering. The Priest explains eloquently that man's suffering is the result of the sin of Adam, but that Christ suffered for man's redemption. Faustus leaps from his hiding place and disputes the Priest's arguments. Now it is Faustus's rhetoric which prevails - he cannot fail when he draws attention to the wealth of the Church and the poverty of the populace. But the Priest reminds his listeners that the works of darkness bring a curse rather than a blessing. The crowd are quick to agree, citing instances of the after-effects of Faustus's benevolence; and it is only the intervention of Mephistopheles that prevents the mounting hysteria of the crowd from destroying Faustus.

One of the main problems of the Faust legend is the tedious series of exploits on which he is supposed to have employed his vast intelligence and freedom from moral restraint. Scene Three begins with an originally lively, but increasingly boring, account of the way in which the twenty-four years that have elapsed since the previous scene, have been squandered. At the same time as Mephistopheles is rehearsing some of the more outrageous features of Faustus's life, he meets the Angel Azrael who is carrying the soul of Lisa, now new born into the Eternal Life of Heaven.

Faustus, who appears throughout this scene as a young man, is engaged in controlling military campaigns against Rome. He has promised the Emperor a vision of the combat; but he is suddenly reminded of the approaching expiry of his lease of life by the presence of the angel. Lisa's death threatens to plunge Faustus into inconsolable grief and it is only Mephistopheles's cunning that diverts his thoughts to the beauty of the Empress. When, however, Faustus demands that the Empress be brought to his bed the following day, he is again reminded sharply of his perilous state, for Mephistopheles replies with awful simplicity: "There will be no tomorrow for you, master." Faustus, growing more deluded each moment, refuses to listen to talk of death for he has convinced himself that his perpetual youth is immortality. Death and Hell have become a fable to him; the futility of his activities on the very brink of his damnation heighten the tragedy.

The action of a battle takes place offstage and, like William's fall in *The Zeal of Thy House*, is seen through the eyes of a group of spectators onstage. Until Ionesco wrote his play *The Leader*, this description of the battle must have been the longest piece of narrated action written for stage performance.

The final moments of the scene contain an ingenious twist and contain the first entirely original idea of the play. Mephistopheles notices that Azrael has the soul of Faustus in a bag and is about to make off with it. When Mephistopheles demands the soul, he produces the bond as evidence, but his confidence is rocked when Azrael agrees that the bond is in order, only to add "Always supposing your client's soul was his to sell!" Mephistopheles attempts to brush this aside as a "legal quibble", but he soon has another shock. Azrael agrees to hand over the soul, declaring that he intends to enter an appeal before the High Court, but when Mephistopheles opens the bag containing the soul, he pulls out a small black dog! Mephistopheles is incensed to find Faustus's soul thus transformed and he becomes more bewildered when Azrael accuses him of not only causing the metamorphosis, but of mistreating the King's property. The bargain which Mephistopheles struck with Faustus has consequences, therefore, that even the Devil could not foresee.

The final scene of *The Devil to Pay* continues without a break from the previous scene as Heaven opens and the Judge appears above. At the beginning of the scene Azrael, haughty and long-winded, and Mephistopheles, childish and with odd flashes of wit, state their case before the Judge. They, in fact, do little more than repeat the substance of their argument at the close of the previous scene, but phrased, now, in legal terms. Mephistopheles has no answer to the question with which the Judge silences his more indignant protestations:

What did you think would happen to the soul
When you did that to it?

The real interest of the scene develops when the Judge decides that it is only Faustus who has a case to answer. And, as time has no significance in the celestial court, Faustus (conveniently for the progress of the play) is able to appear in his own body to hear the charges against him. Faustus wakes from his sleep thinking of the nightmare through which he has passed and, in agony of conscience, calls on Christ whom he has betrayed and denied. The Judge reveals himself as Christ just before Hell-mouth is opened and Faustus passes from sight, gazing on the face that he will see again. Devils below rumble their chorus of "Deep calleth unto deep", Azrael sings *De Profundis* and, finally, there is the exultant singing of the heavenly chorus which closes the play, like Handel's *Messiah*, with the words "Worthy is the Lamb. Amen."[5]

The Devil to Pay is largely concerned with the nature of evil and Dorothy Sayers chose to personify this in the figure of the Devil. She was particularly anxious to avoid what she called "the Promethean set-up",[6] the sense of sympathy or admiration which an audience may feel towards the Devil:

It is notorious that one of the great difficulties about writing a book or play about the Devil is to prevent that character stealing the show. Any actor will tell you that the rôle of the Devil . . . is sure fire.[7]

But, at least according to one press report, she failed in this respect:

It is useless to deny that Frank Napier's Mephistopheles 'steals the play' from Faustus. He dominates the action from the moment when, to the accompaniment of thunder, lightning and peals of Satanic laughter, he springs from the mouth of Hell, in answer to Faustus's incantations, and declares 'And now, sir, what can I do for you, to justify the expenditure of so many big words and this great exhibition of fi-fo-fum?'

That sentence sets the keynote of this magnificent characterisation. Miss Sayers gives us not a stern and sombre demon, nor a terrifying figure of Satan but a Puckish fellow with a sort of Cockney humour and crude wit . . . Mr Napier gives a performance which is almost incredibly good . . . impishness . . . craftiness . . . solemn dignity . . . flawless diction.[8]

Dorothy Sayers's purpose in trying to avoid the "Promethean set-up" was to show that the "Devil is a liar and the father of all lies",[9] a fact which, she claimed, the grandeur of the Devil's language in both Marlowe and Milton had obscured. All the Devil's lies, Dorothy Sayers suggested, derived from "the primary illusion inside which the Devil lives and in which he deceives himself and others."[10] This "primary illusion" is that evil and darkness can exist without the Light and are anything other than pure negation. The Christian view is that only God, the Light, is primary and that time, creation and darkness are secondary. Faustus himself provides an illustration of this principle in the first scene when he explains the eclipse of the sun to Wagner:

> **Faustus:** The moon has no light of herself. When she passes between the earth and the sun she shows but as a mass of dark matter, as your head does, between me and that candle.
>
> **Wagner:** I see. And if the sun were to pass between us and the moon, could he show dark also?
>
> **Faustus:** No; for he is the very source of the light, and in him is no darkness at all. (p.4)

Faustus fails to see the significance of this until the final scene of the play, for in his first disputation with Mephistopheles he is deceived by lies. To his first question, "Tell me, then, thou Evil, who made thee?" Mephistopheles answers that it was God. From this Faustus deduces that the God who made evil is worthy only of contempt, but in the presence of God in the final scene Mephistopheles admits that in the Garden of Eden and ever since, he has aimed to lead men through the "gate that leads them into the circle." He is simple negation - the opposite to the choice of God - the 'not-God' - he can only claim to have been made by God as "the light makes the shadow". He is:

> . . . the price that all things pay for being
> The shadow on the world, thrown by the world
> Standing in its own light, which light God is. (p.19)

Mephistopheles has no value in himself, he simply gives a name to the values of Permanence, Pleasure and Good. When Faustus hears this he recalls his exposition of the eclipse and marvels at his stupidity in being so deluded.

Faustus, in electing to call Mephistopheles at the opening of the play, has therefore passed from the possibility of evil, which Sayers says "exists from the moment that a creature is made that can love . . . because it chooses", to the actuality of evil which "exists from the moment that the choice is exercised in the wrong direction. Sin (moral evil) is the deliberate choice of the not-God."[11]

Figure 21: Harcourt Williams as Faustus and Frank Napier as Mephistopheles. Setting adapted by Frank Napier. *The Devil to Pay* (1939).

Another of the Devil's tricks is to convince Faustus that it is
possible for him to return to a state of primal innocence, to go to a
stage before the Fall in which the knowledge of good and evil do
not exist. Helen of Troy becomes the symbol of this desire and
Sayers explains her intention in her essay *The Faust Legend*:

The illusion of Helen is the illusion that it is possible to go back before the Fall and regain the simple animal innocence which Walt Whitman admired . . . the innocence which does not *know* evil . . . But the years cannot be turned back. We cannot, as Mr Charles Williams has said, return to primal innocence by simply removing our aprons of fig leaves.[12]

The extent of the illusion is cleverly demonstrated by Dorothy Sayers's stage directions for, as the image of the young Faustus embraces the image of Helen, Faustus himself actually embraces Mephistopheles. Helen is therefore shown to be, like Marlowe's Helen, a succubus. Faustus can only possess Helen when Mephistopheles has taken away the knowledge of good and evil in exchange for his immortal soul. Her name, she tells Faustus, was once Lilith (the legendary first wife of Adam) and he must renounce Eve and the sin of Adam before he can obtain her. At the point when he realises what he must do to gain Helen, Faustus reaches a second phase in which he repudiates "the actuality of evil and, with it, the whole personal responsibility for the redemption of evil."[13] In her programme note, the playwright describes this phase more fully in an attempt to demonstrate the contemporary significance of the play:

. . . he falls into despair (or, to use the current term, into 'defeatism') and takes flight into phantasy.

His escape takes a form very common in these terms: it is the nostalgia of childhood, of the primitive, of the unconscious; the rejection of adult responsibility and the denial of all value to growth and time . . . Time and eternity are two different things, and that which exists temporally must admit the value of time.[14]

Twice Mephistopheles suggests the true nature of Helen. When he tells the Emperor that Helen is no longer Faustus's paramour he neatly summarises the point which Sayers has been trying to make:

Man's delight is ever in the unattainable. When he is innocent, he longs for knowledge; when he is grown wise, he hankers after innocence. Between Lilith and Eve, Adam is unfaithful to both, and there is no contenting him.   (p.41)

And finally, when Helen is summoned for the last time, Mephistopheles reveals that Helen is the delusion that leads men on to the fateful bond:

She is the promise
Of golden phantasy, the worm in the brain,
The song in the soul: she is the world's desire.
Gaze on her face . . . She is the unattained.
The unattainable. (pp. 47-48)

Sayers was keenly aware of the attacks made on contemporary Christianity by the humanists and in *The Devil to Pay* she attempts to answer the challenge posed by critics who denied the idea of Original Sin and who cited examples of agnostic, humanitarian reformers. Faustus and Mephistopheles, having deluded themselves that God created evil, represent the world's suffering as God's abdication of responsibility. It was not his fault, Mephistopheles claims, that Adam and Eve had believed that God was all they hoped to be themselves, "all-good, all-wise, all-powerful." Mephistopheles is a "plausible humanitarian, breathing contempt upon the inefficiency of God"[15] and he provides a Tennysonian account of cruelty in nature. Mephistopheles also suggests that God's greatest folly was His attempt to meddle in Creation through the Incarnation, the mission of the Man of Sorrows was a failure and His words have been so misinterpreted as to be divisive.

In response to the false conception of God that Mephistopheles has created Faustus becomes,

. . . the type of impulsive reformer, over-sensitive to suffering, impatient of the facts, eager to set the world right by a sudden overthrow in his own strength and regardless of the ineluctable nature of things.[16]

Faustus makes his resolve clear when he leaves the protection of the magic circle which Lucifer has forbidden Mephistopheles to enter. Surrounded by devils, who have brought him platters of fruit and a goblet of wine and standing in darkness which follows the thunder he announces:

If God's so harsh a stepfather to His sons
Then must we turn adventurers, and carve out
Our own road to salvation. (p.11)

Then, with god-like arrogance, he surveys the Creation of the God he now disowns. It is obvious that Faustus is beginning to equate himself with God, as William of Sens had done. At several points he seems to identify himself with the Man of Sorrows. At the very beginning of the play Lisa said that Faustus "cannot bear to see anyone suffer" and when he looks in the mirror, he attributes his ageing and care-worn appearance to the grief which he has endured for the sufferings of men. He continues to give generously to the poor, but when he visits Rome, he laments that the people "have not even the heart to be grateful". When Mephistopheles tells Faustus that the way of Christ was "folly and failure", Faustus believes this to be true of his own way and he begins to despair of mankind whom he loves but who obstinately "hug their chains".

The most crucial stage in Faustus's development as a humanitarian reformer is reached when he determines to use the power of evil as, "The short cut to a remedy . . . to cast out bodily evil by invoking the power of spiritual evil."[17] Writing some years after the play was first produced Dorothy Sayers adds: "Many builders of earthly utopias and new orders seem prepared to do the like."[18]

Mephistopheles recognises that Faustus has made an irrevocable decision and calls down to Lucifer, "Lucifer, Lucifer! the bird is caught." In contrast to Faustus, Wagner remains deeply concerned for humanity whilst retaining his faith. As he grows older, and Lisa dies caring for plague victims, he comes to realise that "to aim at happiness is to miss the mark." Faustus aims at happiness through humanitarian reform, whereas Wagner, involving himself completely in the needs of mankind, finds happiness as a by-product.

The humanitarian as opposed to the Christian view is always a difficult topic for the writer who is attempting to commend Christianity to a socially-concerned audience. Dorothy Sayers brings the issue to a head in the confrontation between Faustus and the Pope (already discussed on p.241). Faustus claims that, like Christ, he is not afraid to suffer for men if only he can remove suffering from the world; but, having power, he intends to use it to this end. The Pope elucidates the "stony road / To Calvary", and then describes the infinity of God's mercy, explaining that the sin of confusing evil with good is only unforgivable because it makes men incapable of recognising God's pardon. Damnation, therefore, "Is consequence, not vengeance".

Figure 22: Mephistopheles produces the soul of Faustus (a small black dog) from a bag. *The Devil to Pay* (1939).

Interesting as some of the ideas of the play might be, there are three main reasons why *The Devil to Pay* is a most unsatisfactory and, at times, monumentally boring play. The reasons derive from Dorothy Sayers's limitations as a theologian and as an artist, for she seems to have had an extremely restricted view of Christianity and an inability to decide what sort of play she was trying to write.

The first reason for the play's failure is her obsession with the Garden of Eden and the Fall. There is no doubt that Dorothy Sayers was anxious to demonstrate that man's fundamental nature is evil, that he is in need of redemption and that any humanist or rational, socialist answer to man's problems failed to take account of this fact. Nevertheless, she constantly emphasises the Fall both in *The Zeal of Thy House* and *The Devil to Pay* to such an extent that it becomes an historical event rather than an allegorical expression of a truth. Reference to the myth of Lilith was probably as confusing to the average Christian as to any Humanist and when the whole theological content of the play has been examined it is clearly little advanced over *The Zeal of Thy House*. The ideas are presented within a medieval, orthodox structure of belief that admits no debate and was unlikely to inspire a non-believer.

The second area of weakness in the play is the playwright's inability to focus on the main issues involved. She distracts attention from important points by her faulty sense of humour, which leads her to mix comic and serious elements with great uncertainty. The first entry of Mephistopheles is, for instance, ludicrous rather than terrifying and, at the dreadful moment when Faustus embraces the power of evil, Mephistopheles calls to Lucifer:

> You may turn off the lights and put the cat out
> And shut the door and go downstairs to bed.
> I shall not be home for supper. (p.14)

Miss Sayers's wit is very feeble and quickly becomes irritating; there is a great deal of playful banter in the dialogue which fails to advance the action.

The appearance of the small black dog representing the soul of Faustus was a special kind of disaster (see Figure 21). The local press found the use of a live spaniel in very bad taste and it is difficult to imagine how the play could recover from the sense of embarrassed amusement caused by its appearance. The use of the dog had been prepared for earlier in the play when Mephistopheles informs Azrael that instead of primal innocence Faustus has attained primitive brutishness; and again when Faustus behaves like a dog and Mephistopheles treats him as one after the appearance of the Pope's phantom. Dorothy Sayers explained the significance of the dog in her essay *The Faust Legend*, "His soul becomes the soul of an animal, knowing neither good nor evil."[19] But the representation of this idea in the form Sayers chose lacked sensitivity to a dramatic situation and she succeeded only in creating something ridiculous at a serious moment in the play. In the course of the action it is extremely doubtful if the significance of the dog was realised by the audience.

Finally, the language of the play is disappointing. In some respects the play is simply a bad pastiche of Marlowe with additional material from Shakespeare. When, for example, Faustus first sees Helen he exclaims:

> O wonder of the world! O soul! O beauty
> Beyond all splendour of stars!   (p.19)

Which is a feeble imitation of Marlowe's:

> O, thou art fairer than the evening air
> Clad in the beauty of a thousand stars.

Faustus, surveying the suffering world, uses words obviously adapted from the Duke of Burgundy's speech about France in Act V, Scene Two of *Henry V*:

> God's old realm,
> Like an estate farmed by a bankrupt, dwindles
> The sluggard way to ruin; her rank hedgerows
> Drop down their brambles over the sour ditch;
> Bindweed, tough tares, and tangling restharrow choke
> Her furrows, where the plough stands idle, rust
> Reddening the share;   (p.11)

Faustus's last mortal words are "O, I am slain!" (p.49) and Wagner speaks his final lines as if he were rounding-off an Elizabethan scene:

> This thy golden dream
> Shall dwell with me; and I will be thine heir,
> Hoping that hope may yet outdo despair.   (p.19)

At times, Sayers handles the verse with some skill, such as when the characters on stage comment on the unseen battle:

Secretary: No, they give ground!
Empress: Locked to and fro they sway -
Emperor: They are repulsed again.
Chancellor: The town's defenders
Make sortie through the breach.
Faustus sweeps the world for his vision:
Up winds, and send the echo! Let us hear
The terrible voice, the glorious voice of war. (p. 17)

and Mephistopheles invokes the images of the hell of which war is a part:

. . . the inky Styx
Bubbling about their feet: bogs of delusion
Snare them about.   (pp. 44-45)

The verse reaches an alliterative climax as,

A monstrous mine
Bursts in the breach, and blows them all to pieces!
Arms, bodies, stone and fragments, nightmare faces,
And shattered engines tumbled together, falling -   (p.19)

In addition to such energetic verse, Dorothy Sayers can also produce the memorable image. As Helen, gliding with deceptive beauty, comes onto the stage for the last time, Mephistopheles speaks to the accompaniment of unearthly music:

The sun is fled, and darkness folds the earth
Like the chill shade that steals before the eclipse.   (p.47)

But far too often the imagery is contrived and fails to strike by its aptness or originality and when Faustus tries to express his eternal devotion to Helen, he can only manage a blend of Burns and Stephano!

Not till the seas run dry; not till the centre
Kiss the circumference, and time's iron hand
Crack the great axle of the world asunder!
O Helen, Helen, Helen, I have loved thee
Before time was.   (p.29)

The verse of *The Devil to Pay* blends poorly with the colloquial prose. Generally, the verse is reserved for Faustus's great statements and his dealings with Mephistopheles and Helen, whereas the servants converse in prose. Where the supernatural is involved, verse is used and the entire final scene is also conducted in verse. A major weakness of the dialogue is the excess of attempted humour, but the transitions from verse to prose often jar badly and serve no useful dramatic purpose. In style, language and subject matter, *The Devil to Pay* was therefore a strange exercise in archaeology that failed to fulfil the promise of *The Zeal of Thy House*; it was simply a re-working of old material and the public made their judgement clear by allowing it only a brief run in the London theatre.

Notes to Chapter 10

1. E. Martin Browne, *'The Devil to Pay'*, Canterbury Cathedral Chronicle XXXIII (1939), 16.

2. Dorothy L. Sayers, *'The Devil to Pay'*, Canterbury Cathedral Chronicle XXXII (1939), 12.

3. All page references are to Dorothy L. Sayers, *The Devil to Pay* (Acting Edition for the Friends of Canterbury Cathedral, Canterbury 1939).

4. *cp.* above, p. 222.

5. Dorothy L. Sayers, 'The Faust Legend', *The Poetry of Search and the Poetry of Statement* (London 1963), 229.

6. *loc. cit.*, 227.

7. *'The Devil to Pay'*, *Kentish Observer*, 16th June 1939.

8/9/10/11. D. L. Sayers, 'The Faust Legend', *op. cit.*, 229, 228, 230, 238.

12/13. Dorothy L. Sayers, *'The Devil to Pay'*, *loc. cit.*, 11.

14. Dorothy L. Sayers, *'The Faust Legend'*, *op. cit.*, 239.

15. Dorothy L. Sayers, *'The Devil to Pay'*, *loc. cit.*, 11.

16/17/18. Dorothy L. Sayers *'The Faust Legend'*, *op. cit.*, 238.

Part V

Two Post-War
Canterbury Plays

11

Peasants' Priest

The first play to be produced at a Canterbury Festival after World War II was Laurie Lee's *Peasants' Priest* which was given eight performances in the Chapter House between 21st and 28th June 1947. Inevitably, after a lapse of seven years, the event aroused some nostalgia and *The Times* wrote:

The sun shone and visitors were clearly happy to be once again on a pilgrimage which memory had cherished during its wartime suspension.[1]

The choice of play, however, reflected Laurence Irving's continued determination to encourage new writers of verse plays.

Laurie Lee was neither a well-known national or local literary figure. His first collection of poems had appeared in 1944 and during the war he had worked unobtrusively as a documentary filmscript writer for the GPO film unit and for the Ministry of Information. In 1946, he had written a successful radio play, *The Voyage of Magellan*, and as a result was invited to write a play for the Canterbury Festival. [2]

Peasants' Priest was in some ways the least successful of all the Canterbury plays: it has never been performed again and the author has not written another play since. Indeed, Laurie Lee was particularly unhappy about the whole venture, as he explained in a letter to me:

I chose the subject, but it was written under stress and with lack of conviction. It was also sadly derivative of verse plays of that period. I was inhibited by the thought of Canterbury and the Chapter House and tried to produce what I thought they expected.

Quite rightly, it was not well-received. I do not include it in my list of 'authors works'; I would not allow it to be revived: and I do my best to forget it. I hope you will oblige me by trying to forget it too.[3]

Lee's attitude to *Peasants' Priest* is understandable because, in a number of ways, he experienced major problems both in the writing and the production of the play. Lee was still suffering from a recurrent tropical illness and this greatly hampered his progress.[4] The result was that the script was not ready by the printer's deadline, so the cast not only had to use a hastily prepared typescript, but were also allowed insufficient time for rehearsal. The usual Acting Edition was eventually published in time for purchase by the audience, but this did not contain the revisions to the script that were found necessary during rehearsals. Regrettably, the consultations between producer and playwright, that had become a feature of the Canterbury plays, never took place. The typescript, on which I shall base my account of the play, therefore contains a number of additional lines and re-allocation of speeches that are entirely the work of the producer, E. Martin Browne.[5]

A second problem was the absence, in 1947, of all but two of the local actors who had taken part in previous Chapter House productions. In an address to the Friends, Laurence Irving reminded his audience:

With the example of the few faithful professionals and the training by visiting producers, our Canterbury amateurs became more and more accomplished and well-versed in the idiom peculiar to our Chapter House plays.[6]

But for *Peasants' Priest* a cast had to be assembled from a variety of sources. It included some of the Pilgrim Players, the touring company founded by E. Martin Browne;[7] pupils from the King's School; soldiers from Canterbury barracks; and the well-known actor Bernard Miles.[8] Under the normal conditions that had existed at Canterbury before the war it was possible to weld such a varied collection of individuals into an efficient cast - Masefield had demonstrated this brilliantly. But on this occasion, the short time available and the lack of experience in verse drama of many of the cast, created impossible demands on the producer.

Figure 23: The opening scene. Setting by Harald Melvill.
Peasants' Priest (1947).

261

To add to E. Martin Browne's difficulties, the permanent setting devised by Irving had been destroyed by bombing during the war and there was no money to pay for a replacement. All that was available was the simple platform erected at one end of the Chapter House, but *The Times* noted that the producer made "ingenious use of tapestries on the stage beneath the bomb-damaged East Window".[9] The "tapestries" were cheap fabric, skilfully painted to provide a number of evocative backcloths by Harald Melvill, one of the foremost exponents of design for small theatres.[10] The backcloths, however, provided no effective side entrances as Irving's screens had done and conditions were extremely cramped.

Undoubtedly, Laurie Lee was hampered by the notion that there was a particular idiom appropriate for a Canterbury play and, although this may have been conveyed to him unintentionally, he was clearly uneasy about the existence of a tradition that he had to preserve. He had neither the experience as a playwright nor the opportunity for consultation that would have helped him to overcome his inhibitions and the unsatisfactory production of his play merely added to his sense of frustration. This is particularly unfortunate, for the play's reception by the critics was by no means as hostile as he has since suggested and *Peasants' Priest*, though obviously unpolished, is a work of considerable originality and promise that stands out brightly against the backdrop of dreary verse plays of the same period with such unpromising titles as *This Way to the Tomb*.

For the theme of his play, Lee returned to an event in the history of Canterbury: the peasants' uprising of 1381, which took place when Simon Sudbury was Archbishop. The play focuses attention on the priest, John Balle, who shared the leadership of the revolt with Wat Tyler and inspired the peasants by his preaching of a classless society. Wat Tyler's rebellion had been the subject of two previous plays: Southey's *Wat Tyler* (1817), described by Allardyce Nicoll as "an unfortunate mistake on the part of a very young man",[11] and the melodrama *Wat Tyler and Jack Straw* by "R. A." (1834). The story continued to attract writers who, like Southey, had socialistic ideas and Laurie Lee may well have used William Morris's *The Dream of John Ball* (1888) as a source. In 1972, the Half Moon

Theatre group, an ensemble with a strong socialistic commitment, presented another play on the same theme: Steve Gooch's *Will Wat? If Not, What Will?*

Peasants' Priest is certainly more concerned with the social and behavioural consequences of Christian belief than with worship and the play has no liturgical content or any resemblance to a Morality. It is really a series of dramatic fragments linked by the words of the chorus. The six scenes, of roughly equal length, show different stages of the peasants' uprising, from its secret beginnings to its failure, and each is set in a new location. The action of the scenes is naturalistic in intention, though the characters speak in verse, but important events are presumed to have taken place between the scenes and these are reported by the chorus or by the characters themselves.

The first scene shows the growing discontent amongst the English peasantry coalescing into organised rebellion, inspired by the egalitarian preaching of John Balle. These themes are suggested by the conversation of three main characters: Barfoot, Skelp and Flint and the location is a Kentish Forest.

Barfoot, an escaped serf, is surprised as he crawls through the woods by the two outlaws, Skelp and Flint. Quickly Barfoot drops his aggressive front when he realises that he is among friends and explains to the inquisitive outlaws how he came to run away. Gratefully he accepts some food and is assured of support by Skelp's "you have run to the right place, we've need of your kind". He expounds his discontent and makes the first mention of the "preaching priest" (p.4).

There are several, stark reminders that the action of the play is set during the period when the effects of the bubonic plague were making terrible inroads into peasant life throughout Britain and Europe. The most powerful of these occurs when the action is punctuated by the ringing of a plague bell; but this is being used as a secret signal to inform the peasants of further support and the scene ends with the peasants running to Canterbury.

The second scene is unquestionably the finest in the play:

The play is most alive when priest and priest, Balle with his burning sense of social injustice, and the orthodox Friar, clash in bitter argument.

wrote *The Times*.[12] The Friar is Balle's jailor and the scene takes place in a cell in Maidstone Jail. During the dispute between the two priests, Balle sets out clearly the ideas that lie behind the peasants' grievances, whereas the Friar represents the views of the privileged classes. The most startling moment comes when the Friar tells Balle that it would take a miracle to make him accept Balle's ideas. Balle, obviously aware that his rescuers are at hand, times the entrance of Flint, Skelp and Barfoot to seem like a miracle.

Balle's rescuers tell him that Maidstone, where he is imprisoned, has fallen to the peasants and the Mayor has sworn for the Commons and King Richard. Dartford and Canterbury have been captured, the Archbishop fled to London and his house smashed. Wat Tyler is the "leading sword" and Balle is to be "the sceptre".

The whole of Scene Three is located in the Tower of London. The impatient Earl of Kent laments to Mayor Walworth the lack of fight which has driven them to virtual imprisonment. No news filters through the advancing ranks of peasants; the boy King Richard is at a loss to know the best course of action. Kent's only solution is to meet the rebels with force of arms but Walworth councils patience. The time is not ripe for reprisal, it would be futile anyway for the peasants are too strong.

Young Richard (played at Canterbury by a schoolboy, Neil North, who became a successful professional actor) is desperately anxious about his mother who had undertaken a pilgrimage and not yet returned. He is unable to listen to Kent's dramatic description of the country's plight which "like a storm-hit raft/Is overturned" and dismisses both Kent and Walworth to find information of his mother's fate. The King's mother, however, appears almost at once. The Black Prince's widow recovers her composure, after a moving reunion with her son and, in replying to his enquiries, gives a graphic account of her experiences during her pilgrimage to her husband's tomb at Canterbury. *The Times* records the impact of the speech at the first performance: "Miss Josephine Wilson, as the Black Princess, describes a hazardous journey through the rebels' encampment with a fine vivacity".[13] *Punch* also commented on Josephine Wilson's performance.[14]

Figure 24: Douglas Wilmer as Salisbury, Neil North as Richard II,
Josephine Wilson as the Black Princess. *Peasants' Priest* (1947).

Scene Four takes place on Blackheath where, separated from the city by the "neutral river", the peasants await the promised appearance of the King. Already the delaying tactics employed by Richard and his advisers are having their effect for, as Skelp, Flint, Barfoot and Bowman gather around the Banner of St George, they calculate that only one more day of hunger can be endured before the impetus is lost. With tempting smells of the city and its luxuries vivid in their imaginations, the peasants are in danger of losing sight of their original objectives. Impatiently, they wait for Balle to give them further inspiration. The mid-point of the play, as in *Murder in the Cathedral*, is a sermon. Balle's exhortation to the peasants to achieve equality and freedom with mercy and without unnecessary violence occupies most of this scene after the preliminary discussion amongst Skelp and his friends.

Scene Five shows Richard in consultation with Salisbury, Kent, Archbishop Sudbury, Mayor Walworth and Treasurer Hales in the Tower. By reference in the discussions a considerable amount of detail of the actual historical events emerges: London is on fire, the particular targets for the rebels' ire blaze fiercest - Hales's house, John of Gaunt's Savoy Palace, the Inns of Court. Traitors have opened London Bridge to the peasants of Kent; others from Essex have taken Aldgate. Now wandering the streets in amazement, the peasants are under orders not to loot and have behaved with considerable discipline. They have camped on Tower Hill and are calling for the death of Hales and Sudbury. The most poignant part of the play occurs towards the end of this scene. The callous and unscrupulous Walworth suggests that, while the King should accept Salisbury's plan and ride out to meet the rebels with false promises, Archbishop Sudbury and Treasurer Hales should be left to satisfy the rebels' desire for blood. Laurie Lee directs that "*All look at Hales and Sudbury*" and then, with cruel irony, Richard asks that all kneel to receive the Archbishop's blessing.

When the Archbishop and Hales are left alone on the stage, with the mob's cries clearly audible, Sudbury declares with moving simplicity that death would be no stranger to him: he has been spiritually dead for years. As Hales kneels to receive the last rites, the shouting outside becomes distinguishable as taunts and threats.

PEASANTS' PRIEST

There is no hope of escape and (for the fifth time in a Canterbury performance) an Archbishop goes to his death, walking with Hales towards the insistent voices.

For the final scene, Lee shows the events in a tavern after the meeting at Mile End between the peasants and the King. The historical fact is that the outcome *was* an anti-climax and the playwright can claim some justification for ending the play in this way. Flint, celebrating his new liberty with a wineskin as companion, speaks enthusiastic prose through a haze of drink. Clutching the deed of liberation from bondage that every peasant has received from the King, he announces himself as one of the Great Company. The barmaid is not impressed because she has seen the murder of clerks and Flemings which has tarnished the peasants' record of mercy.[15] There is already a sense of sourness in the success of the peasants; but worse is to come.

Skelp, Barfoot and Bowman enter the tavern in great agitation and lay the lifeless body of Wat Tyler on the floor. The victory which Flint had stolen away prematurely to celebrate, is lost, the peasants are leaderless in battle, the Lords are scattering them and rounding up the ringleaders. Speculation as to the fate of Balle does not last long, for as the peasants stare in dismay at one dead leader and pray for the safety of the other, the peasants' priest knocks at the door.

Balle insists that the peasants should not look upon their defeat as final nor their efforts as wasted and he sends them away to hide the body of Tyler and then find their own safety. Balle is finally alone on the stage. For a few moments Balle ruminates on what has been achieved: he senses the end is near but he knows that for a brief while he has helped create a vision of heaven on earth. "Like foxes creeping from our holes" the uprising of the peasants has made a point which cannot be ignored and now they must return to dark-ness until faith strengthens them for another attempt. Soldiers then arrive and Balle, the peasants' priest, is taken away. The play ends with a simple couplet:

Rebellion's bread was leavened by this yeast;
Take him away, he was the peasants' priest.   (p.55)

267

Figure 25: John Balle (Bernard Miles) with the body of Wat Tyler.
Peasants' Priest (1947).

Linking the scenes are two chorus figures: a black-robed figure wearing a yellow tragic mask and a red-robed figure with a green comic mask.[16] Before each scene these figures provide an evocative introduction to the setting and universalise the significance of the action. Whilst providing essential information for the understanding of the play, they also create an atmosphere in which the action can take place. Lee's use of the Chorus compensates for the absence of scenery but, unlike the various chorus figures in previous Canterbury plays, the figures take no part in the action of the play and their contribution constitutes a number of interludes. The choric verse is spoken antiphonally by the two masked figures; there are similarities with the ritual qualities of Yeats's *Plays for Dancers* and, perhaps, some echoes of Eliot's *Four Quartets* as the speakers begin:

> It was yesterday, it was today,
> A black winter and a red summer;
> A blackened death, a crimson birth:
> It was today, and yesterday. (p.1)

The masked figures never attempt, however, to create a ritual; they constantly remind the audience that they are to witness a play of real events with universal significance:

> Behind the mask my visage sweats,
> Behind the play the flesh already breathes. (p.1)

As the masked figures introduce the scenes, they comment on man's activities, remaining detached and inviting the audience to consider the events and their significance, dispassionately. When the peasants march on London and set fire to some of the buildings the Chorus remarks:

> All this we've seen before.
> What scarlet cities, lost Jerusalems,
> Were razed and broke to raise some buried God
> Whose tomb was found already robbed and bare. (p.37)

No particular doctrinal position is suggested, the deeds of men are shown as falling short of the ideals of individual compassion and mercy and so, time and again,

> the dream was God's, the deed the Devil's.

The most interesting feature of Laurie Lee's Chorus is the quality of the verse and a comment in *The Times* suggests that it was the

Chorus verse which made the strongest impression in performance:

> Mr Lee's blank verse is vivid, but descriptive rather than dramatic ...
> There is some excellent descriptive verse. It is admirably spoken ...[17]

The language of the Chorus shows Lee's ability to create what Stephen Spender described as "a sharp, sunlit impression ... almost untouched by thought."[18] The verse is at its finest when the Chorus establishes the scene:

> The bearded trees are gods,
> The sun is dark.
> To this green gloom,
> The mind's mediaeval web,
> There comes a man,
> Half-beast, half angel . . .   (p.2)

Or when Yellow Mask comments on the aftermath of the revolt:

> Now the dawn wind blows powdered night away,
> The rich sun drips from summer's heavy husk,
> And night's delirium ends.   (p.46)

Such lines are not only rich in imagery and superbly atmospheric, they are just as dramatic as they are descriptive and serve the same purpose as,

> Now entertain conjecture of a time
> When creeping murmur and the poring dark
> Fills the wide vessel of the universe.   (*Henry V*, Act III, Sc. 6)

especially when spoken on a bare stage. Sometimes Lee's Chorus suggests the movement and rhythm of larger forces than can be contained on the stage:

> There they go in all their merry buzz,
> Leaping to feel the wind sing in their ears . . .
> But look again at what the city shows.   (p.37)

Laurie Lee achieves this "clear and unpretentious verse"[19] in short stanzas loosely based on four or five major stresses to the line. The verse is sometimes, though never obtrusively, alliterative and consistently avoids archaism.

By contrast, the dialogue of the scenes generally consists of fairly long speeches and there are few quick interjections or sudden responses. Like the Chorus, however, there is a suggestion of the iambic, five-foot line as the prevailing mode, though this never obtrudes. As in the choric verse, Lee prefers the brief image or sudden emphasis of alliteration to achieve effect:

Great roots and bogs whose scrubby pits and traps
Have thrown me on my face these fifty hours.
A very fiend of forests! (p.6)

A more striking example of the use of alliteration occurs when King Richard is ruminating what disaster has overcome his mother, "murdered with her maids" or "piked on a pole". The speech with which the princess describes her journey is equally vivid in impact, it is a marvellous tapestry of impressions: great halls and abbeys ablaze; "monks flying like crows into the woods"; heads upon posts; peasants marching and leaping onto the wagon asking for a kiss from the Black Prince's widow; crude weapons; deserted fields; unforgettable faces; and simple loyalty to the crown.

Inevitably perhaps John Balle's famous couplet:

When Adam delved and Eve span
Who was then the gentleman. (p.34)

is woven into the fabric of his longest speech in the play, but the verse is never simply derivative and it always carries the argument of the play forward; although the peasants are clearly far too articulate, the language throughout the action does give the impression of real conversation.

The language of the *Peasants' Priest* is totally lacking in display for its own sake; there is no attempt at a grand style and it demands sensitive, rather than declamatory, speaking. Unfortunately, the only critical comment on the verse that has appeared since the original press reports is J. C. Trewin's inept observation that masquerades as a definitive statement: ". . . it wants heat and light and sound, the trinity without which a poet's play must inevitably collapse."[20] Trewin, an admirer of Stephen Phillips and a devotee of Masefield's "loveliness", could hardly be expected to find Lee's restrained and uncomplicated verse to his taste.[21] Trewin certainly failed to recognise that *Peasants' Priest* probably came nearer than any other post-war play to establishing a successful type of modern dramatic verse; an achievement largely overshadowed by Christopher Fry's superficial verbiage.

The main theme of *Peasants' Priest* is John Balle's fight against social injustice based on his belief in the equality of man. Balle himself does not appear until the second scene of the play, but in the first scene Lee provides a detailed picture of the social inequality that has led to deep discontent among the peasants and suggests the effect of John Balle's preaching. There are two particularly effective statements of the peasants' grievances in Scene One: the first is made by Barfoot who contrasts the luxurious lifestyle of the master from whom he has escaped with the wretched condition of the serfs who, under the feudal system, are bound to their master by birth. While Barfoot describes his own condition as:

> Cracking our winter's teeth on cricket's meat
> Or sharing roots with sheep, (p.5)

he describes his former master as:

> A man so sick with evil
> He kept a dozen friars to shrive him daily.
> His very dogs wore silk, were diamonded,
> and nibbled peaches from his milky hands. (p.5)

When Skelp and Flint recognise in Barfoot a recruit to their cause, they join together to establish the reasons for their intended rebellion in a series of antiphonal speeches.

> **Flint:** Look to our masters. Look to their estates,
> Castle and abbey, hall and monastery,
> Like bulging clippers, stuffed with meat and cloth,
> Sailing the hungry land.
> **Skelp:** Look to the fattened fathers of our church,
> Bowing the bloody dukes, forgetting Him
> Their just and holy Master.
> **Flint:** And those red friars that peddle asses' bones
> And call them saints;
> That shrive the rich of murder for a pension,
> Pay pardons for a dinner,
> And drag our wenches with their double talk
> Into a devil's ditch of lechery!
> **Skelp:** Look to those Abbots who keep men in bond
> To bear them capons, cream and honey butter,
> While they, poor peasants, bite upon a husk
> And starve their souls of promises of heaven. (p.8)

This very clear and powerful statement forms the background against which the other scenes are played and is recalled especially in the scene where the King consults Kent, Walworth, Sudbury and Salisbury as to his best course of action. Kent and Walworth, inevitably, recommend violence, arguing that the peasants will soon be drunk and drowsy and could easily be taken by surprise. Salisbury dismisses the suggestion as a gross understatement of the peasants' discipline and purpose:

> They are the country hands of England,
> Joined in a solemn purpose to redress
> A list of ancient wrongs. (p.41)

He is forced to admit that there is justification for a well-ordered strategy behind the uprising. He observes especially how the peasants take no spoils but stoke the fires with "the deeds and rolls of advocates and clerks" - the symbols of serfdom and taxation.

Two main factors have taught the peasants to form ideas of equality and liberty: the plague, which has not discriminated between men; and Balle's preaching. The play contains two major scenes in which Balle's teaching and charismatic influence are seen at first hand. In Maidstone Jail, Balle is shown as a humble man, content with his dark prison and calm in the moment that would bring most men to despair. His sadness is reserved for the blindness and hypocrisy of his persecutors who are as much the Catholic Church as the corrupt State. Balle is formidable in argument, contemptuous of the idolatry and ritualistic trappings with which the Church has obscured the pure gospel of Christ and has used as a means of power and money-raising. With powerful insistence and colourful imagery he points to the malpractice of the monasteries, the pomp of popes and bishops and the Latin mumblings which pass for prayer.

Balle, for all his ruthless exposure of the corruption within the Church, does not lack compassion: he deplores its absence in his jailor, the Friar, whom he once knew as a sensitive boy. Christian compassion is the basis of his gospel. He sees the Kingdom of Heaven on earth as a society without hatred or class. The Word of God, he maintains, was first preached to the peasant, and it is in

273

spite of, not because of, the Church that it survives and still has the power to change the world.

The Friar, on the other hand, lacking Balle's eloquence and intellectual bite, can afford to ignore Balle's social gospel because he is convinced of his heresy. Arrogant and unable to see that Balle outmanoeuvres him at almost every turn, he takes refuge behind the "Pope's instruction" and plods remorselessly on with the jargon of damnation. Once he is nearly overwhelmed by Balle's passionate plea for the restoration of the essential gospel of Christ to the central position in the life of the Church, and he cries "Stop! Stop!" But the idea that he should join in declaring,

Christ's Kingdom new,
Where each is free, each serf Christ's son,
Each pope a peasant and each peasant pope!   (p.15)

is too much for him and he reverts to seeing only hatred and heresy in Balle's words and, as he hardens his position, will not even face the truth of Balle's criticisms of monastic life.

Unlike Balle, who sees every man as equal, the Friar maintains that his prayers carry greater weight than a peasant's for "by life and dedication" he is "dearer to God than ordinary men". Similarly, he justifies the sale of relics to the simple and ignorant as merely the activity of sheepdogs driving a foolish flock into position. He cannot hide his essential class-consciousness for long and appears to despise Balle more for his dealings with the peasantry than for the content of his preaching.

The most impressive feature of the scene is the sheer energy of Balle's language, the colour and nimbleness with which he conveys the essential simplicity of his message. He is quick to acknowledge a point from his opponent, but his main device is to turn the Friar's own words against him. For example, as the Friar mocks Balle with the security of the dungeon,

Friar: If your men come, then Glory be,
They must move Heaven and earth to get you free.
Balle: If heaven has moved them brother,
T'will not be hard for them to move the earth.

or the Friar declares his awareness of heresy:

Friar: Also I've here the image of Our Lord,
New blest, whose wounds weep actual blood
When faced before a fiend.
Balle: Also you've there the image of a man
Whose eyes should weep to look upon that Christ
Whose wounds you friars betray!   (pp.13-14)

Balle is not beyond combining this devise with powerful scorn:

Prayer! What do you know of prayer?
The supplication on a rustic's lip,
Muttered to stone or spirit,
Lies to Christ's ear with more directness
Than all your ordered groans.
Think you your doggerel Latin bears
A greater weight than his unlettered cry?   (p.16)

An equally impressive, though more orthodox display of Balle's verbal skill is given in his address to the peasants on Blackheath. Balle's sermon, delivered with considerable power by Bernard Miles at Canterbury,[22] has some of the resonance and form of the preaching of Jesus in the thirteenth play of the *Chester Cycle*. It moves from idealistic statement "Brothers! you are the sons of heaven", through the grief of the preacher

O mortal exiled flesh
What evil has been done to you!

to the colourful declarations and repeated rhetorical questions, which include the famous couplet (pp. 34-35). Then Balle moves on to more explicit statements concerning the brotherhood of man and ends by challenging the peasants to respond in action. He delivers a final exhortation with: "let no man stand alone!" and the peasants erupt into cheers as a rebel runs in to announce that London Bridge has been taken and Wat Tyler had ordered the march to begin.

After this climax Balle remains for a moment and, slowly crossing himself, wonders how many of his words will have been in vain. Lee provides a similar glimpse of Balle's quiet resignation at the end of the play. He is left alone with the girl who urges him to hide; she becomes a temptress, describing the horrors of the torture he will surely face; challenging him to confess his heresy; and, when these fail, offering herself as an end to celibacy and

275

priesthood. But Balle cannot now be deflected from martyrdom. The sufferings of Christ have taught him the way to life, to discount the flesh and save the soul. The Church is nothing but a body of men and women, it is not a thing which can "call us outcast" for it is composed of us. Balle's activities have taken too many to the grave; he cannot take the girl to further burden his conscience. Gently, he sends her away.

The sympathetic view of the peasants and of Balle's ideas that is shown in Lee's play is contrasted with the duplicity and malice of the ruling classes. Salisbury's answer to the problem of rebellion has a familiar ring in international and industrial relations:

They ask for stars, we'll give them paper stars.
All this costs nothing. What we give
We can take back again,
In easier times. . .   (p.42)

Peasants' Priest does not contain specific social comment but it is certainly there by implication. It is in this respect, particularly, that Lee's play differs from all the other Canterbury plays: there is no spiritual journey for the protagonist or devotional ending; there is, instead, a simple but effective statement of the brotherhood of man as a direct consequence of the fatherhood of God.

This complete change of approach by a Canterbury dramatist was, no doubt, partly responsible for the rather lukewarm reception given to the *Peasants' Priest* by the Friends, a rather right-wing body who, like the Chapter, were frequently in dispute with the so-called "Red Dean", the socialist Dr Hewlett Johnson (Dean of Canterbury, 1931-1963). Nevertheless, there is sufficient, obvious potential in the existing text of *Peasants' Priest* to leave one wishing that, almost alone amongst Canterbury dramatists, Laurie Lee had been given another and better opportunity to write a play.

Notes to Chapter 11

1. 'Review of *Peasants' Priest*', *The Times*, Monday June 23rd 1947, 6.
2. I. R. Willison, ed., *The New Cambridge Bibliography of English Literature* (Cambridge 1972) IV, gives 1948 as the date of the broadcast of *The Voyage of Magellan*, but Laurie Lee in a letter to me dated 16. ii. 76, says he "had written a successful radio play the year before", i.e. 1946.
3. Letter to K. W. Pickering 16. ii. 76.
4. See 'The Address by Mr L. Irving at the gathering in the Chapter House, 28th June 1947', *Canterbury Cathedral Chronicle* XLII (1947), 17-20.
5. All page references are to the typescript produced by May Hemery Ltd, (London 1947). Pencilled additions appear in all copies. Gouldens published the usual Acting Edition.
6. 'The Address by Mr Laurence Irving' *loc. cit.,* 18.
7. See above, p. 111.
8. See Appendix.
9. The *Times, loc. cit.,* 6.
10. See Appendix & Figures 22 and 23.
11. Allardyce Nicoll, *A History of English Drama IV: Early Nineteenth Century Drama* (Cambridge 1955), 102.
12/13. The *Times, loc. cit.,* 6.
14. 'Review of *Peasants' Priest*', *Punch,* July 2nd 1947.
15. The Flemings, introduced into England during Edward III's reign to advise on the wool trade, were a particular target of prejudice and hatred.
16. E. Martin Browne played the part of Green Mask.
17. The *Times, loc. cit.,* 6.
18. Quoted in J. Wakeman, ed., *World Authors 1950-1970* (NY 1975), 849.
19. 'Review of *Peasants' Priest*', *Punch* July 2nd 1947.
20. J. C. Trewin, *We'll Hear A Play* (London 1949), 90. Also quoted in D. Donoghue, *The Third Voice* (Princeton 1959), 138.
21. See above, p. 56.
22. The *Times, loc. cit.,* 6.

12

Thor, with Angels

Christopher Fry was invited to write the Canterbury Festival play for 1948 and he responded with *Thor, with Angels*, the last new play to be performed in the Chapter House until 1951. Fry was an obvious choice for, by 1948, he was established as a well-known, Christian verse-dramatist with nine previous plays to his credit. Of these, *The Boy with a Cart* (1939), *A Phoenix Too Frequent* (1946), *The First-born* (1946) and *The Lady's Not for Burning* (1948) had brought him a considerable reputation in the commercial theatre and Fry was generally being hailed as a new and exciting talent. Furthermore, Fry had already co-operated with E. Martin Browne by writing a play for the Tewkesbury Festival and had had early associations with George Bell and therefore the Friends, no doubt, had every confidence in turning to him.[1]

Since the play was specially written for the Festival, it was not surprising that Fry chose material that centred on Canterbury. *Thor, with Angels* fits into the general scheme of Canterbury history plays and initiates a story which is continued in *Becket* and *Murder in the Cathedral, Cranmer of Canterbury, Peasants' Priest, The Young King* and *The Zeal of Thy House*.[2] By selecting material from a period before the appointment of the first archbishop, Fry was able to concentrate on more primitive and basic Christian ideas,

278

rather than on issues specific to Canterbury or to the Anglican communion. There is no clear evidence as to what sources Fry used, but it seems likely that he derived the main idea from Bede's *Ecclesiastical History of the English People*. The play is set in the sixth century,

> in and around a Jutish farmstead on the site of Canterbury, in late winter weather and a desolate landscape, where the old Christian churches, built in the time of the Roman occupation, have become pagan temples, and Thor and Woden ride about in the hollow skies.[3]

King Ethelbert of Kent, the most powerful king in England, had, however, married Bertha, the Christian daughter of a Frankish ruler. Queen Bertha had been permitted to bring her own priest to England and she had ordered the restoration of St Martin's Church, which still stands in Canterbury, the oldest church in England in which Christian worship has been continuously offered. When Pope Gregory sent Augustine to England, the situation was less hostile than he feared. Augustine was received by Ethelbert and Bertha and the spread of Christianity was rapid. It was from these events that the Cathedral at Canterbury came into being. These events are recorded in Bede.

No doubt Fry wanted his play to have special relevance to Canterbury, but the result was not entirely satisfactory. The reference to the play's setting in Canterbury and to the arrival of St Augustine are so marginal as to seem contrived and dispensable. It is possible that Fry was distracted by a concern to make the play suitable for production elsewhere, for all the characters are imaginary and the action could have taken place almost anywhere. As it proved in practice, the setting of *Thor, with Angels* was one of the weaknesses of its first production as it was completely out of keeping with the Chapter House stage. Fry directed that the scen-ery should depict a number of farm buildings and trees and Harald Melvill accordingly designed and built a realistic setting. Not only did this look absurd on the small stage and in its ecclesiastical surroundings, it also posed great difficulties of construction. The absence of any permanent arrangement for fixing scenery in position meant that a series of ugly and incongruous wires had to be stretched across the stage to provide rigidity for the set.

Figure 26: Taken during rehearsal. *Thor, with Angels* (1948).

Fry, an experienced producer, directed the play at Canterbury with an almost entirely professional cast. Most of the cast were newcomers to the Festival but it included Frank Napier, the veteran actor from the Old Vic who had appeared in the plays of Eliot, Williams and Dorothy Sayers, both in the Chapter House and any subsequent productions.[4] The part of Colgrin, the old steward, was played by the radio actor Norman Chidgey whose voice became familiar to thousands in the popular *Mrs Dale's Diary*.

Thor, with Angels was first published at Canterbury in an Acting Edition and was re-issued unaltered by the Oxford University Press in 1949. Not surprisingly, Fry made no cuts in his text for performance,[5] but *Thor, with Angels* is the shortest and simplest in form of all the Canterbury plays. It consists of one act and the action is continuous; the events shown take place in a single day, though the play opens in winter and ends with the coming of spring, thus emphasising the passage of time.

In keeping with a tradition at Canterbury, the programme for the Festival contained 'The Argument of the Play' and Fry himself contributed this summary of the action:

An old steward is asleep in a barn, supposed to be guarding the household against surprisal while the menfolk are away fighting King Ceaulin and his West Saxons. Now they return after a long night's march, Cymen (the head of the family), his sons and his brothers-in-law all in a disagreeable mood, for not only have they been defeated in battle, but Cymen has been the victim of an attack by some supernatural will which drove him to rescue a British slave who was fighting for the West Saxons. He brings the Briton back with him as a prisoner, and the brothers-in-law believe that their defeat is due to this incomprehensible action. Cymen is alarmed by the violence of the mood of mercy which came upon him unexpectedly in mid-battle, and when the morning sun at last breaks through the mist he is determined to become a good pagan again, to be accepted again by Thor and Woden, and raises his cup to drink a toast to the gods and the god-like sun; but the inexplicable spirit which ravages him twists his words to its own ends.[6]

At this point, Fry's résumé of the action acquires a less specific nature as he indicates the spiritual discoveries made by Cymen before and after the arrival of St Augustine. Fry obviously wished to conceal from his audience that the play culminates in the ritual killing of Hoel, the Briton, by crucifixion.

Judgement of *Thor, with Angels* is complicated now by the atmosphere of general critical hostility that has increasingly surrounded all of Fry's work. While it is sometimes conceded that Fry's plays had an exuberance that was welcomed in the years of post-war depression, Denis Donaghue's contention that "his permanent contribution to the theatre is likely to be slight" is probably typical of the prevailing view.[7] Eliot apart, the reputation of other Canterbury dramatists - Williams, Dorothy Sayers, Lee - rested mainly on their Festival plays; but Fry's work did attract very considerable attention during the forties and early fifties and extravagant claims were made for him, rather as they had been for Stephen Phillips. Great theatrical talents such as Gielgud, Olivier and Edith Evans helped to boost Fry's reputation by their performances in his plays, but his fame faded rapidly with the theatrical revolution of 1956 and after.[8]

J. L. Styan states clearly and fairly the need for, and the difficulties of, reaching a balanced evaluation of Fry's plays:

> Christopher Fry's work was doubtless overrated in the fruitful years of *The Lady's Not for Burning* and *A Sleep of Prisoners*; it is most certainly underrated today . . . It is as if Becket and the Theatre of the Absurd had not existed, nor Brecht . . . nor Osborne.[9]

Later Styan adds:

> Eliot notwithstanding, Fry's is the most sustained attempt in English to write an undogmatic Christian drama in modern times.[10]

One of the main reasons why much of Fry's work seems unacceptable today is that it depends upon the playwright's manipulation of a number of largely Christian ideas and symbols. This can be clearly seen in *Thor, with Angels* which was never one of Fry's most successful plays, though it was performed at the Lyric Theatre, Hammersmith, in 1951.

In *Thor, with Angels*, Fry examines the Christian ideas of love for the enemy and of "the nature of suffering and sacrifice".[11] The Jutes had come to Britain with Utopian visions; they had heard of the white villas and fertile valleys and risked their lives to conquer the land. Cymen's forefathers had:

... pitched themselves on the narrow, shuddering sea
To deal and duck death under the hanging chalk.   (p.9)
But their courage and ferocity had only been rewarded by the harsh
reality of cold mists, ruined buildings and the need to coax a living
from the soil. The mist, which surrounds and dampens the Jutes'
lives, is a persistent image in the first part of the play; it represents
the disillusionment of early dreams and the superstitions and hatred in which the characters flounder.

The desperate fight for survival and the moral darkness which
surrounds them, cause the Jutes to hate the former possessors of the
land - the Britons, their enemies. Their negation of the Christian
precept is total, understandable and familiar. Anna, Colgrin's wife,
states the position clearly, she is speaking of the Briton, Hoel:

> He's caused a lot of trouble
> Having to be conquered, and that's enough from him.
> I shall probably get to be fond of him, but I'll never
> Like him. It wouldn't be right if I did, when you think
> Of all our men who've been killed killing these heathen.   (p.16)

The cruelty of the Jutes is shown with considerable force; and
when the wolves come to rob the flock, their indiscriminate cruelty
is a parallel to the human behaviour of the Jutish warriors
Quichelm, Cheldric, Tadfrid and Osmer. The difference, however,
is that the humans try to justify their cruelty and hatred. Martina,
Cymen's daughter, who forms a sympathetic relationship with the
prisoner, tells Hoel that she is forced to hate him because he is a
Briton. She admits the blind prejudice of her attitude, and high-
lights its ab-surdity by saying that, had he been a Saxon, the warriors would still have been obliged to kill him - but "with consideration", thinking of him as a brother. Martina justifies this savagery
by pointing to the harshness of the existence which they all endure:

> We have existence on such hard terms,
> As though birth into the world had been a favour
> Instantly regretted.   (p.38)

But she comes much nearer to a perceptive comment on human
conduct when she observes that hatred is an act whereby men
maintain their self-esteem.

The Jutish conception of the gods as demanding and malevolent is merely an extension of their idea of human conduct. Woden and Thor apparently require constant appeasement by sacrifice; the initiative must always be made by man: the gods' cruelty must be satisfied by man's cruelty. When Cymen prays at the altar he refers to the insatiable appetites of the gods for sacrifice and suffering:

> The deed of death is done and done and always
> To do, death and death and death; and still
> We cannot come and stand between your knees.　　　(p.33)

But the results of sacrifice are only "despair and desperation" and the acts of cruelty (so constantly done in the name of religion) are made more dreadful for being, apparently, passionless.

When the warriors eventually determine to kill Hoel in Cymen's absence, their cold-heartedness is terrible:

> Let's not rage.
> We do what's demanded of us, with solemnity,
> Without passion.　　　(p.43)

The callous death ritual has already been foreshadowed by Tadfrid who claims that Hoel "died" at the moment when he earned death by killing a Jutish earl in the battle. All that remains is formality and ceremony. Even when Hoel saves the Jutes by killing the leader of the attacking wolves with his bare hands, his actions are interpreted as stemming from some evil power and the Jutish warriors are even more determined to sacrifice him.

The view of the gods represented in *Thor, with Angels* can be interpreted as a commentary on some crude, anthropomorphic Christian attitudes, particularly "blood theology". The crucifixion is not to be understood as a sacrifice made to placate God, angered by the world's sin. Nor is the idea of original sin, which estranges man from God, to be confused with the idea that men must for ever suffer for an act once committed: "They can't expect sons to carry the blame for fathers" says Quichelm, "Would they make us suffer because of our blood?" But Hoel seizes upon the danger of understanding God in terms of man's nature - "Yes", he replies, "Or from whose example would men have learnt that trick."

Fry never labours a theological point, normally being content to imply his message, but he does seem anxious in this play to present a clear interpretation of the vicarious sufferings of Christ. Cymen's gradual enlightenment involves an exploration of the necessity of suffering. His acts of mercy are contrasted sharply with the cruelty of the Jutes, whose theology totally lacks compassion. He is unable to account for his behaviour in the battle and claims that his sword was broken by a force of blinding light. Cymen is determined to discover the source of the light; the moment is re-echoed when the light of the sun falls on the spear which is about to kill Hoel.

The play moves from darkness towards light, from winter to spring and from hatred towards love. There are two particularly effective moments when Cymen moves suddenly nearer to the Truth. When he is refreshed by sleep after the battle, he feels his strength returning and he proposes his toast to the gods. The pagan toast becomes a figure of the last supper at which Christ gave his new commandment, "Love one another", for Cymen finds these words drawn involuntarily from his lips. In the confusion which follows this negation of pagan values, distinctions become blurred, man's differences have no consequence and Cymen nearly kills his own son. Fry wrote in his programme note:

From now on his soul is under the plough, being prepared for the sowing, which is to come towards the end of the play, with the land-ing of St Augustine. No-one can help him in his struggle against the spirit, not Clodesuida his wife, a devout and orthodox pagan, nor Martina his daughter, whose interest in the supernatural is one of popular superstition . . . [12]

The circumstances in which Cymen learns of the coming of Augustine provides the second highly dramatic twist in his search for the Truth. He kneels at the altar of the gods and challenges them to come down, but there is no answer and Cymen pulls the stones of the altar apart. In the horrified silence that follows, a distant cry calls Cymen's name. It is not the voice of the gods, but a messenger from King Ethelbert ordering his people to come and hear the preaching of Augustine. Cymen is determined to respond, he rejected the way of the gods when he first shouted in the battle "Let 'em learn of us", the still, small voice calls him to his new understanding:

> We're in the path
> Of change. And I must go to meet the change,
> Being unable to live unaltered.

His soul is prepared by the evidence of the power of love which burns in him; and in a rich image of the fierceness and beauty that awaits him, he goes to hear Augustine:

> I go to dare my arm into the thicket
> To know what lifts its head there, whether rose
> Or tiger, or tiger and rose together. (p.36)

Cymen's final understanding is expressed in his long speech when he returns to find Hoel dead, crucified by the Jutish warriors. In striking contrast with his speech at the altar, when he has speculated on the need for sacrifice, he now sees that the initiative has been taken by God. The perfect sacrifice has been made by God on the Cross. The act of reconciliation involved God entering human suffering, and man has only to accept God's grace. Cymen delivers his sermon-like speech with the crucified figure of Hoel behind him - this is a striking image.

Much of the Christian doctrine in the play is reinforced by the images and statements of Hoel and Merlin. God acts through Hoel though he is unaware of it. Hoel retains memories of Christianity and has been baptised, he remembers only that in the One God there are three - "Father, son and brooding dove", but his faith is too mingled with superstition to be effective. He is, however, the only character to have some sense of transcending the differences between men:

> What simple-witted things the affections are,
> That can't perceive whether people are enemies
> Or friends. (p.42)

Hoel becomes both a figure of David and of Christ. When the wolves come Hoel, "Like a shepherd/With a lion", kills the fiercest as did David the Shepherd, but the image suggests that Hoel is also like the Good Shepherd, son of David, who cares for the sheep and protects them against the wolf. The Good Shepherd values the individual, in compassion he searches out the one lost among the ninety-nine; he takes the initiative in his saving act. Cymen senses that the unknown force is generated through Hoel:

As though a spirit in you, like
A wild fowl hiding in the mere of your flesh,
Heard the sound far off and flew up clamouring
Rousing a spirit in me.   (p.36)

It is almost inevitable, therefore, that Hoel must die by crucifixion. Moelwyn Merchant draws attention to the sensitivity of the moment:

Hoel is to be killed, 'Bring him to the tree.' In the succeeding lines, Martina's cry to her human father is joined to a direct invocation of God by Hoel, the two simple speeches united in a dramatic trinitarian statement.
'**Martina:** Father! Father!'
'**Hoel:** Son and the brooding dove.
Call him again.'
These are the moments, when creed is crystallised into dramatic speech, that give specifically religious drama its validity.[13]

Hoel's cry is, an echo of a line he has spoken earlier in the play, and the full force of his death is only achieved when Cymen enters, delivers his exposition and only then sees the crucified man. Holding the body in a type of pieta, Cymen assures his family that God's original sacrifice was brought about by man's anger and that forgiveness, mercy and compassion are the only basis for life.

Merlin is, in some ways, a warning to Christianity and Canterbury that a misty faith based on traditions is weak and dangerous. His understanding of life is usually presented as nebulous and dreamlike, his long speeches have a tendency to be an accumulation of images, none of which clarifies the meaning of its predecessor. Cymen sees Merlin's weakness, which typifies the Christian land the Jutes invaded, and contrasts it with the strength of the force which is now upsetting him. Nevertheless, Merlin is able to view Cymen's struggles from a background of Christian pantheism and sheds a "watery light" on the issues involved,

Be lost
And then found. It's an old custom of the earth
From year to year.   (p.22)

he tells Hoel. Throughout the play he likens Christian ideas to their parallel in nature. He welcomes Spring and the coming of Augustine simultaneously and he had acquired an insight into man's conduct because he is aware of broader currents.

Merlin asks Cymen,

> Who, apart
> From ourselves, can see any difference between
> Our victories and our defeats, dear sir?   (p.24)

then he extends his argument to include an image of specifically Christian origin, but cloaked in the ideas of nature:

> Much more so you gods
> Who live without the world, who never feel
> As the world feels in springtime the stab of the spear
> And the spurt of golden blood,
> Winter's wound-in-the-side, the place where life begins.   (p.24)

Both Merlin and Hoel convince Cymen of the existence of a spirit within that drives men to seek the transcendent. An "obdurate pressure edging men toward a shape beyond" is the only definition which Merlin can offer. The old man has come to realise that rage and anger are self-defeating because they are always turned inwards; instead, he insists that man should strive towards a goal "shaped by the gods".

Many of the Christian ideas in *Thor, with Angels* are intrinsically very interesting, especially if interpreted as Fry's account of the difficulties facing the minority who find faith in hostile surroundings. Nevertheless, the gradual conversion of Cymen is achieved through a number of unusual and supernatural events that are not presented with sufficient dramatic force in the play and the development of the main themes are far more obvious in the study than on the stage. In performance, *Thor, with Angels* seems disjointed and the more interesting, underlying ideas are secondary to dull theatrical qualities.

A good deal has been written concerning the shortcomings of Fry's verse as dramatic dialogue, most of it pointing to verbal excess. Frederick Lumley speaks of "a bacchanalia of words" and "a thesaurus of fine phrases";[14] Bamber Gascoigne says "it is all a sophisticated form of exhibitionism";[15] and John Russell Taylor talks of "the bubbling poetry of Fry".[16] Donoghue, Fry's severest

288

critic, designates his dramatic verse "a wanton prancing of words".[17] Critics, indeed, appear to delight in finding new, dismissive descriptions for Fry's verbal luxuriance.

Thor, with Angels may have some excuse for excess; it is an "alliterative pastiche of Old English"[18] and has some of the qualities of a wordy and dull saga. Fry gives his warriors vigorous lines to speak, such as those in which Quichelm describes Cymen's strange behaviour in the battle:

> Burst in among us, blaspheming against Woden,
> Broke his sword in the air - he swore it broke
> Against a staggering light - and stood roaring. (p.5)

and this ingenious poetic technique is reinforced by some colourful imagery and sensitive atmospheric verse:

> The sky is clear,
> The sun still shines, but there's little doubt
> Their indignation is mounting under the self-control
> Of the horizon. (p.35)

There are some speeches, especially Merlin's welcome to Spring and Sleep, which can rivet the attention of an audience; and there are passages of gentle, free-moving verse which have a certain lyrical, mystic flavour. But *The Times*, commenting on the "rich sonority" with which Michael Golden, as Cymen, spoke his lines, indicated one weakness of the verse:

> . . . it is good to hear and even better to read. It is true that Mr Christopher Fry has an Elizabethan relish for words, but he has not . . . the Jonsonian trick of making their meaning plainer to the ear than to the eye . . .
>
> We think we have understood a speech, realise we have not, and take a surreptitious glance at the text which instantly makes all clear.[19]

Thor, with Angels undoubtedly shows ingenuity, but as J. C. Trewin remarked, "verbal ingenuity by itself is not really enough to carry an evening."[20] The effect of Fry's verse quickly palls because it is neither effective as dialogue nor as powerful statement. It is a series of speeches occasionally interrupted by stage direction; the language itself rarely gives cues for stage action nor does it show any emotional range. Perhaps the most irritating feature of the language is Fry's apparent desire to be witty. There are long passages of attempted light humour, particularly at the very beginning of the play. Apart from their dismal failure as wit, the passages of playful banter prevent the building of any real tension, create an atmosphere of inappropriate triviality and distract from the serious issues of the play. Large portions of the dialogue are wasted in verbal gymnastics and feeble humour as, indeed, they are in Dorothy Sayers's *The Devil to Pay*, but the situation is all the more serious in *Thor, with Angels* because of its comparative brevity.

Another result of Fry's failure to create dramatic verse is the absence of rich and varied characterisation. The language never creates the illusion of real characters in conversation and *Thor*, unlike the majority of the Canterbury plays, has no memorable characters and no actor created a great rôle at its first performance. Frank Napier as Merlin and Norman Chidgey as Colgrin apparently made everything possible of their parts but *The Times* reported that Michael Golden "found too little of an edge"[21] in the part of Cymen. The women of the play are, as Colgrin expresses it, "devout and dismal"; the warriors remain undelineated as individual characters; and only the young girl Martina and the Briton Hoel, who form the one sympathetic relationship in the play, develop characters that can interact. Even this most successful aspect of the characterisation fails finally for, as Gerald Weales has pointed out, Fry leaves no time for the audience to regret the death of Hoel, the play's most likeable character.[22]

It is impossible to know what audience response Christopher Fry hoped to achieve with *Thor, with Angels*. Reaction could, no doubt, range from mild amusement to enjoyment of the best speeches as lyric verse. Emotional involvement in the action of the play or the lives of the characters is prevented by the playwright's style and, by deliberately avoiding the liturgical elements of many of the previous Canterbury plays, Fry obviously precludes a devotional response.

Notes to Chapter 12

1. See above, pp. 112-3.
2. The two later plays - Robert Gittings's *The Makers of Violence* (1951) dealing with St Alphege (circa 1012 AD) and Hugh Ross Williamson's *His Emminence Of England* (1953) on the life of Cardinal Poel - also fit into this scheme.
3. Christopher Fry, *Thor, with Angels*, Canterbury Festival Programme (Canterbury 1948), 7.
4. See Appendix.
5. All page references in this chapter are to Christopher Fry, *Thor, with Angels* (Acting Edition for the Friends of Canterbury Cathedral, Canterbury 1948).
6. Christopher Fry *Thor, with Angels, loc. cit.*, 7.
7. Denis Donaghue, *The Third Voice* (Princeton 1959), 192
8. Frederick Lumley, *New Trends in Twentieth Century Drama* (London 1967), 284: "It was almost in reaction to all this that the public listened to John Osborne thumping on the door."
9/10. James Vinson, ed., *Contemporary Dramatists* (London 1973), 273.
11. Moelwyn W. Merchant, *Creed and Drama* (London 1965), 101.
12. Christopher Fry, *Thor, with Angels, loc. cit.*, 7.
13. Moelwyn W. Merchant, *op. cit.*, 101-102.
14. Frederick Lumley, *op. cit.*, 283.
15. Bamber Gascoigne, *Twentieth Century Drama* (London 1962), 67.
16. John Russell Taylor, *The Rise and Fall of the Well-Made Play* (London 1976), 161.
17. Denis Donoghue, *op. cit.*, 182.
18. Michael Anderson, et al., *A Handbook of Contemporary Drama* (London 1972), 166
19. '*Thor, with Angels*', *The Times*, Monday June 21st, 1948, 7.
20. J. C. Trewin, *Drama 1945-1950* (London 1951), 27.
21. *The Times, loc. cit.*, 7.
22. Gerald Weales, *op. cit.*, 214.

Fig. 27: Bill Maynard as God in the 1988 production of *Mystery Plays* at Great Malvern. Courtesy of the *Malvern Gazette & Ledbury Reporter*.

organisation representing a large number of local amateur dramatic societies asked Browne to direct a mystery cycle in the ruins of the old Cathedral. The ensuing production was, perhaps, innovative for two main features: firstly, it was a promenade performance in which the audience moved from location to location to see the next episode. Cast members moved through the audience, leading them and focusing their attention. Secondly, Browne called his compilation of plays, taken from the erroneously named *Ludus Coventriae, The Mysteries* - a title which would become very familiar to British theatre audiences.

A relatively small cast undertook the production and its flexibility and use of differing perspectives and settings, together with the sense of gathering round by the audience created an intimate and moving experience. The performance of the Coventry mystery plays was also established as a regular event and, after some years, the responsibility for the production was transferred to Coventry's Belgrade Theatre. Fragments of a once entire *Coventry Cycle* had been discovered and these were made into an entirely new script by Keith Miles in 1978. The series of all-professional productions in association with the Cathedral provided some spectacular and technically accomplished pieces of theatre. But, by the 1990s the financial burdens had become too great and the plays reverted to the amateurs under the direction of of a talented local clergyman.

Chester pioneered the idea of a more extensive cycle, dividing the plays into two sections: the *Old Testament* and the *New Testament* plays, to be presented on consecutive evenings. In Chester, the usual setting has been the Cathedral Green and the productions have seen some of the most experimental and controversial work of a succession of outstanding directors, two of whom have documented their work in a particularly fascinating way. James Roose-Evans, playwright, director, mystic and non-stipendiary priest, had a formidable reputation as a leader of drama workshops, using a range of techniques drawn from Oriental, East European and North American theatre and was recognised as a major figure in the London theatre. His deep interest in ritual and his personal faith, coupled with an ability to provide profound insights for his actors, made him an inspired choice to break the mould of previous productions in Chester.

Utilising a big-top tent, rather than the traditional Cathedral Green, and a small cast of thirty drawn from the hundreds who had auditioned (and, perhaps, expected to take part), Roose-Evans embarked on a period of preparation which required intensive exploration of the ideas and text, often through periods of Quaker-like silence. His version of the text abandoned the two halves and created a single, nightly performance which included the words of the *Lord's Prayer* and the *Beatitudes*, neither of which actually appear in any of the original texts. He concentrated on a sense of community with his actors, exemplified by having all the men play Adam and all the women Eve simultaneously in the temptation scene. From the centre of the large circular stage a thirty-foot 'Cosmic Tree' arose, around which an elaborate theatre ritual was acted out. Roose-Evans's book *Inner Journey, Outer Journey*, in which he describes the production, remains one of the most perceptive explorations of the re-discovery of ritual as a central element of theatre, religion and life.

When Bob Cheeseman came to direct the *Chester Cycle* in 1987 he encountered the, now familiar, opposition of at least one leading clergyman who maintained that to play God was blasphemous. Cheeseman had successfully combined the careers of academic and director and had directed a long-running, major production of *Godspell*, the stage musical version of *St Matthew's Gospel* written by two graduates from the American University where E. Martin Browne had held his first professorship. He now addressed the two issues: how to re-create that sense of involvement of a large community in the plays and how to represent God. He decided to hand responsibility for each individual play to different organisations in the town.

I decided to revisit the National Theatre production and, in a conversation with one of the actors after the show, an important seed was planted in my mind. I had been struck by his commitment as a performer and when I complimented him upon his work, he suddenly told me he hadn't principally concentrated upon portraying the various characters he had been assigned (Adam, Isaac, etc.): the one character he had focused on was a fictitious butcher from Wakefield who (the actor imagined) had been asked to play various cycle characters. Hearing that piece of information was the beginning of a process which eventually led me to a hugely exciting production concept. As I pondered upon that theatre-bar conversation, I realised that a real butcher (or baker) from Wakefield (or Chester) was something which a truly authentic revival could uniquely provide. I ceased wondering about how a contemporary production could be sufficiently artistically impressive and, instead, I started to look very carefully at the original texts.

It was only then that a concrete production concept hit me: and it wasn't even original, it was medieval! Here before me were separate plays written for separate casts, the original medieval people. None of the official mystery play 'revivals' of this century (Chester, Coventry, Wakefield and York) had attempted to reactivate that very basic concept: instead of regenerating what in medieval times would have been a kind of one-act play festival incorporating many and various kinds of people of the locality, each revival had chosen to present a single continuous production - the National Theatre had also taken this approach. At last I realised that we in Chester could endeavour to mount something which no normal theatre company in the world could ever attempt.

After hundreds of years, this fascinating material could once again be handed over to individual performers and companies of the community of Chester and its surrounding areas. Various contrasting approaches could be taken to the separate plays, and their accompanying entertainment, resulting in a festival of biblical drama, a festival which realised once again the enormously diverse range of those original plays (comedy, earthiness, majesty, tragedy and worship) through circus skills, dance, drama, fireworks, music, participation, visual art, etc., in a total production which could be spread out over the equivalent of three whole evenings of entertainment.

How, then, was this production to represent God? I combed *The Bible* (the overwhelming inspiration of the Cycle) for any reference to God's 'appearance' and, after extensive searching, I found three relevant statements: 1) 'No man has ever seen God' - *1 John 4*, 12 - that would indeed be a problem on stage; 2) *Psalm 18* is more graphic about the invisibility: 'Darkness he made a veil to surround him' - something more tangible, but still a problem for dramatic representation, because most of the production would take place in daylight (and sometimes bathed in sunlight); 3) *Exodus 34, 29* gives a completely opposite indication of God's appearance: 'When Moses came down from the mountain of Sinai (where he had been allowed to glimpse only the back of God) the skin on his face shone'. And there is a parallel reference in the very first play of the *Chester Cycle* when God says: 'Behold the beams of my bright face'.

Here then was a fascinating and an apparently unresolvable para-dox - darkness coupled with dark beams! At the time of this research I happened to be employing a mirror-ball within a college production of a completely different play, and while watching one of the per-formances of that production, a possible image occurred to me: if God were played by an actor with a very black skin, pieces of mirror on the skin could reflect intense light and cause God to appear to be invisible and glorious simultaneously. Thus it was that the Canon's original misgivings eventually led to a concept for depicting God on stage. I decided to offer the part of God to an impressive black actor who had just played Othello at the Gateway Theatre (I was convinced he was able to convey the essential authority of the Cycle's King of Kings with-out resonance of a white ruling-class); at the same time, through care-fully designed costume, imagery and lighting, the actor's appearance could transmit aspects of mystery, darkness and illumination.[2]

When Bob Cheeseman returned to direct the *Chester Mystery Plays* in 1992 he emphasised the concept of the Trinity by having three actors play the part of God simultaneously. The city has continued to present its Cycle regularly and more recently has invited tenders from production companies to undertake responsi-bility for the project. This reflects a trend in the 1980s in which professional companies involved themselves in developing large-scale, community productions, drawing on local issues, traditions and amateur performers. As the term 'mystery' derives from a word meaning 'the know-how' we can see that this process is appropriate for the mounting of medieval cycles.

The medieval mystery plays are among the great treasures of Europe. Like the scriptures which inspired them, they present a tapestry of memorable characters: tyrant kings, talking donkeys, rough shepherds, loose women, comely damsels and criminals; and at any moment a life can be transformed by an encounter with God, His Son or an angel. The mysteries were written by men who never allowed piety to swamp their humanity: the plays abound with humour, music, pathos, dancing, tension, refinement and vulgarity. They show the story of God's Creation and subsequent involvement in that Creation so that the events seen in performance represent the most important events in the world's history seen through medieval eyes.

By the late 1950s and early 1960s the performance of medieval mystery plays had become established as part of the curriculum of drama colleges: Goldsmith's College of London University chose to open its new theatre with a production of *Heaven's New-Born Heir*, a compilation of mystery plays made and directed by Honor Matthews, the Head of the Drama Department and whose book, *The Primal Curse*, derived from her interest in the play of Cain and Abel. Martial Rose, the Principal of Bretton Hall College in Wakefield, made a fine acting edition of the *Wakefield Cycle* and there was hardly a drama course in the country that did not include *The Second Shepherds' Play* from that Cycle.

A generation of actors and directors, made aware of the robust and economical style of medieval drama, became anxious to explore its commercial potential. The actor and ITV newsreader, Gordon Honeycombe, made a selection of plays from various cycles about the life of Christ which he entitled *The Redemption* for a presentation by members of the Royal Shakespeare Company at Southwark Cathedral. The great stumbling block to any further development in the commercial theatre, however, was the Theatres' Act of 1843 which had established the office of Lord Chamberlain to license plays for public performance. It had become quite clear that no play in which God or Christ appeared, or which contained nudity, would be granted a licence. Plays written before 1843 were exempt but, as E. Martin Browne observed, any competent lawyer could show that the texts of mystery plays being used were not entirely medieval. But in 1968 the Act was repealed and with the abolition of the censor's office the theatre was liberated from a period of stifling restriction.

The commercial theatre was quick to realise the box office potential of nudity and Jesus Christ with the rock musicals *Hair, Jesus Christ Superstar* and *Godspell*. These latter attracted the inevitable protests and charges of blasphemy, particularly as *Superstar* focused on the manhood rather than on the divinity of Christ and *Godspell* portrayed him as one of a troupe of clowns. However, for those who saw the performances, moments such as Christ's agony in Gethsemane in *Superstar* and the inventive retelling of the gospel parables in *Godspell* were, arguably, not only moving but 'sacred' theatre by any standards.

Andrew Lloyd-Webber, the composer of *Jesus Christ Superstar*, was the son of the organist and composer W. S. Lloyd-Webber whose compositions included a cantata *The Saviour*, a setting of the Passion in the tradition of Bach and Stainer. Familiarity with such music may well have provided a basis for the rock musical. It is, however, quite certain that with their two seemingly indelible biblical musicals, *Joseph and the Amazing Technicolour Dreamcoat* and *Jesus Christ Superstar*, the lyricist Tim Rice and the composer Lloyd-Webber established themselves as the most successful partnership in the British musical theatre since Gilbert and Sullivan.

In 1981, London theatre audiences were provided with a much more conventional, but wholly remarkable, view of the life of Christ with Alec McCowan's solo performance of the entire *Gospel of St Mark*; and a similar experience was enjoyed by television audiences in Peter Barkworth's version of *St Matthew*. These were not simply astounding feats of memory, they exposed the humour, irony and sheer humanity of the Gospel accounts, even in the Authorised Version, and they rid the text of *The Bible* of any trace of the cloying piety that had so often dogged its reading in church.

It took eight years for the National Theatre to develop its production of *The Mysteries*, first seen at the Cottesloe Theatre in 1985 where it established itself as one of the great theatrical landmarks of the decade. Using a script adapted from various cycles by the poet Tony Harrison, the National Theatre conceived a massive production in three parts: *The Creation*, dealing with events from the Creation of the universe to the birth of Jesus; *The Passion*, dealing with the life of Christ; and *Doomsday*, covering the Resurrection, Ascension and Last Judgement. Thus audiences who attended all three performances were able to see a considerably larger sweep of the drama of redemption than in any previous 'revival' of mystery

choice of settings. The performing area in the Water Garden was conceived as a more rustic staging, built of rough timber and having a stencilled hessian backcloth, while the stages in the Nave and Chapter House were painted and decorated to look more jewel-like and highly coloured, both to contrast with the grey stone of the buildings and to resemble medieval *Books of Hours*.[8]

An area of the Nave was identified which could provide an 'arena' whilst enabling the great steps and the organ loft to be used as Masefield had done. Large pieces like the 'Mansions', 'Hell-mouth' and 'Earth' (from which Adam and Eve appeared) could be trundled in and out of the arena by costumed members of the cast and in this part of the Cathedral, the five hundred people who could be accommodated sitting on the carpeted floor or standing, never knew where the next piece of action would take place among them. By leading them through the magnificent cloisters, it was possible to take the same audience to the open, grassed area partially surrounded by ancient archways and the water tower. Fortunately, the enclosing buildings created good acoustics and the heavy wooden stage a superb setting for the construction of the Ark or for the Crucifixion. A ramp from that area led to the Crypt in which a complete 'theatre-in-the-round' was achieved by a simple arrangement of chairs and benches.

Another walk through the cloisters led to the Chapter House but it was discovered that, like the Crypt, this space could only accommodate an audience of two hundred and fifty gathering around the acting area. It was decided, therefore, that once the initial audience of five hundred had seen the plays in the Nave and the Water Garden it would then be split in two: one half being taken to the Crypt and the other half to the Chapter House to witness simultaneously plays of exactly equal length and then be taken to the other venue before being re-united to re-enter the Nave. The division of the initial audience necessitated the selection of plays where the sequence was immaterial for the smaller venues.

A further problem, however, led to the decision involving the most risk. An audience of approximately one thousand per night was needed to make the project viable. It was decided, therefore, to have one audience of five hundred arrive at 7.00 pm and begin its

311

progress around the Cathedral while another audience of the same size would arrive forty-five minutes later and follow the same pattern. This meant that those plays shown in the Nave and Water Garden were performed twice each night and those in the Crypt and Chapter House four times. In the case of *The Creation* this involved complex and precise timing to ensure God's omnipresence, whereas *The Passion* required two actors in the major rôle of Christ and a third playing one play four times to enable the main actors to be elsewhere!

Nevertheless, the excitement generated by audiences moving around the Cathedral in changing light and aware of other audiences and performances in the distance was to prove one of the most memorable qualities of the production. For the cast, there was no offstage, for they mingled with the audience, leading them, seating them and performing in the midst of them without warning. Deprived of the security of wings and the conventions of up- or downstage and the certainty of where the audience would be, many of the amateurs were initially sceptical and uneasy, but once live audiences were pressing in on them they responded by creating their own spaces and appropriate timings.

Before rehearsals began, the directors pondered the need for a leading professional actor to play the part of God. This was not only a means of attracting audiences, but a source of constant inspiration for the rest of the cast, continuing the Canterbury tradition of co-operation between the professional and amateur stage. In many ways, it is the voice of God which is so important in *The Mysteries* and a particularly haunting voice was that of Marius Goring who had narrated the massive television history of the Great War. His acceptance of the rôle lifted the production onto an altogether higher plain and his contribution to the development of the text during rehearsal was invaluable and rooted in profound knowledge of Scripture. Electing to emphasise the notion of God as 'The Ancient of Days', Goring astounded the cast by his nimbleness and power: his curse to Satan was terrible; his attention to Noah gentle. As Helga Wood relates, he also had strong ideas about his own costume:

As far as costuming the Mystery Plays, my greatest problem was the sheer size of the cast, and the rather limited budget. I decided that my guiding principle would be that the actors would all be considered to be medieval townsfolk, in their basic everyday costume of wool tunics, hoods, wimples and dresses and overdresses, and that they would then add special costumes when they played a specific character; for example, the actor playing Lucifer in the opening sequence, in his green, snake-like hood and gown, would re-assume his woollen tunic and cape for the rest of the plays when he reverted to being a member of the Company. For many characters, such as Noah and his family, or Abraham, no additional costume was needed; but for others like Adam and Eve, Moses, the Angels, Mary and Jesus, I used a generally medieval image as an inspiration for the costume. God himself, the most crucial player in this drama, was to be played by our only professional actor, and one of immense experience and standing, Marius Goring, and he had his own strong vision of his character and costume which befitted his rôle - he was not seen as a medieval townsman dressed up to play his part but more as a benign headmaster watching over his often unruly children. Needless to say, the work was all completed in time, the performers all experienced a tremendous feeling of achievement, and some reached heights of performance no one thought possible; audiences came in large numbers and were visibly moved by their experience, and we all came to a great knowledge and love of the Cathedral building that is rarely possible for the casual visitor. That, and the wonderful feeling of comradeship in working to recreate what had lain dormant since the Middle Ages, to see the plays as vibrant, humorous and moving now as they obviously were then, are the memories that will always endure for me.[9]

Much of the feeling of community was generated by participation in the music and dancing. A score by the Kentish composer Keith Cole enabled large choral moments to punctuate the action, whereas he also created moments of pathos and tension with instrumental movements. These were supplemented by music played on medieval instruments under the direction of Will Ward, who also devised the dances. Music and dancing involved large numbers of performers who might, at any moment, act a part. This flexibility was typified by the two main actors to play Jesus: drama teacher, John Hole, who as Adam was buried in earth, as Mak was tossed in a blanket and as Jesus carried aloft and hung on a cross;

Peter Brooks, on the other hand, combined a charismatic Jesus with a delicate performance as Abraham, both of which belied his amateur status.

Archbishop Runcie took a great interest in the production and attended a launch at which he was able to meet the cast, but constant negotiations with the Cathedral authorities were needed to deal with the movement of scenic items, storage, construction, rigging of lights and the very limited space and time for rehearsal in the Nave. Watching the solemn audience led from the scene of the Crucifixion by a drumbeat and a haunting shawn melody, then to be confronted with a blinding light emanating from the risen Christ as they re-entered the dark Nave, it was clear that something of abiding value had been created. After the performance the Archbishop, who had sat on the floor with the rest of the audience wrote:

> I want to thank you before I go off to America for *The Mysteries*. They were a triumph. It's impossible for me to do justice to my feelings in this letter; but I was so impressed by the spirit of the company, and the way in which it all seemed to flow out of the buildings and yet give something raw and amusing and poignant back to the buildings again.
>
> The children that we brought were quite enchanted and enthralled to the end. In fact, four of them had just arrived with us from a continental holiday and were fairly exhausted. They came with the idea that they would just stay for part of it all. In fact, at the end they were chattering away and asking the most amazing questions about God and some of them were very fast balls for Archbishops. It was fascinating to see how alive they were on their return and I couldn't help comparing it with some children that I have known to return from Church Services![10]

Such reactions and many other signs of success at Canterbury led the directors to offer their project and way of working to other venues, although not all of the original team was involved in subsequent productions. In 1987, *The Mysteries* were staged at the Orchard Theatre at Dartford in North Kent, the stage and front section of the auditorium of this modern theatre being transformed into a huge arena. The cast was drawn from local people, but the part of Jesus was played by the well-known actor and television presenter, Peter Duncan, and a benign God by Bill Maynard, better known, perhaps, as a comic. Without the enormous spaces or crowd move-

314

saturated the theatre with mystery plays. Canterbury experienced similar problems to other cities: rising costs and a quest for novelty exerted enormous pressures on production teams; a cast of over two hundred with three directors in 1986 had decreased to ninety-eight actors and one director in 1992. The elaborate logistics of two nightly-performances had become virtually impossible with such diminished forces. Amateur actors, who had regarded the huge commitment as a once-in-a-lifetime opportunity to work with professional directors, designers, technicians, choreographers, musicians and famous actors, were content for it to be just that. The small core of local actors who returned for a third time were, like their forerunners in the Canterbury Festival Plays, increasingly aware of their standing and resistant to change. It was clear that a further production of *The Mysteries* was not viable.

But the experience gained and the continuing involvement of the Cathedral authorities were exploited by Channel Theatre Company in their remarkable community production of Shakespeare's *Romeo and Juliet* in 1995. This project, directed by Claudia Leaf and Philip Dart, attracted a new and younger cast alongside some of the *Mysteries* players. By having two Romeos and two Juliets it was possible to follow the established pattern of presenting two nightly promenade performances using the Nave, Crypt, Water Garden and Chapter House. The sense of movement in the opening scenes in the Nave was wonderfully contrasted with the stillness of the tomb in the Crypt. By seating the audience in the Water Garden on the spot where the *Mysteries* stage had been, the directors were able to use the structures of the Cathedral itself for the balcony scene and created a feeling of magic with the warmly lit stone in the moonlight.

Birmingham Cathedral was still enthusiastic for a further production of the *Mysteries* in 1997, particularly as this large city was able to replenish constantly its supply of performers. However, the impetus and resources of the original productions were no longer available and in this difficult situation I turned to friends in Images Theatre Company based, as Laurence Irving had been, in Whitstable. Previous co-operation on their touring production of *Vita and Harold* enabled me to work easily with the company's director, Anthea Preston and her husband, Harry, one of their leading actors. It was decided to create a somewhat minimalist production using a new translation of the 'N' Town Cycle (Ludus Coventriae) commissioned from Douglas Sugano, Professor of English at Whitworth College in Spokane, Washington, USA.

The Midlands' Mysteries, as they came to be known, were staged on an elevated, traverse stage in Edwardian costume for a seated audience. Both halves were played entirely inside as the disruptions and security affecting the outdoor plays had become intolerable. The production opened with a carnival procession, Harry Preston played God as an impresario and Lucifer, a new rôle for Steve Lloyd, was a showman. Joseph wheeled Mary to Bethlehem on his delivery bicycle and Derek Willis, a young doctor, created an engaging Jesus in blazer and flannels, drawing on his considerable experience in physical theatre. There was no onstage crucifixion, the terrible event was seen through the eyes of the onlookers; the knockabout fun of the midwives at Christ's Nativity contrasted starkly with the darkness of the Courts and Herod's soldiers. The action was supported and punctuated by a rich collection of folk tunes and songs arranged by Andy Casserley and a Hellmouth furnace was a reminder that these Mysteries were being presented in an industrial city.

Birmingham Cathedral, maintaining a policy of encouraging drama, hosted a performance of my play about Cardinal Newman, The Parting of Friends, first performed in 1994 in St Mary's Church, Oxford, where Newman had ministered. In 1988, the same Cathedral also staged the production of Murder in the Cathedral which had been performed in the Crypt of Canterbury Cathedral for the Lambeth Conference by Canterbury Festival Productions. But however many versions of The Mysteries or revivals of Murder in the Cathedral were presented, they did not constitute a dynamic form of new Christian drama. Indeed, the use of cathedrals as theatres had probably become inhibiting rather than liberating and workers in the field of drama were constantly confronted with a Church which, while pouring enormous resources into music, gave virtually nothing to drama.

Tony Jasper, the remarkable actor, broadcaster, music journalist and writer, created a professional theatre company to tour churches with plays exploring more recent aspects of Christian history. Jasper, who is also a Methodist lay preacher, has effectively challenged the antipathy of the Non-conformist churches by presenting them with facts about their own traditions through the medium of highly-polished musical theatre.

The closing years of the twentieth century, in an increasingly pagan Britain, also saw an urgent reawakening by Christians to the fact that the transcendent may be explored and revealed through drama. Thus drama is seen both as a potential element of teaching and worship *and* as a form of outreach. Significantly, much of the emphasis has been on taking drama out of churches rather than on enticing audiences into churches. Among the most substantial contributions to these developments have been two Christian theatre companies: Riding Lights and New Directions, both of which have tended to draw their impetus from the evangelical wing of the Church.

Riding Lights, founded in York in the 1980s, initially devised material for use in worship, but quickly its all-professional membership extended its work to touring. Using techniques drawn from 'agit-prop' and Theatre-In-Education, the company has devised many challenging programmes dealing with serious issues from a broad, Christian perspective. More recently, Riding Lights have been presenting Shakespeare and running extensive courses on playwriting and aspects of production. In these developments and in the book *Theatrecraft*, written by one of the directors, Nigel Forde, one senses a determination to avoid the charges of amateurism and mediocrity so often levelled against the writing and performance of religious plays.

New Directions Theatre Company, founded in 1994 by Robin Meredith, perhaps comes nearest to George Bell's vision. Their policy is to develop new Christian playwriting through professional workshops and then to find a production company willing to take the work into the commercial theatre. Participating playwrights explore their craft in a mutually supportive atmosphere but remain emphatic that their plays are not intended for a specifically

Christian audience. If they are successful we shall no longer need Cathedrals as playhouses, but, ironically, in the year 2000, the *York Mysteries* were finally presented inside the Minster.

Notes to Chapter 13

1. E. Martin Browne, *Two in One* (Cambridge 1981), 235.
2. Bob Cheeseman, 'Searching for God: Directing the *Chester Mystery Plays'*, *Speech and Drama II*, VII No.1. (1998), 29-34.
3/4. Kenneth Pickering, David Bradby and Philip Thomas, *Studying Drama* (Beckenham 1983), 237-238.
5. Browne, *op. cit.*, 237-238.
6. Shirley Bennetts (ed), The *Mysteries at Canterbury Cathedral* (Worthing 1986), x.
7/8/9. Helga Wood, a personal account. Unpublished (1999).
10. Robert Runcie, a personal letter to K. W. Pickering (1986).
11/12. *Metro News*, Birmingham (1991).

Appendix

Actors, producers, designers and other personalities contributing to drama at Canterbury.

This appendix demonstrates the extent to which the professional theatre combined with local amateur talent in the production of the Canterbury plays. In the case of each entry, the plays to which the person contributed are listed before their biographical details. The main sources used in compiling this appendix were: *The Oxford Companion to the Theatre* (*OCT*), *Who's Who in the Theatre* (*WWT*) and *The Dictionary of National Bibliography* (*DNB*). Other sources are acknowledged where appropriate, but may include personal reminiscence. In some cases this appendix supplements information already given in the text.

RONALD ADAM - (b. 1896). Played Henry II in *Becket* (1932 & 1933), Henry II in *The Young King* (1934). Manager of the Embassy Theatre 1932-39 where he was responsible for one hundred and fifty productions and appeared in many of the plays in their West End transfer. He acted at the Garrick (1950) and the St James (1951) and subsequently took important parts in most major British theatres and in the USA. Director of the Wyndham's season in Edinburgh and Glasgow. Laurence Irving refers to Adam's magnificent voice which, "as one of the most trusted controllers at Fighter Command, was to guide, warn and position our outnumbered pilots fighting over Kent in the Battle of Britain." *WWT*; Laurence Irving, *The Canterbury Adventure* (Canterbury 1959).

MARGARET BABINGTON - (Steward and Treasurer of The Friends of Canterbury Cathedral 1928-58). Played Queen Eleanor (1932 & '33). The tall, trim figure of Margaret Babington on her ancient bicycle was likened to Boadicea. She had a genius for organisation and for securing volunteers and always marked her letters to the Dean "Urgent". "She knew she had the power to appeal to the romantic in the common man," said Hewlett-Johnson, "and she did it in a brilliant way." Laurence Irving writes: "Her fervour may have exasperated the sluggards, her ruthlessness may have shocked the timid, but she was a person to whom it was impossible to say 'no' and she held together the vast numbers of volunteers needed for the Festival for thirty years."

Her death in 1958 was the final blow to the Festival and John Masefield wrote a poem in her memory. She lectured widely and her book *The Romance of Canterbury Cathedral* ran into many editions. By the time of her death, Miss Babington had enrolled over 6,000 Friends of the Cathedral and had helped to raise over £100,000 for the restoration of the building. Hewlett-Johnson, Sermon, Sunday 24th August 1958; Laurence Irving, *The Canterbury Adventure* (Canterbury 1959).

PETER BARKWORTH - Played God in *The Mysteries* (1989 & '92). An extremely popular actor with Kent connections and many theatre and film credits. He had a large number of major television rôles, including that of Edward VIII in *Crown Matrimonial*. His book *First Houses* describes his early career in Folkestone and he distilled the results of his teaching at RADA into two excellent books on acting. His interest in religion was obvious in his televised work on St Matthew's Gospel and his performance as C. S. Lewis in *Shadowlands*.

E. MARTIN BROWNE (b. 1900) - Produced and played Fourth Knight and Fourth Tempter in *Murder in the Cathedral* (1935) and in the subsequent Mercury Theatre production; produced and played Skeleton in *Cranmer* (1936); produced and played Green Mask in *Peasants' Priest* (1948); produced revival of *Christ's Comet* (1958). Browne probably contributed more to the development of Christian verse drama in this century than any other person. He was trained as a theologian at Oxford, but held a Professorship of Speech and Drama in the United States before being appointed by George Bell as Director of Drama to the diocese of Chichester.

APPENDIX

Ronald Jasper's *George Bell* (London 1967) contains Browne's account of his first meeting with Bell, and Browne's own *The Making of T. S. Eliot's Plays* explains how Browne and Eliot came to be associated with Canterbury. Browne, a strict disciplinarian in rehearsals, achieved his results in remarkably short rehearsal periods. After the success of *Murder in the Cathedral*, Eliot insisted that all his subsequent plays should be produced by Browne, both in London and on Broadway.

During the war Browne and his wife, Henzie Raeburn, founded the Pilgrim Players and after the war Browne directed a series of plays by poets at the small Mercury Theatre. He became director of the *British Drama League* in 1945 and held the post until 1957 when he inaugurated the Program in Religious Drama at New York Theological Seminary where he was visiting Professor until 1962. In 1951, 1954 and 1957 he produced the *York Cycle of Mystery Plays* in York for the first time since 1572 and in 1963 he became Drama Adviser to Coventry Cathedral. He directed *Murder in the Cathedral* in Canterbury again in 1970 and died in 1980 as his autobiography was going to press. *OCT*; see also Bibliography under E. Martin Browne.

ANN CASSON (b. 1915) - Played Queen Margaret (1934). Daughter of Lewis Casson and Sybil Thorndike, she first appeared as Tiny Tim in *A Christmas Carol* at the Lyric Theatre (1921) and in 1924 was seen in *Peer Gynt* and *The Trojan Women*. She played in the 1936 Old Vic Shakespeare season and at the Tewkesbury Festival in 1939. During the war she joined the Pilgrim Players and after the war acted with the Birmingham Repertory Theatre. From 1950-4 Ann Casson taught at LAMDA before going to live and work in Stratford, Ontario. *WWT*.

CHRISTOPHER CASSON (b. 1912) - Played Angel of the Tree and Melchior (1938). Son of Lewis Casson and Sybil Thorndike, toured the USA with Ben Greet in 1932 and the following year appeared with his parents in *Ghosts* and *St Joan*. He acted in the first full English production of *Peer Gynt* at Sadlers Wells in 1936 and in 1937 was the Third Priest in *Murder in the Cathedral* at the Old Vic (and in New York in 1938). He directed a 14-part recording of Shakespeare's plays 1963-64. *WWT*.

MARY CASSON - Played Rosamund (1932 & '33). Mary did not take happily to the stage and she did not appear regularly after her early, adolescent rôles.

DRAMA IN THE CATHEDRAL

VERA COBURN-FINDLAY - Played Queen Eleanor (1934), Queen Mary (1936), Lady Ursula (1937), Empress (1939). Vera Coburn had been a professional actress, but on a tour of South Africa she met and married Colonel Findlay and retired from the stage. When she came to live in Canterbury she became a very active member of the amateur dramatic society and of the *Friends*. She had a powerful personality and had something of a love-hate relationship with Margaret Babington. After the war, she supervised the wardrobe for the Festival plays.

PHILIP DART - Directed *The Mysteries* at Canterbury (1986) and Birmingham (1994). After gaining a degree in Drama at Hull University, Philip's early directing career took him to the Nuffield Theatre, Southampton, the Plymouth Theatre Company and the Soho Polytechnic Theatre in London. He was a founder member of Channel Theatre Company, and took over the position of Artistic Director in the late 1980s, immediately introducing a new and critically acclaimed programme of work. Channel came to be one of the country's leading theatrical organisations and the company's small scale, community operations developed at a remarkable pace. Work as a freelance director included the Pavilion Theatre and the English Theatre in Vienna. In addition, he enjoyed success as a playwright-adapter: His play *Sugar and Spice* toured Austria, while his adaptation of *Jane Eyre*, which toured nationally in 1998, was produced by Northampton's Royal Theatre touring company.

WILLIAM FORDYCE - Played King Louis (1932), York (1933), William Marshall (1934), Second Priest (1935), Preacher (1936), Martin (1937), Nicolaus (1938), Priest (1939). Fordyce joined the Canterbury Dramatic Society in 1925, the year after its foundation, and appeared in *Mr Wu* (the play which brought fame to Matheson Lang, a cousin of the Archbishop of Canterbury, Cosmo Lang). He was so enthusiastic that he cycled to rehearsals from Sandwich, some ten miles away, and frequently amused his colleagues, as he worked at his lathe in the workshops of the East Kent Road Car Company, by declaiming his lines loudly. He was a strong and impressive actor with a fine, resonant voice.

CHRISTOPHER FRY (b. 1907) - Wrote and produced *Thor, with Angels* (1948). Fry became an actor after a short period as a schoolmaster and in 1934 he was appointed director of the Tunbridge Wells Repertory Theatre. In 1936 he toured in Ivor Novello's *Howdo, Princess?* and two years later his play *The Boy With A Cart* was first produced. He was

APPENDIX

director of the Oxford Playhouse during 1940 and from 1944-6 he also directed several plays at the Arts Theatre, London.

Since writing *Thor, with Angels* for Canterbury, Fry has maintained a steady output of plays, including translations of Anouilh, Giraudoux and recently of Ibsen. Fry's *A Yard of Sun* (1970) was produced at the Notting-ham Playhouse and the Old Vic during 1970; he has written a number of successful, biblical-spectacular filmscripts including *Ben Hur* (1959), *Barabbas* (1960) and *The Bible* (1964). *WWT*; bibliography in *Tulane Drama Review* (New Orleans, March 1960); James Vinson, ed., *Contemporary Dramatists* (London & New York 1973).

MICHAEL GOLDEN (b. 1913) - Played Cymen (1948). Made his first appearance on stage at the Abbey Theatre, Dublin in 1932. He remained in Ireland playing in Shakespeare and Shaw until 1942 when he joined the Oxford Repertory when Christopher Fry was its director. During 1947 he was in the company at Stratford-on-Avon Shakespeare Memorial Theatre and played in *Dr Faustus, Measure for Measure* and *Richard II*. When he came to Canterbury he had just appeared as Montague in *Romeo and Juliet* and Orsino in *Twelfth Night* at His Majesty's Theatre. His first film appearance was in 1944 in *The Canterbury Tale*. *WWT*.

MICHAEL GOODLIFFE (1914-1976) - Played William of Sens (1949). Goodliffe was a schoolboy at St Edmunds School, Canterbury where Philip Hollingworth was teaching. He joined the Liverpool Repertory Company after graduating at Oxford, and between 1936 and 1939 acted at Coventry and Stratford-on-Avon. During the war, Goodliffe was taken prisoner and spent most of his time organising play productions in the prison camp. His first production was *Hamlet* for which he wrote out the script from memory; distemper from the walls was used as make-up. His productions became so popular with prisoners and guards alike that he was driven in a German staff car to Stuttgart to select costumes from the wardrobe of the Opera House. After the war he appeared at the Mercury and Lyric Theatres before his performance at Canterbury. He made many appearances in London, New York and on television. *WWT*.

MARIUS GORING - Played God in *The Mysteries* (1986). One of Britain's leading classical actors who made his stage debut at the Old Vic in 1927. He joined the Compagnie des Quinze to tour Europe performing in French and then returned to the London and Stratford stage. During the war he supervised BBC broadcasts to Germany and then toured, playing

DRAMA IN THE CATHEDRAL

in German. He had a succession of major TV rôles and appeared in many films. He contributed a final speech to the text of *The Mysteries* based on the *Book of Revelation*.

SIR PHILIP BEN GREET (1857-1936) - Produced *Henry IV, Part 2*, and *Henry V* (1930). This energetic but blunt actor-manager, friend of Headlam and pioneer of the open-air Shakespeare productions in 1886, provided many actors and actresses with their early training and experience in his Woodland Players. Among those who toured with Greet were Laurence Irving's parents, H. B. Irving and Dorothea Baird and, later, Sybil and Russell Thorndike. Sybil Thorndike remembers him entering the compartment of the railway carriage where she and another young actress were making their first journey from home. He said, "Well, you two little duffers, what are you crying for? Go and eat some sandwiches and then go to sleep!"

Greet took over Poel's production of *Everyman* and toured the USA with it. He also founded an Acting Academy, started the Regent's Park Open Air Theatre (1901), was jointly responsible for founding the Old Vic (1914) where, between 1915 and 1918, he produced twenty-four of Shakespeare's plays; in the 1920s and '30s he organised the London County Council Children's Shakespeare performances which Headlam had negotiated. Greet was knighted in 1929. *DNB*; *OCT*; Elisabeth Sprigge, *Sybil Thorndike Casson* (London 1971); F. G. Bettany, *Stuart Headlam* (London 1926); Laurence Irving, *The Successors* (London 1967); W. F. Isaac, *Ben Greet and the Old Vic* (London 1964).

ELIZABETH HAFFENDEN - Designed costumes 1935-39 and 1947. Laurence Irving writes:
Elizabeth Haffenden was a student at the Royal College of Art during the late '20s. I met her when working after she won her diploma in costume design, she designed the dresses for a film *Colonel Blood* written and directed by W. P. Lipscomb on which I was working as production designer. I was deeply impressed by her talent and skill and recommended her to T. S. Eliot to design the dresses for *Murder in the Cathedral*. However, he had a friend that he asked us to invite to do the work (as you know in those days all the artists contributing to the Festivals made an offering of their work). So Elizabeth Haffenden's first designs for the Friends were those for *Cranmer* (except for the 'Figura Rerum' which I drew and was used for the jacket for the published play). Thereafter she designed all the Festival plays until

330

after the war, when the local volunteer seamstresses could no longer carry out her designs and the London costumiers' costs were beyond our resources, she supervised the selection of the most fitting she could find in their stock. Her first *succès d'estime* was her dressing of a superb tableau that was the finale of an entertainment given by our King and Queen to President Lebrun of France in 1939, when Edith Evans as the Spirit of France declaimed a poem by Masefield against a background of beautiful girls dressed to represent the provinces of France. After and before the war she collaborated in several theatrical productions and she designed the dresses for the film *Uncle Silas* which I produced in 1947. By then she had become the leading costume designer in films of that time. Soon after the war she went into partnership with Joan Bridge, who was an expert on technicolour. Together they worked on many films including, I think, *Dr Zhivago* and was still actively so engaged when, alas, she died a few months ago. Letter to K. W. Pickering, dated 01/08/76.

CHRISTOPHER HASSALL (1912-63) - Author of *Christ's Comet* (1938 & '58). Produced *The Zeal of Thy House* (1949). Played voice of God (1960). Christopher Hassall read music and English literature at Oxford but a financial crisis at home cut short his university career and he joined a touring theatrical company led by Nicholas Hannon. When he was playing in *Henry VIII* at the Old Vic he was invited to understudy Ivor Novello in *Proscenium* and Novello read Hassall's first volume of verse, *Poems of Two Years*. Novello convinced Hassall that he was not a good actor but that he had the poetic talent to become his chief librettist.

Hassall's verse was influenced by Sir Edward Marsh and Walter de la Mare, both of whom gave him encouragement. His sonnet sequence, *Bell Harry*, written in memory of his friend Francis Cornford, is built around the single symbolic image of the central tower of Canterbury Cathedral. John Wakeman, *World Authors 1950-1970* (New York 1975). See also *Bibliography* under Christopher Hassall.

PHILIP HOLLINGWORTH - Played Knight (1928), York (1932), Bertrand de Born (1934), Third Tempter & Third Knight (1925), Henry VIII (1936), Prior (1937), Strabo (1938), Wagner (1939), Theodatus (1949). Produced *Everyman* (1960). The Canterbury Dramatic Society was founded in 1924 and gave performances in the Theatre Royal; Hollingworth, a classics master at St Edmunds School, married a founder-member of the Society and himself joined in 1925. A great enthusiast for verse-speaking,

Hollingworth played important rôles in nearly all the Canterbury plays and received good notices in both local and national press reviews. He remained a leading figure in Canterbury dramatic circles and made strenuous efforts to revive the Chapter House plays after the war. He felt that the war prevented the revival of poetry in the English theatre and, as a drama critic for a local newspaper, continued to take a lively interest in modern developments still insisting on the central importance of dramatic language: in a recent review of *Abelard and Heloise* he concluded:

The rapt attention of the audience served to strengthen . . . my long-held conviction that the essence of theatre is the spoken word finely used to show man's spirit in all its complicated ramifications. All else is at its best embellishment, at its worst gimmickry. *The Kentish Gazette*, February 26th 1976.

Author of a parody *The Young Thing* (see *Bibliography*). He died during the preparation of the first edition of this book.

LAURENCE IRVING (b. 1897) - Played Caspar (1928), designed set and costumes (1934) and designed set (1935-'8). Laurence Irving was one of the key figures of the Canterbury Festival, he represented the interests of drama on the Council of the Friends, placed his extensive experience of the theatre and his skill as a designer at the Friends' disposal and negotiated new plays for the Festivals. Irving designed the Festival posters and frequently entertained the playwrights in his home. He was trained as an artist and, after the First World War, he held four exhibitions of his work at the Fine Art Society (1925, '28, '36, '50). He was Artistic Director to Douglas Fairbanks in 1928 & '29 for the films *The Iron Mask* & *The Taming of the Shrew*, and between 1926 and 1955 he produced many remarkable stage designs, including *Hamlet* (1950), *Pygmalion* (1953) and *The Wild Duck* (1955).

Irving has made a significant contribution to theatre history by establishing and acting as first Chairman of the British Theatre Museum and by the writing of his biographical and autobiographical accounts of his family's involvement in the theatre. His *Henry Irving: The Actor and His World* (London 1951) is unlikely to be surpassed as a detailed and vivid picture of his famous grandfather and Laurence Irving hoped to include the text of his address *The Canterbury Adventure* as the appendix of a further work which will complete the trilogy of which *The Successors* (1967) and *The Precarious Crust* (1971) form the first two parts. *Who's Who 1976*; *OCT*; see also *Bibliography* under Laurence Irving.

APPENDIX

CLAUDIA LEAF - Directed *Romeo and Juliet* (1995). Trained at the Rose Bruford College of Speech and Drama. On leaving drama school she worked as an actor for a number of years before turning her attention to directing and writing. She directed for a number of touring companies, including Pumpkin Theatre and Q20 Theatre Company in Bradford, and worked as a guest director at Christ Church College in Canterbury and the School of Continuing Education at Kent University. She has written and directed extensively for Channel Theatre Company and one of her Theatre-In-Education scripts, *Radical Will,* has recently been published.

MICHAEL MACOWAN (b. 1906) - Produced *Christ's Comet* (1938). Acted in many of Shaw's plays (1925-31) and appeared as Little Billy in *Trilby* (1927). Trained at RADA. His first production was *Judgement of Dr Johnson* at the Arts Theatre (1932); he was director of Hull Repertory Company (1933-4) and Croydon Repertory (1934-5). From 1935-6 Macowan was assistant director of the Old Vic Dramatic School and as director of the Westminster Theatre he was responsible for a series of plays by Ibsen, Strindberg, Tchekov, Shakespeare, Shaw and O'Neill. In 1945 he was appointed Drama Director of the *Arts Council of Great Britain* but resigned in 1946. He directed Fry's *A Sleep of Prisoners* (London & New York 1950) and *A Phoenix Too Frequent* and *Thor, With Angels* (London 1951). He was appointed Principal of LAMDA in 1954. *WWT.*

HARALD MELVILL - Designed setting (1947-9). Melvill was an expert in designing for small stages and was therefore in great demand by leading amateur companies. He could create the impression of varying textures by the use of simple stage-painting techniques and produced a considerable number of practical handbooks for amateur stage managers and theatre technicians. See *Bibliography* under Harald Melvill.

SIR BERNARD MILES (b. 1907) - Played John Balle (1947). Miles first appeared in *Richard III* (1930) but also devoted much of his time to making theatre properties and building stage sets. He made the props for the 1935 Mercury Theatre Production of *Murder in the Cathedral.* During the war he joined the Old Vic Company and played Iago and after a number of productions at the New Theatre including *Men in Shadow* (which he co-produced) he rejoined the Old Vic and, during the year in which he came to Canterbury, he was seen as Christopher Sly in *The Taming of the Shrew,* the Bishop of Carlisle in *Richard II* and Robert de Baudricourt and the Inquisitor in *St Joan. WWT.*

333

DRAMA IN THE CATHEDRAL

NUGENT MONCK (1875-1958) - Produced *Everyman* and *Dr Faustus* (1929). Monck was a disciple of William Poel and began a career as an actor shortly before WWI. After the War he became producer to the Norwich Players, an amateur group which he founded in 1911, and for this group he bought and reconstructed a dilapidated theatre building which became the famous Maddermarket Theatre. The Elizabethan stage of Monck's small theatre has seen the production of all of Shakespeare's plays and the amateur company still plays there, achieving a remarkably high standard. Monck, a member of the original cast of Poel's *Everyman*, was involved in the revival of many medieval plays. *OCT*; June Ottaway, 'Nugent Monck of Norwich', in *Christian Drama* Vol. II, 22.

FRANK NAPIER - Played Second Knight and Second Tempter (1935 and at the Mercury Theatre), Second Lord and stage manager (1936), Theodatus and co-director (1937) and in commercial productions, Mephistopheles and stage manager (1939) and in London, Merlin (1949). He was Stage Director at the Old Vic from 1931-4 and appeared in many productions there, notably as Flute in *A Midsummer Night's Dream* (1938) and as Aslaksen in *An Enemy of the People* (1939). Napier was an enthusiast for verse-drama and as early as 1930 he had produced Gordon Bottomley's *Midsummer Eve* at the Old Vic. He had a magnificent voice and a great gift for comic acting. He was the author of *Curtains for Stage Settings* (London 1939) a useful book for those working with small stages and simple scenery, such as at Canterbury. Audrey Williamson, *Old Vic Drama* (London 1948).

CHARLES RICKETTS (1866-1931) - Designer for *The Coming of Christ* (1928). Described by Masefield as "that witty, smiling, satanic looking man with a knowledge as profound as it was varied and beautiful!"
A pre-Raphaelite painter greatly admired by Bottomley, Shaw, Sturge-Moore, Wilde and Yeats, Ricketts introduced a richness and care in the design of stage costume that was unprecedented. He designed costumes and settings for many of the last romantic verse plays as well as for the historical plays of Shaw and the new poetic drama of Bottomley and Yeats. Ricketts pioneered the use of moveable screens for stage settings and may well have influenced Laurence Irving, his pupil, in this respect. When Ricketts was due to arrive in Canterbury, enquiries were made as to when he would like to be met at the station, but he replied by telegram from London, "Am walking to Canterbury." His one extravagance was a passion for flowers, and his Canterbury designs confirm this. *DNB*;

Johnson, Hewlett, 'Sermon on Sunday, 24th August 1958', *Canterbury Cathedral Chronicle, LIII,* October 1958, 3-6.

Jones-Evans, Eric, 'Henry Irving in Kent', *Kent Life, X,* 11, 1971, 29-30.

Jones, David E., *The Plays of T. S. Eliot,* London, Routledge and Kegan Paul, 1960.

Jones, Henry Arthur, *The Renaissance of the English Drama: Essays, Lectures and Fragments Relating to the Modern English Stage, Written and Delivered in the Years 1883-94,* London, Macmillan, 1895.

Kennedy, Andrew K., *Six Dramatists in Search of a Language,* Cambridge, CUP, 1975.

Kernodle, G. R., 'England's Religious Drama Movement', *College English, I,* 1940.

Kierkegaard, Soren, *Philosophical Fragments,* ed., Williams, C., London, OUP, 1936.

Kunitz, Stanley J. and Haycraft, Howard, eds., *Twentieth Century Authors,* New York, H. W. Wilson, 1942.

Lewis, Cecil, ed., *Self Portrait: Taken From the Letters and Journals of Charles Ricketts, R.A.,* London, Peter Davies, 1940.

Lewis, C. S., ed., *Essays Presented to Charles Williams,* London, OUP, 1947.

Leyson, Peter, *London Theatres: A Short History and Guide,* London, Apollo Publications, 1970.

Littlewood, S. R., 'Dramatic Notes', *English, VI,* 33, 1946, 135.

Littlewood, S. R., 'Great Chances for New Playwrights', *English, VI,* 34, 1947, 202.

Littlewood, S. R., 'Poverty, Poetry and Plays', *English, VI,* 31, 1946, 25-27.

Lloyd, Roger, *The Church of England, 1900-1905,* London, SCM Press, 1966.

Lobb, K. M., *The Drama in School and Church,* London, Harrap, 1955.

Lumley, Frederick, *New Trends in Twentieth-Century Drama,* London, Barrie and Rockliff, 1967.

Marshall, N., 'The Plays of Masefield', *The Bookman, LXXXIX,* 1930.

Masefield, John, *Grace Before Ploughing,* London, Heinemann, 1966.

Masefield, John, *Recent Prose,* London, Heinemann, 1924.

Masefield, J., *Some Memories of W. B. Yeats,* Dublin, private printing, 1940.

Masefield, John, *Speech at a Festival in Honour of W. B. Yeats,* private printing, 1930.

Masefield, John, *Thanks Before Going: With Other Gratitude for Old Delight, Including 'A Macbeth Production' and Various Papers Not Before Printed,* London, Heinemann, 1947.

Masefield, John, *William Shakespeare*, revised edition, London, Heinemann, 1954. Originally published 1911.

Masefield, John, *With the Living Voice: An Address Given at the First General Meeting of the Scottish Association for the Speaking of Verse, 24th October 1924*, London, Heinemann, 1925.

Mason, Eugene, 'John Drinkwater', *The Bookman, LVI*, 332, 1919, 70-72.

Megroz, R. L., 'Gordon Bottomley', *The Bookman, LXIV*, 382, 1923, 177-78.

Meisel, Martin, *Shaw and the Nineteenth Century Theatre*, Princeton, NJ, Princeton University Press, 1963.

Melvill, Harald, *Complete Guide to Amateur Dramatics*, Lon., Rockliff, 1957.

Melvill, Harald, *Historic Costumes for the Amateur Theatre and How to Make Them*, foreword by Christopher Hassall, Lon., Barrie and Rockliff, 1961.

Melvill, Harald, *The Magic of Make-up*, London, Rockliff, 1957.

Melvill, Harald, *Stage Management for the Amateur Theatre*, London, Barrie and Rockliff, 1963.

Merchant, W. Moelwyn, *Christianity and the Arts*, Penarth, The Church in Wales Council for Education, 1957.

Merchant, W. Moelwyn, *Creed and Drama*, London, Society for the Promotion of Christian Knowledge, 1965.

Michigan, Stanley, *Christopher Fry: A Critical Essay*, NY, Eerdmans, 1970.

Milne, A. A., 'Attila, My Attila', *Punch*, September 11th, 1907, 186.

Monkhouse, A. N., 'The Words and the Play', *Essays and Studies by Members of the English Association, XI*, collected by Oliver Elton, Oxford, The Clarendon Press, 1925, 32-48.

Morison, Mary, ed., *The Correspondence of Henrik Ibsen*, London, Hodder and Stoughton, 1905.

Muir, Kenneth, 'Verse & Prose', *Stratford-upon-Avon Studies, 4: Contemporary Theatre*, London, Edward Arnold, 1962, 97-115.

Myers, H. A., 'New Poetic Drama', *Times Literary Supplement, XXIV*, 1935.

Napier, Frank, *Curtains for Stage Settings*, London, Muller, 1939.

Nicoll, Allardyce, *British Drama*, London, Harrap, 4th edition, 1947.

Nicoll, Allardyce, *English Drama: A Modern Viewpoint*, London, Harrap, 1968.

Nicoll, Allardyce, *English Drama 1900-1930: The Beginnings of the Modern Period*, Cambridge, CUP, 1973.

Nicoll, Allardyce, *The English Stage*, London, Ernest Benn, 1928.

Nicoll, Allardyce, *A History of English Drama 1660-1900, V: Late Nineteenth Century Drama, 1850-1900*, Cambridge, CUP, 1907.

BIBLIOGRAPHY

Nichols, Wallace B., *The Speaking of Poetry*, Preface by Gordon Bottomley, London, Methuen, 1937.

Ottaway, June, 'Nugent Monck of Norwich', *Christian Drama, II*, 1953, 22

Parker, John, ed., *Who's Who in the Theatre*, 15th edition, Lon, Pitman, 1972.

Parsons, Eric, *Dramatic Expression of Religion*, Lon., Epworth Press, 1947.

Peacock, Ronald, *The Poet in the Theatre*, London, Routledge, 1946.

Poel, William, *Monthly Letters: Essays on the Drama*, arranged by A.M.T., London, T. Werner Laurie, 1929.

Poel, William, 'Poetry in Drama', *Contemporary Review, CIV*, 1913.

Potter, Robert, *The English Morality Play*, London & Boston, Routledge & Kegan Paul, 1975.

Purdom, C. B., *Harley Granville-Barker*, Cambridge, Massachussetts, Harvard University Press, 1956.

'Review of *The Acts of St. Peter*', *The Times*, March 21st 1934, 12.

Reynolds, Ernest, *Modern English Drama: A Survey of the Theatre From 1900*, Connecticut, Greenwood Press, 1974.

Roose-Evans, James, *Inner Journey, Outer Journey*, London, Century Hutchinson, 1987.

Ross, Robert H., *The Georgian Revolt: Rise and Fall of a Poetic Ideal*, London, Faber & Faber, 1965.

Roston, Murray, *Biblical Drama in England*, London, Faber & Faber, 1968.

Rouse, Rand & Neill, S. C., eds., *A History of the Ecumenical Movement*, London, SPCK, 1954.

Rowell, Geoffrey, *Hell and the Victorians*, London, OUP, 1974.

Rowell, George, *The Victorian Theatre*, London, OUP, 1956.

Rumsey, H. St. J., *Clear Speech for Platform and Pulpit*, Lon., Muller, 1938.

Russell Taylor, John, *The Rise and Fall of the Well-Made Play*, London, Methuen, 1967.

Sayers, Dorothy L., *The Mind of the Maker*, NY, Meridian Books, 1956.

Sayers, Dorothy L., *The Poetry of Search and the Poetry of Statement*, London, Gollancz, 1963.

Scholes, Percy A., *The Oxford Companion to Music*, London, OUP, 1955.

Scott, Clement, *From the Bells to King Arthur*, London, Macqueen, 1896.

Scott, Reverend W. S., *Worship and Drama: An Enquiry Into the Nature and Interpretation of the Dramatic Element Inherent In All Forms of Liturgical Worship, With Especial Reference To its Place in the Anglican Liturgy*, London, Allen Lane, 1938.

Shaw, George Bernard, *Dramatic Opinions and Essays*, 2 volumes, New York, Brentano, 1907.

Shaw, G. B., *Our Theatre in the Nineties*, 3 volumes, Lon., Constable, 1932.

Shaw, G. B., *Pen Portraits and Reviews*, London, Constable, 1949.

Shelley, Percy Bysshe, *Poetical Works*, London, Warne, 1890.

Shrubsole, Stanley & Beddow, Seaward, *Dramatic Production: A Practical Guide for Free Churchmen and Others*, London, Independent Press, 1932.

Smith, Carol H., *T. S. Eliot's Dramatic Theory and Practice*, London & Princeton, OUP, 1963.

Smith, Jean and Toynbee, Arnold, eds., *Gilbert Murray: An Unfinished Autobiography*, London, George Allen & Unwin, 1960.

Smith, Nowell, 'Review of Dante's *Purgatorio* translated by Laurence Binyon', *English*, *II*, 9, 1939, 181.

Smith, Nowell, 'Thoughts on Laurence Binyon's Poetry', *English*, *IV*, 23, 1943, 144-5.

Spanos, William V., *The Christian Tradition in Modern British Verse Drama*, New Jersey, Rutgers University Press, 1967.

Speaight, Robert, *Christian Theatre*, New York, Hawthorn Books, 1960.

Speaight, Robert, *William Poel and the Elizabethan Revival*, Cambridge, Massachussetts, Harvard University Press, 1954.

Speaight, Robert, 'With Becket in *Murder in the Cathedral*', *T. S. Eliot: The Man and his Work*, ed., Allen Tate, London, Chatto & Windus, 1967.

Speckbaugh, P. F., 'Poetic Drama', *Spirit*, *VIII*, 1941.

Sprigge, Elizabeth, *Sybil Thorndike Casson*, London, Victor Gollancz, 1971.

Stanford, Derek, *Christopher Fry: An Appreciation*, Lon., Peter Nevill, 1951.

Stanford, Derek, 'Christopher Fry', *Writers and Their Work: 54*, ed., Dobrée, Bonamy, London, Longmans Green, 1962.

Steiner, George, *The Death of Tragedy*, London, Faber & Faber, 1961.

St. John, Christopher, ed., *Ellen Terry and Bernard Shaw: A Correspondence*, London, Constable, 1931.

Strong, L. A. G., 'John Masefield', *Writers and Their Work: 24*, ed., Dobrée, Bonamy, London, Longmans Green, 1952.

Tate, Allen, *Reactionary Essays on Poetry and Ideas*, NY, Scribner, 1936.

Tennyson, Hallam, *Alfred Lord Tennyson: A Memoir*, two volumes, London, Macmillan, 1897.

Thorndike, Sybil, 'The Theatre as a Service to the Community', lecture delivered on June 12th 1934, *Canterbury Cathedral Chronicle*, *XVIII*, July, 1934, 15-17.

Thouless, P., *Modern Poetic Drama*, Oxford, Basil Blackwell, 1934.

Tolley, A. T., *The Poetry of the Thirties*, London, Gollancz, 1975.

INDEX

The Single Source of All Filth

The Jeremy Collier Controversy

David Self

In 1698, Revd Jeremy Collier, a Non-Juror, "venom'd priest" and outlaw, published his pamphlet, *A Short View of the Immorality and Profaneness of the English Stage*. It gave rise to a vicious and hilariously bad-tempered debate, with the dramatists defending themselves in print and Collier responding with more attacks on the stage - "the single source of all filth". As a direct result of this protracted spat, the literary careers of Vanbrugh and Congreve were aborted, red-blooded Restoration drama gave way to innocuous sentimental comedy, Collier became a hero of the emerging middle-class and the Lord Chamberlain was appointed censor of the English stage - a position he held until 1968.

Since the original publications are not readily accessible, *The Single Source of All Filth* is as much an anthology of those writings as a critical survey. As well as the most pertinent sections of Collier's writings and Vanbrugh's response, it includes extracts from other commentators and from *The Stage Beaux Toss'd in a Blanket* - the play which mocked Collier's zealous, if intemperate, efforts.

The *Jeremy Collier Controversy* is far more than a footnote in the history of English literature. Because Collier articulated the mood of the new, moral middle-class, his ill-argued outpourings were highly effective. His *Short View* changed the course of English drama and David Self provides a cogent account of this neglected debate which will be of great interest to students of English theatrical history.

David Self lectured in drama at *Bede College* and was a BBC producer. He has had several of his own plays produced. He has also written and broadcast extensively on the theatre, including programmes for the *Open University*, and regularly reviewed for *Kaleidoscope, Plays International* and the *Times Educational Supplement*. He has contributed to the *Guardian, Independent on Sunday, Punch* and was a columnist on *The Listener*. His many books include *Classic Drama* (Stanley Thornes), *The Drama and Theatre Arts Course Book* (Nelson) and *Television Drama* (Macmillan).

ISBN: 0 85343 626 6
Price: £10.50

Saints and Their Emblems

Robert Milburn

Each figure of a saint in a church, whether in stone, glass or wood, depicts a particular person, but they are rarely named, so the interested visitor is dependent on guidebooks to identify them. St George and a few others are well-known, but in medieval times images were often used to convey identity, so many other saints were given an emblem or object as a common identifier.

This book lists over 250 saints, including all the common saints and many uncommon ones, each of whom is connected with at least one English church. The author gives a brief history of the saint in fact or legend and describes the identifying emblem. The commonest emblems are illustrated by small drawings.

Robert Milburn was an Honorary Fellow of Worcester College, Oxford and was Dean of Worcester from 1957-1968. His other works include *Early Christian Interpretations of History* and *Early Christian Art and Architecture*.

ISBN: 0 85956 064 3
Price: £8.50

J. Garnet Miller also publish a wide range of theatrical textbooks, including books on choreography, costume, make-up, musical productions and stage management, as well as plays for every theatre - amateur and professional, all-women, mixed and youth casts, sketches, one acts and full length plays.

Religious Plays

Christmas Plays

One-act Plays

The Angels at Bethlehem - Freda Collins
Dark Noël - L. E. Thomas
Fit For a King - Barbara Willard
Jesus of Nazareth : This is Your Life - Andrew Taggart
The Journey of the Star - Edward Murch
The Light in Darkness - T. B. Morris
Lonely Road - T. C. Thomas
No Room - Freda Collins & Alison Graham-Campbell
Time to be Born - P. D. Cummins

Full Length Plays

Christmas in the Market Place - Henri Ghéon, adapted by Eric Crozier
Emmanuel - James Forsyth
Journey of the Three Kings - Henri Ghéon

Easter Plays

One-act Plays

Fine Linen - H. M. Richards
I Will Arise! - T. B. Morris
Mary's Son - Sylvia Davidson
On the Hill - Edward Murch
Road to Calvary - Robert Duce
Sorrow Into Joy - Dorothy Myring
Stranger On the Road - Beatrix Carter
They Wanted a Leader - Sam Bate

Full Length Plays

Behold Your King - Thomas Doran
Eyes Upon the Cross - Don Mueller
Innocent Blood - Thomas Doran
Look Back to the Hill - Don Mueller
Pontius Pilate - Gordon Lea
Road to Emmaus - James Forsyth
Spark in Judea - R. F. Delderfield

General Religious Plays

One-act Plays

The Answer - Phoebe M. Rees
Farce of the Devil's Bridge - Henri Ghéon
The Fortieth Man - Freda Collins
Mine Enemy My Friend - T. B. Morris
The New Jerusalem - Phoebe Rees
The Trumpet Shall Sound - Phoebe Rees
The Waters of Lethe - Frank Sladen-Smith

Full Length Plays

An Army of Innocents - Keith William
The Boy With a Cart - Christopher Fry
Brother Ass & Brother Lion - Barbara Willard
The Hopeful Travellers, - G-M. Martens, adapted by A. Obey, translated by
I. Capell
Immortal Garden - H. Stevens
The Ingoldsby Legends - Kenneth Pickering
Jonah - David Campton
The Midlands' Mysteries - K. Pickering & D. Sugano
Noah Gives Thanks - Eric Crozier
The Parting of Friends - Kenneth Pickering
The Song of the Morning - T. B. Morris
Tyndale's Dream - John Stuart-Anderson